Near the Banks of the River

CELEBRATING HARDING SCHOOL OF THEOLOGY IN MEMPHIS

EDITED BY MARK E. POWELL & STEVE CLOER

Near the Banks of the River
CELEBRATING HARDING SCHOOL OF THEOLOGY IN MEMPHIS

Copyright © 2024 Regnum Media.

All rights reserved. No portion of this publication may be reproduced or transmitted in any form by any means—except for use in teaching contexts or brief quotations in published reviews—without prior written permission.

Names: Powell, Mark E., editor. | Cloer, Steve, editor.
Title: Near the Banks of the River: Celebrating Harding School of Theology in Memphis / Mark E. Powell and Steve Cloer, editors.

Scripture quotations marked NIV are taken from The Holy Bible, New International Version®, NIV®, copyright © 1973, 1978, 1984, 2011 by Biblica, Inc.® Used by permission. All rights reserved worldwide.

Scripture quotations marked NRSV are taken from New Revised Standard Version Bible, copyright 1989, Division of Christian Education of the National Council of the Churches of Christ in the United States of America. Used by permission. All rights reserved.

Regnum Media is the publishing imprint of the **Center for Christian Studies**
12407 N. Mopac Expy. Ste. 250-530
Austin, TX 78758

www.christian-studies.org

TABLE OF CONTENTS

A Word from the Publishers — 5

Introduction — 9
Steve Cloer

The Story of Harding School of Theology in Memphis — 15
Mark E. Powell

Biblical Studies: Old Testament — 29
Nathan Bills

Biblical Studies: New Testament — 43
Garrett Best

Theological Studies — 59
C. Leonard Allen

Library and Theological Scholarship — 75
Carisse Mickey Berryhill

Preaching — 87
Matthew D. Love

Congregational Ministry — 101
Carson E. Reed

Global Missions — 117
Craig Ford

Urban Mission *Jim Harbin*	131
Counseling *Erika Carr*	147
Spiritual Formation *Grant Azbell*	163
African American Church Leadership *Edward J. Robinson*	175
Chaplaincy *Dorn Muscar, Jr.*	193
Campus Ministry *Chris W. Buxton*	209
Bivocational Ministry *R. Mark Wilson*	223
HST and the Changing Landscape of Theological Education *Mark E. Powell*	239
Pictures	247
Administration, Faculty, and Staff	253
Alumnus/Alumna of the Year	255
Alma Mater	257
Contributors	259

A WORD FROM THE PUBLISHERS

Except for a brief time in high school, I (Kevin) never expected to be a minister. Looking back, it is somewhat surprising that, to my knowledge, no one suggested I should consider ministry; it is surprising because I was active in my high school's Christian Student Union, I occasionally led devotionals in youth group, went on all the mission trips I could, attended every youth rally and retreat I could, and asked my parents to buy me Christian non-fiction books. I even bought my own Greek-English interlinear (alas, we all do foolhardy things when we're young!) New Testament to teach myself some basic Greek. Despite the (now) obvious signs that God was preparing me for some kind of ministry, I majored in History at Harding University and graduated in 2008 with a degree and a plan to get another degree, a Master's of Science in Education with an emphasis in social studies for secondary education. Like both of my loving and supportive parents, I planned to teach. While I was a History major I minored in Greek because, in my own words, "That sounds like fun." Sadly, I was that slow on the uptake, but by God's grace I eventually sensed there was something missing during my M.S.E.—it was studying Greek. What could I do? Where could I study God's word at that level? The last Greek professor I had in undergrad was Dr. Paul Pollard; a year later he and I were talking one fateful afternoon and he gave me a simple yet life-changing piece of advice: "Kevin, you should really check out the Grad School." Long story short, after much prayer and discernment, I began my MDiv at HST (still HUGSR then) in the Fall of 2010, and quickly fell in love with my courses, the school, and even Memphis.

I went to HST with a mission, too: to finish strong so I could be accepted into a PhD program to study New Testament. As I like to say, I "majored" in Allen Black and Rick Oster at HST, and largely due to their teaching and guidance I was accepted at Asbury Theological Seminary (graduated in 2020) where I was blessed to study with internationally-respected scholars and extraordinary peers (three of whom were also HST alumni). Because "to whom much is given, much is expected," I knew I had a holy obligation, a sacred duty, to use the education God was blessing me with; so, while at Asbury I had put my world-class education from HST and Asbury to good use by serving in congregational ministry. I continue to serve God's church by taking the tools and training I received at HST and equipping the faithful with whom I work to live their faith more genuinely and discuss their faith more intelligently.

Kevin B. Burr, PhD
(MDiv, HST 2014)

My path to a life of ministry was a winding one, largely characterized by me trying to avoid a series of open doors that God had placed before me while I sought to do something else with my life. Eventually, I got the message, and once I set my face toward the vocation of ministry, I realized that I needed training and began my time at HST. I am deeply grateful for the many years that I spent there (I was on the eight-year MDiv plan, so it was *many years* for me!). I have very fond memories of my intensive course weeks in Memphis, which were some of the most challenging weeks of my life, but also some of the best weeks of my life. I had many professors who poured into me and became deeply influential in my life—Dave Bland, Allen Black, Rick Oster, Mark Powell, Phil McMillion, and others—and met lifelong friends as well.

As I reflect on my time at HST, I realized that HST gave me the twin gifts of humility and confidence. I showed up in Memphis with an unhealthy amount of arrogance, but my graduate school training quickly helped me to understand how little I actually I knew, and convinced me of the need to be a lifelong learner. I realized that I was never going to master the study of Scripture, or doing ministry, or discovering God. But amidst that new posture of humility, HST also helped me develop confidence through the construction of a solid foundation for a life of faith and ministry. For all that I didn't know, there were some things I *did* know, really important things about the Triune God, Scripture, and God's Church through the centuries that I could build my life around. And even though I am never going to master Scripture or ministry, I developed skills to study Scripture well and do ministry faithfully. Humility and confidence are wonderful gifts that I received from HST and which I have tried to use faithfully in two churches as well as other contexts. I can confidently say that I would not still be in ministry today without my training at HST.

Luke Dockery
(MDiv, HST 2018)

We were honored when Mark Powell asked Regnum Media to be involved in the publication of a collected volume dedicated to the work and impact of Harding School of Theology. It is our pleasure to play a role in honoring HST's legacy of faithful stewardship, rigorous scholarship, and love for God and his church. It also seems appropriate, because Regnum Media simply would not exist without HST.

You have already read of the deep influence HST has had on each of us, and its role in guiding us to lives of service in God's church through congregational ministry. The creation of Regnum Media is another means of equipping God's church—together, we have ministered for a combined length of nearly thirty years, and during that time we have come to see just how important it is to find trustworthy teaching material, and how difficult it can be to do so. Regnum Media is proud to offer quality, affordable Bible study curriculum for church classes, small groups, and individual study—but none of this would be possible without the deeply formative years we spent at HST.

INTRODUCTION

Steve Cloer

*"Near the banks of the river that flows down through our land
Is a school for Christian service forever may she stand..."*

In 1811-1812, a tremendous series of earthquakes hit the bootheel of Missouri.[1] These quakes were felt as far east as Washington DC, as south as Mexico, as north as Canada, and as west as the Rocky Mountains. These significant tremors, occurring in a brief five-month span between December 1811 and April 1812, devastated the city of New Madrid, Missouri and surrounding areas and dramatically impacted the Mid-South region. Three earthquakes during this span are estimated to register near 8.0 on the Richter scale and constituted the severest earthquakes to hit the contiguous 48 states in recorded history. Historians claim that these earthquakes were so disruptive that the Mississippi River flowed backward.[2]

Stories have been told about boatmen trying to save their boats during the quakes, only to find themselves floating north to St. Louis. Enormous sections of the riverbank collapsed, as the river receded violently from the shores, leaving standing boats on sand. Then, the banks would overflow again as the river crashed back toward the shores. As a result, the topography around the Mississippi river changed. Sunklands were created. Forests became submerged in water, as chasms developed in the ground. Where once there were trees, there were now swamps and lakes. Where there were existing lakes, there

---

[1] I am indebted to Jason Knight (MA, 2001) for the use of this metaphor. Knight introduced this metaphor at the last Convocation for Harding School of Theology in Memphis on August 14, 2023.

[2] To read more on the phenomenon of the New Madrid earthquakes, see Jay Feldman, *When the Mississippi Ran Backwards: Empire, Intrigue, Murder, and the New Madrid Earthquakes* (New York: Free Press, 2005).

were now hills and ridges. The route of the river adjusted to the changing and unstable earth and its flow became different.

The time in American history was a significant one. Governments were pushing Native Americans further west in order to settle more land. This oppressive move created a desire for rebellion and war among the Shawnee chief Tecumseh and other tribal leaders. The Mississippi delta was experiencing a tense time and the anxiety felt among the inhabitants was lived out within the tremors in the land. Jay Feldman wrote, "The US was at a turning point, one of those defining moments in history when forces converge so powerfully that something has to give. This was true geologically as well as historically—it was almost as if the earthquakes were a symbol of the turmoil of the times."[3]

On August 4, 2023, another earthquake occurred in the Mid-South region. This earthquake was not a geological occurrence, but one in theological education, when the Harding University Board of Trustees made the decision to relocate Harding School of Theology from Memphis, Tennessee to Searcy, Arkansas.[4] Like the New Madrid quakes, this decision was felt by alumni in the north, south, east, and west. But it was felt most keenly in Memphis, as the place where HST has resided for the past 66 years. Like the New Madrid quakes, this decision is a defining moment in theological education, where forces have converged so powerfully that something has to give: a combination of online education, decline of residential students, minister shortages, and institutional sustainability. This is not the place to debate this decision, but it is the place to acknowledge its impact. Like the Mississippi River, HST will not look the same from this moment. A significant change has occurred and there is no going back. Whenever significant changes occur, there is always a sense of loss—a loss of what once was, a loss of knowing things will not be the same, a loss of a courageous dream started 66 years earlier. When God's people

---

[3] Feldman, 14.

[4] While Harding School of Theology has been referred to by various names and nicknames (e.g. "the grad school") through its history, throughout this book the recent name of Harding School of Theology (adopted in 2011) will be used. The affectionate acronym, HST, will appear regularly.

face a critical bend in the road, such as this, it is appropriate and helpful to pause, reflect, and notice God's work up to this point.

Often in the Old Testament, the people of God were exhorted to remember (Deut 6:4-11). Various forms of memorials were utilized, including altars, offerings, and Sabbath days to help the people recall the hand of God in their life up to this point. As the New Covenant people of God, we gather each Lord's Day and share the Lord's Supper as a moment to remember the covenant we share in the body and blood of Jesus (1 Cor 11:23-26). Remembering is important and necessary. It keeps us grounded, thankful, and mindful of God's hand at work.

Another example of remembering appears in 1 Samuel 7. The people of Israel had just received back the ark of the Lord after a 20-year absence. They had gathered together in renewal before the Lord, confessing their sins, and directing their hearts to God. But as they did, the Philistines attacked them. Samuel demonstrates his priestly leadership by taking a lamb, offering a sacrifice, and calling upon the Lord for deliverance. And the Lord came to their aid. He thundered on that day, confusing the Philistines and allowing the Israelites to defeat them. After this defeat, Samuel decides to set up a memorial stone and name it Ebenezer, or "stone of help," proclaiming, "Thus far the Lord has helped us" (2 Sam 7:12).

This stone was an exercise in memory. God had just done something incredible for Israel. A new season was beginning: one of peace and safety and one where Samuel was judge (2 Sam 7:13). Samuel did not want the people to forget how they had arrived at this place, so he names a stone and commemorates it. Scholars have noticed the ambiguity in the phrase "Thus far."[5] The phrase could denote a geographical or spatial meaning, "As far as this geographical spot." Or it could carry a temporal meaning, "Until now." Perhaps the writer wanted both meanings to carry force. Something had occurred in Israel's *past* and in this *place*. This stone, or marker, was an

---

[5] Joyce Baldwin, *1 and 2 Samuel*, Tyndale Old Testament Commentaries (Downers Grove, IL: InterVarsity Press, 1988), 80. David Toshio Tsumura, *The First Book of Samuel*, New International Commentary of the Old Testament (Grand Rapids: Eerdmans, 2007), 238.

acknowledgment of that fact. From the idolatrous path that Israel had traveled until now and from the oppressed past that Israel had journeyed from until now, the Lord had helped them. This stone was a chance for Israel to stop, pause, and remember God's goodness.

This book is a "stone of help" for HST. For 66 years, God has been at work in this geographical spot of Memphis to train Christian ministers and prepare leaders. God has been good to HST and has been faithful in providing for this institution. A new season is starting—one that I hope will be full of peace and stability. So it just seems right and appropriate to stop, pause, and reflect on what God has done. This book is a simple way to acknowledge that "thus far" the Lord has helped us.

The genesis of this book began, actually, last summer (though we did not know it). HST applied for a *Moving Forward in Mission* grant from the Association of Theological Schools and received it in July 2023.[6] The original intention of this grant was to organize a special event in April 2024 to highlight the Doctor of Ministry program. When the board decision occurred in August, we pivoted and determined to use this grant as a moment to celebrate HST in Memphis by hosting an HST reunion, where we invited back alumni and guests for a special weekend. It was determined that a unique way to commemorate this occasion would be to commission a *Festschrift* in honor of HST in Memphis.

Current and former faculty and staff were invited to identify key theological areas or disciplines that have been significant during HST's time in Memphis. These would be areas that received significant attention over the decades either because of HST's context in Memphis or HST's mission as a school. Then, we invited the same group to nominate distinguished alumni in each area to offer a brief essay. The essays reflect on the unique contribution that HST in Memphis has offered to their field and look forward to key opportunities and barriers in the future for their field and for HST. Each essay seeks to catalogue this unique moment in HST's history and to notice the "ripples on the pond" that this school, in its present location, has had, while also keeping

---

[6] See https://www.ats.edu/files/galleries/ats-requests-proposals.pdf.

an eye to the future. After considerable discussion, fourteen areas were selected: Biblical Studies (Old Testament and New Testament), Theological Studies, the Library and Theological Scholarship, Preaching, Congregational Ministry, Global Missions, Urban Mission, Counseling, Spiritual Formation, African-American Church Leadership, Chaplaincy, Campus Ministry, and Bivocational Ministry. All of these authors, like myself, benefitted greatly from their educational experience at HST in Memphis, as is demonstrated in each essay. In addition, current dean Dr. Mark Powell has included a special history of HST and a description and evaluation of the changing landscape of theological education.

Within these pages, you will read about the ministry of study, stories of faculty gone by, the treasured library, and many other things. But mostly, you will hear gratitude. Gratitude for how God has faithfully worked through this institution to train and equip leaders for the Kingdom of God. There was a six-month period between the conception of this project in October 2023 and the publication of this book in April 2024. Obviously, this book would not have been possible without the support of the alumni who contributed chapters, most of whom are quite busy themselves. Two other alumni, Kevin Burr and Luke Dockery at Regnum Media, prioritized this project to help us meet the April 11, 2024 deadline, when HST hosted the HST Reunion on the Memphis campus. Mark and I are grateful to all of these alumni and their labor of love on behalf of HST. We hope and trust that this book will contribute to the continuing scholarship that emanates from Harding School of Theology, while also declaring a testimony of faith, so that as we look back on 66 years in Memphis, we can truly say, "Thus far the Lord has helped us."

Two significant results of the New Madrid earthquakes of 1811-1812 symbolize what I hope for HST in the future as it transitions from Memphis to Searcy. First, the Mississippi River is still flowing. Despite the twists and turns, the topographical changes, the sunklands, the dried-up lakes, and even the river running backward for a time, the Mississippi River continues to flow steadily and smoothly. It flows a little differently. The path has changed somewhat. But it still flows. That is my belief for the future of HST. HST is changing its address, but it is not changing its mission. The mission is still "to challenge Christian leaders to develop deeper faith in God and higher standards of ministry and scholarship." Now, the path to do so may look a little different. The flow of this mission might feel a little different. But I believe and trust that the river of theological education will continue to flow, just like "the 'ol mighty Mississipp'." Second, the largest sunkland that was created through the earthquakes became filled with water and developed into a lake. It is called Reelfoot Lake. It covers 15,000 acres and is the only natural lake in Tennessee. Tourists regularly travel to this lake for boating and other recreational activities, located in a state park around 100 miles north of Memphis. Out of the devastation of earthquakes has come a new and unexpected place of joy. I believe that the same is in store for HST. Despite the earthquake of a geographic move, I anticipate various Reelfoot Lakes to appear that may not have ever appeared without the move. These new developments will bring about continued training and equipping for church leaders for years to come. The challenge, then, is having eyes to see the new things that God will do.

Mark and I believe these truths about HST's future, not because of our faith in human ingenuity or the power of organizational restructuring, but because of the God that we believe in. Israel was at a crossroads in 1 Samuel 7. Previously, Eli's leadership had dwindled away, ending poorly. The ark of the covenant had previously been captured. The people were weary from oppression. On the other side of the chapter, Israel will demand for a king to save them from their troubles. But in the middle—between a failed judge and a desire for a king—is a memorial stone. A stone that declared that all Israel needs is the reign of God. As David G. Firth put it, what Israel needed to do was to "remain faithful to Him and recognize that He indeed has been their help, their Ebenezer."[7] With this book, we endeavor to do just that. I close my reflection with this line from a hymn written by Joseph Hart that perfectly sums up the heart of this volume, "We'll praise Him for all that is past, and trust Him for all that's to come."[8]

---

[7] David G. Firth, *1 and 2 Samuel*, Apollos Old Testament Commentary Series (Downers Grove, IL: InterVarsity Press, 2020), 109.

[8] Joseph Hart, "How Good is the God We Adore."

CHAPTER ONE

The Story of Harding School of Theology in Memphis

Mark E. Powell

Hallowed ground.

These are the words alumni use more than any other to describe the Harding School of Theology (HST) campus in Memphis. Just as the presence of W. C. Handy, Elvis Presley, and B. B. King can be felt on Beale Street, so the presence of W. B. West, Jr., Jack P. Lewis, Annie May Alston Lewis, and Jane Tomlinson can be felt at 1000 Cherry Road.[1] When one considers the administrators, faculty, and alumni who have come through HST in Memphis over the last 66 years, it is impossible to provide a complete account of the school's history in this brief chapter. Rather, by focusing on these four figures who represent the administration (W. B. West), faculty (Jack Lewis), library (Annie May Lewis), and staff (Jane Tomlinson), I will attempt to convey the spirit of the school, as well as how God's Spirit has worked through the school. I will also interweave key events from the school's history in the narrative. W. B., Jack, Annie May, and Jane did more than establish a school in the face of strong opposition; they also forged a culture of excellence combined with humility, all in service to the church and for the sake of the world, that continues to this day.[2] As the school prepares to move back to the main campus of Harding University in Searcy, Arkansas for

---

[1] Marc Cohn's song "Walking in Memphis," released in 1991, captures the experience many have when visiting the historic sites of the city.

[2] After I had already settled on these four individuals as the "Mount Rushmore" of HST, I learned that Allen Black also identified these four as "the school's founders... who led the way in four areas" of administration, teaching and research, the library, and staff. See Allen Black, "Reflections from the Dean: A Tribute to Jane Tomlinson," in *The Bridge* 60, no. 2 (Winter 2020): 3.

the fall 2024 semester, it is important to remember and to celebrate what God has done through HST in Memphis.[3]

W. B. West, Jr. (1907-1994)

The history of HST and the history of theological education in Churches of Christ are deeply interconnected. During World War II in 1944, W. B. West, Jr., who held a ThD from the University of Southern California (1943), established the Master of Arts program in Religion at Pepperdine. It was the first graduate program of any kind for a school associated with Churches of Christ. In 1951, George Benson invited West to chair the Bible Department at Harding and start a graduate program in Bible and Religion; the graduate program began in West's second year in 1952. Extension courses were offered in Little Rock at the Central Church of Christ educational building in 1954, and in Memphis at the Union Avenue (now Midtown) Church of Christ educational building in 1955.[4] In 1958, Harding's Board of Trustees approved the Memphis program to be a branch campus, and West became the founding dean of Harding College School of Bible and Religion.[5]

People often ask why HST is in Memphis, and there are three primary reasons why the school moved.[6] First, Memphis was viewed as

---

[3] The best sources for the history of HST include Bill Flatt, *Harding Graduate School of Religion: 25 Years in Memphis* (Searcy, AR: Harding University, 1983); Jack P. Lewis, *As I Remember It* (Nashville: Gospel Advocate, 2012), especially chapter 8; Evertt W. Huffard, "HST Sixtieth Anniversary Celebration Speech" (unpublished, 2018); HST newsletters, first called *The Bulletin* and later called *The Bridge*, that date back to 1962; and academic catalogs for the graduate program in Religion at Harding that date back to 1952. I have taught at HST for 22 years, or one-third of the school's existence, and have consulted several people who have been here much longer, especially Don Meredith, who came to HST as a student in 1963 and began a 49-year career in the library in 1968.

[4] See the back cover of "Graduate Department of Bible and Religion 1956-1957 Information Bulletin," (Searcy: Harding College, 1956).

[5] Some people still call HST "the grad school" because of the many years the school was named Harding University Graduate School of Religion. Interestingly, the word *graduate* was not part of the original name of the school, and was dropped in 2011 when the name was changed to HST. In the second academic catalog, for years 1963-1964 and 1964-1965, the school was called Harding College Graduate School of Religion.

[6] My three reasons are a consolidation of seven reasons listed by Flatt, 4, 6.

a better location for graduate studies. Memphis is more accessible than Searcy and provides more opportunities for employment, ministry, research, and cultural exposure. Enrollment nearly tripled, going from 31 to 91, the year the school moved to Memphis.[7] Since 1958, the growth of HST has been a result of the partnership between Harding in Searcy and the churches in Memphis. W. B. West worked hard in the early years to establish trust between HST and local churches. Today, many Memphis-area churches and individuals support the school much like they do local non-profit organizations, and HST faculty, staff, alumni, and students are active leaders and participants in Memphis-area churches and the broader community.

Second, Harding was presented with a unique opportunity in Memphis. In 1952, Memphis church leaders purchased a Georgian mansion and the surrounding property for Memphis Christian School, an elementary and high school. The mansion was formerly the home of C. Leroy King, step-son of J. R. Watkins and head of the Memphis branch of the J. R. Watkins Company. Memphis church leaders asked Harding to take over the property and run the school in 1957, after which the school was renamed Harding Academy of Memphis.[8] Harding leaders viewed the mansion as an ideal location for the new graduate school.

Third, members of Churches of Christ were suspicious of theological education when Harding began its programs in the 1950s. Detractors feared that graduate theological education would inevitably lead to liberalism, the professionalization of ministry, and a loss of mission zeal. Some of the undergraduate faculty in Searcy were suspicious of the graduate faculty, most of whom were not Harding graduates.[9] West's proposal to begin a three-year program—today called the MDiv—was rejected by the Harding faculty. With an

---

[7] Interestingly, George Benson and the Harding Board seriously considered moving the entire college to Memphis from 1945-1947.

[8] Harding Academy of Memphis became an independent school again in 1978 but retained the name.

[9] According to Jack Lewis, "West, Rotenberry, Barton, Sime and I were imports and not alumni of Harding.... Some seemed to lack confidence in West. One person ordered a copy of West's thesis to examine." *As I Remember It*, 196-97.

administrative structure that made HST a distinct school in Memphis, Benson and West would not need the approval of Harding faculty to begin new programs. The Harding Board approved the establishment of the school in Memphis by one vote. The decision was so contentious, some Board members resigned after that meeting. Those of us in Churches of Christ who have been blessed by and are committed to theological education are indebted to the tireless efforts of George Benson, W. B. West, and the founding faculty of HST. They were determined to begin a graduate program in theological studies during a time when such programs faced strong opposition.

The 1958-1959 academic catalog lists West, Jack P. Lewis, John A. Scott, and Donald R. Sime as the first faculty in Memphis. James D. Bales, W. B. Barton, William M. Green, Rayburn W. Johnson, and Earl West are also listed, but they were part-time or adjunct faculty. E. H. Ijams appears as faculty in the 1959 graduation picture, and Velma R. West, W. B.'s wife, was Instructor of Greek. The academic catalog states that the school's mission was "to serve by teaching the Bible and closely related subjects to its students on an advanced academic level, and by helping them prepare for maximum Christian service.... Service rather than professionalism will be emphasized."[10] Offices, classrooms, chapel, and even some student housing were in the mansion. The library was first located in the carriage house of the mansion (from 1959-1999, the bookstore was located in the carriage house). For the second year, the library was moved to the mansion basement, which leaks water after a heavy rain to this day.

Jack P. Lewis (1919-2018)

From the beginning HST has been associated with high academic standards, and no one exemplifies this more than Jack P. Lewis, a renowned biblical scholar and translator. With his dry wit, humble lifestyle, and two PhDs—one in New Testament from Harvard University (1953) and one in Hebrew Bible from Hebrew Union College (1962)—Lewis set the bar high when it came to academic

---

[10] *1958-1958 Bulletin* (Memphis: Harding College School of Bible and Religion, 1958), 8.

expectations and research. Lewis's early work on the Council of Jamnia discredited a prevalent view that the council determined the books of the Hebrew canon.[11] He served as a translator for the New International Version and wrote the notes for Hosea and Joel in the *NIV Study Bible*.[12] Lewis is credited with writing over 220 scholarly and popular articles and publishing more than 25 books. He wrote widely, including on both the Old and New Testaments, Bible translations, the history of the English Bible, archeology, and issues facing the church of his day.[13]

In his short but influential article "The Ministry of Study," Lewis gives timeless advice in his own amusing style:

> One of the rabbis said, "A man can only obtain knowledge by sacrifice." You must apply the seat of your pants to a chair for long periods of time.
>
> The preacher needs to plan for a life which involves a ministry of study. Yet one of the preachers in our town openly states that he does not like to study, and all about him would say that his preaching reflects it.
>
> It is much easier to spend your time in "administrivia," in counseling, in gabbing, and in coffee drinking than in honest labor—"the ministry of study."
>
> There is a great deal of difference in getting a degree and getting an education.... [Education] is absorbing all you can absorb and then still thirsting for more."[14]

In honor of his retirement in 1989, the Student Association began to award the Jack P. Lewis Ministry of Study Award to an MA or MDiv

---

[11] Jack P. Lewis, "What Do We Mean by Jabneh?" *Journal of Bible and Religion* 32 (April 1964): 125-32.

[12] *NIV Study Bible*, ed. Kenneth Barker (Grand Rapids: Zondervan, 1985).

[13] See Jack P. Lewis, "Published Works" in *As I Remember It*, 243-269, for a list of published works through 2012.

[14] Jack P. Lewis, "The Ministry of Study," in *Leadership Questions Confronting the Church* (Nashville: Gospel Advocate, 1985), 101-106. The article originally appeared in *The Campus Journal* 12 (Spring 1972): 6-8. The rabbinic quotation is from T. B. Berakoth 60:3.

graduate who took the tougher courses at HST, even if doing so meant a lower GPA. Since fall 2001, HST has granted three full-tuition endowed scholarships to "Lewis Scholars" who exemplify Lewis's high academic achievement and commitment to ministry.

HST pioneered many *firsts* in the history of theological education in Churches of Christ. Three in particular stand out. In 1958, HST was the first school in Churches of Christ to offer a three-year graduate degree, the MTh or MDiv. In 1977, HST was the first to offer the Doctor of Ministry degree, a professional doctorate degree. And in 1997, HST was the first to be accredited by the Association of Theological Schools (ATS).

The one significant goal that HST in Memphis did not accomplish was starting a PhD in Biblical Studies that would match the academic standards of the other degree programs. Twice David Burks, President of Harding University, announced that HST would begin a PhD program. The first time was in 1992 after HST survived the first major attempt to relocate the school to Searcy. The Board voted to continue the program in Memphis and add a PhD program by fall 1993. Instability in the Dean's office—HST had three deans overs a three-year period—and the mansion fire in July 1993, put these plans on hold.[15] The mansion did not open again until January 1995, and the school had to raise $175,000—with insurance covering most of the $1.4 million for repairs. The second attempt was in 2006, when Burks and the Board again approved the development of the PhD degree. $2.5 million was needed to endow the program for two additional faculty members, scholarship funds, and the enrichment of the library collection. A looming recession and declining enrollment thwarted this second attempt.

---

[15] Edward Myers was appointed by David Burks in June 1992 and resigned for health reasons in February 1993. See "Myers Named New Executive Director/Dean," *Harding University Graduate School of Religion Bulletin* 33, no. 4 (July 1992), 1. "Myers Resigns as Executive Director/Dean in February," *Harding University Graduate School of Religion Bulletin* 34, no. 2 (March 1993): 2. Myers was preceded by Philip Slate and succeeded by Bill Flatt.

Annie May Alston Lewis (1917-2006)

The L. M. Graves Memorial Library at HST is affectionately called "the house that Annie May built." Annie May Lewis is the chief architect of the collection, along with Don Meredith who worked at the library for 49 years. Annie May's connection to the library goes back to the very beginning, when she was the head librarian on the Searcy campus. One day, a graduate Bible faculty member was tasked by W. B. West to choose a beginning collection of 3000 books for the program in Memphis. Annie May, always a fearless advocate for the library, learned what he was doing and told him to go back to his office—which he did! That professor was Jack Lewis, and the two of them married 20 years later on Thanksgiving Day 1978, three days shy of her 61st birthday.[16]

In 1962, Annie May accepted West's invitation to be the librarian for HST. She already had an MA from the University of Chicago (1952) and later earned an MA from HST (1967). She was the first theological librarian in Churches of Christ and the first from Churches of Christ to join the American Theological Librarian Association. Annie May developed a course in the 1960s to teach students writing and research skills, and today Advanced Theological Research is one of the few such required courses offered by seminaries.[17] She was the only person to receive the HST Alumnus/Alumna of the Year award twice (1993, 2006), and she impacted the lives of countless people. Harold Hazelip—the second Dean of HST, President of Lipscomb University, and the one for whom Lipscomb's Hazelip School of Theology is named—said this about Annie May: "She changed the direction of my life. I came [to Memphis] to preach and teach; that's all I ever intended to do. When Dr. West retired, I became Annie May's candidate for dean. I owe the administrative experience in my life, both at Lipscomb and at Harding, to Annie May."[18] Jack and Annie May Lewis lived a frugal yet generous life, and when they passed they left a considerable endowment that continues to support the library.

---

[16] Don Meredith, "A Legacy of Holiness," *The Bridge* 47, no. 2 (Summer 2006): 1.
[17] Ibid.
[18] "Annie May Lewis Named Alumna of the Year," *The Bridge* 46, no. 2 (Summer 2006): 7.

Today, HST's Graves Memorial Library is the largest theological library in Churches of Christ and the largest theological library in the Mid-South. The initial 3000 volumes from the Searcy collection has grown to over 171,000 volumes including e-books. The number of catalogued items in HST's library is 84% the size of the Brackett Library collection, which supports all of Harding's programs in Searcy. Further, because of several large endowments, the book-buying budget for HST's library is over twice that of the Brackett Library, although the Brackett has a much larger budget for database and journal access. One of the reasons the graduate program moved to Memphis was so HST students could access other libraries. Today, faculty and students from the University of Memphis, Rhodes College, Christian Brothers University, Memphis Theological Seminary, and other institutions, as well as leaders from a variety of faith traditions, are regularly seen in HST's library and make use of the collection. It will take an estimated 22 tractor-trailer loads to move the HST library collection to Searcy.

Jane Tomlinson (1928-2019)

The story of HST cannot be told without acknowledging the staff, who have fostered a culture of professional excellence, humble service, and care for students. Harold Hazelip observed, "[HST] is more than buildings and books; it is people. This School places high priority on the personal. Faculty, staff and students form a real community. They move among each other teaching, bearing burdens, sharing joys and experiencing the benefits of being joint-heirs of the grace of God."[19] When I came to HST as a faculty member in 2002, the friendliness and helpfulness of the staff was striking. At first, I thought they treated me so well because I was a faculty member, but I soon learned that this high level of care and service is extended to students, community members, and to everyone who needs the assistance of the HST staff.

Jane Tomlinson, who exemplifies the traits that have characterized the staff, started at HST in 1959 and served for a total of

---

[19] Harold Hazelip, "Building on a Heritage," *Harding of Memphis Graduate School Bulletin* 12, no. 12 (March 1974): 1.

40 years. She worked five years in the business office and bookstore, five years in the registrar's office, 15 years as faculty secretary, and 15 years as administrative assistant to five deans.[20] She brought excellence to her work, and even became proficient in proofreading guided research papers, theses, and dissertations. Her knowledge of the English language and Turabian's *Manual* was such that she helped Don Meredith write, and update, the HST Supplement to Turabian. She continued to work part-time on fundraising projects for two years after her retirement. The reason she excelled at fundraising is because she loved HST and she loved the school's graduates—she got to know the students, their families, and their ministries.[21] The HST staff have made a noteworthy contribution to the culture of the school and the experience of faculty and students.

What do W. B., Jack, Annie May, and Jane have in common? A deep faith in God, the pursuit of excellence, humility, love for the church, and care for all people. The desire has always been that these same traits would be passed on to HST's alumni. These four are exceptional figures, but they are also representative of the impressive list of HST administrators, faculty, librarians, and staff through the years, many of whom have made their own significant achievements and received their own richly-deserved accolades.

Since 1958, HST has trained over 1800 graduates who currently serve in 47 states, 20 other countries, and every continent except Antarctica. HST has a national and global reach; the fall 2023 student body comes from 20 states and 16 other countries. HST graduates have served as university presidents, preachers, missionaries, academic administrators, professors, counselors, youth ministers, campus ministers, chaplains, and more. A large percentage of influential ministers, academic thought-leaders, and innovative practitioners in Churches of Christ trace their roots back to HST.

One of these alumni is David Decker, a 1983 MAR graduate who

---

[20] Jane Tomlinson did not work at HST for a five-year period (1973-1978) because her family moved from Memphis.

[21] Allen Black, "Reflections from the Dean: A Tribute to Jane Tomlinson," in *The Bridge* 60, no. 2 (Winter 2020): 3.

later preached at the Fairview Church of Christ in Stockbridge, Georgia, southeast of Atlanta. When I was in middle and high school, David baptized me, mentored me, and encouraged me to go into ministry. I remember his HST diploma being displayed on the wall of his office, and him speaking highly of the school and that accomplishment. Little did we know then that one day I would serve at HST for 22 years as a faculty member and dean. Since that time, I have been blessed to know, and be impacted by, countless HST alumni. In my mind, though, David represents the selfless service of HST's 1800-plus graduates and the impact they have had on the lives of others.

One more comment on HST's early years deserves attention and reflection. Recently, George Benson's defense of racial segregation has been highlighted and rightly criticized. Benson's support of segregation occurred during the same time the graduate program in Religion was beginning in Memphis. James D. Bales, a popular professor and Benson's chief apologist for defending segregation, taught in the graduate program in Searcy from the beginning and continued part-time when HST moved to Memphis.[22] Jack Lewis, though, regularly claimed that HST was integrated from the start. He states, "From the first we have been open to all races, to both sexes, and to all creeds."[23]

The actual situation was more complex than Lewis suggests. In his autobiography, Lewis tells of teaching an extension course in Little Rock before the integration of Central High School in 1957, and he was instructed to ask if the rest of the class would object to the admission of an African American preacher. Even after the school moved to Memphis in 1958, it was still four years until the first four

---

[22] See Barclay Key, *Race and Restoration: Churches of Christ and the Black Struggle for Freedom* (Baton Rouge: Louisiana State University Press, 2020), 69-102 (especially 82-90). Bobby Ross, Jr., "After George Floyd's death, petition to rename Harding auditorium gains support," *Christian Chronicle*, June 5, 2020, https://christianchronicle.org/after-floyds-death-petition-to-rename-harding-auditorium-gains-support/. Audrey Jackson, "'I thank the God of our weary years,'" *Christian Chronicle*, November 16, 2021, https://christianchronicle.org/i-thank-the-god-of-our-weary-years/.

[23] Jack P. Lewis, "The Graduate School As I Remember It," *Harding Graduate School of Religion Bulletin* 19, no. 2 (February 1979): 3. See also Lewis, *As I Remember It*, 196.

African American students were admitted in 1962, one year before the University integrated. One of these four students, Nokomis Yeldell, was a prominent minister at the Norris Road Church of Christ in Memphis.[24] It was nine years after the school moved to Memphis, in 1968, before Bennie Green completed the MA degree and became HST's first African American graduate. The desire of Lewis and other faculty members for integration, and the role HST played in integrating Harding, should be acknowledged, but a more nuanced and somber picture emerges when the experience of African American students and the resistance of the cultural context is considered.[25]

Although the majority of HST's students have been men, women have been instructors and students from the start. Velma R. West taught Greek from 1958-1973, and in 1975 the Greek award was named in her honor. In the second graduating class of 1960, Nancy Shelburne Codner and Mirian Lee Mieher both completed the MA degree and became the school's first female graduates. In that same year, Yung Jin Lee from South Korea completed the MA degree and became HST's first international graduate.

Deeper Faith, Higher Standards

In July 2011 Evertt Huffard, HST's sixth dean, led a process to rename the school from Harding University Graduate School of Religion to Harding School of Theology. With the new name came an updated mission statement and a new logo. This process involved the Memphis-based consulting firm Tactical Magic and included the input of numerous stakeholders, so the results provide insight into the culture of HST during its final 12 years in Memphis.[26]

The old name, Harding University Graduate School of Religion, was too long and did not clearly communicate that HST is a Christian school training Christian leaders. In the broader academic world, the term *religion* is typically reserved for the academic study of religion

---

[24] Lewis, *As I Remember It*, 196.

[25] I am thankful to Ed Robinson for sharing his experience as an HST student in chapter 12.

[26] See Mark Parker, "Harding School of Theology" and Evertt W. Huffard, "More About God," *The Bridge* 52, no. 1 (Summer 2011): 1, 2.

broadly-conceived, including the use of different methodologies for the study of world religions. The term *theology* is used for the study of a particular religion, and often within the context of a faith commitment. HST emphasizes the study of the Christian faith and exists to train Christian leaders, so *theology* is the better term.

HST's early leaders likely avoided the term *theology* because it carried negative connotations in Churches of Christ, alluding to human traditions rather than authentic Christian beliefs grounded in God's word (see Mark 7:6-13). By the time I joined the faculty in 2002, however, the term *theology* had become more acceptable. Huffard also liked to note that *theology* emphasizes God (from the Greek *theos*). For the alma mater, the first line of the chorus was changed from "O Harding Graduate School" to "O God you are our God."[27]

The mission statement now reads, "HST challenges Christian leaders to develop deeper faith in God and higher standards of ministry and scholarship." Nearly every word of this new statement is significant. HST *challenges* Christian leaders because we want our students to pursue excellence in everything they do—God deserves nothing less. Further, God can use challenges to develop character and maturity in our students (see James 1:2-4). *Deeper* faith and *higher* standards are a reminder that we never arrive. HST wants students to continue to go deeper with God and grow as Christian leaders, even after graduation. The terms *faith*, *ministry*, and *scholarship*, and the order of the terms, are significant. It would be a tragedy if students grew in ministry skills and academic ability, but relied on themselves rather than God or digressed in faith. *Ministry* appears next because HST exists, not for the academy *per se*, but to train leaders for the church. God has called HST's faculty, staff, and students to different forms of ministry, but we see all of our work as being in service to the church and for the sake of the world. *Scholarship* is the final word, but HST has always been committed to, and associated with, high academic standards as a graduate school of Harding University. The tagline "Deeper Faith, Higher Standards," which is used on the website

---

[27] The alma mater is included in the appendices of this book.

and in promotional materials, comes from the mission statement. The mission statement is updated, but also it is in keeping with the founders' original desire to train students "on an advanced academic level" and "for maximum Christian service."

The new logo uses the letters H, S, and T to form both three crosses and a torch. The letters H and T are stylized as columns, evoking stability and academic rigor. The letter S is stylized as a flame, alluding to the Spirit.[28]

HST in Memphis is still the largest theological school associated with Churches of Christ east of the Mississippi River, and second to Abilene Christian University overall. Still, our enrollment has declined by one-half since I arrived, from 225 total students in fall 2002 to 112 students in fall 2023. The rise of distance education, especially in graduate programs, brings additional financial challenges for schools like HST. Distance students are typically part-time students, so they take less credit hours; plus, distance students do not require campus housing. Therefore, HST has a smaller student body, taking less classes, with less students living on-campus. HST has done well financially thanks to the generosity of our donors and income from our endowments, but deferred maintenance, unused space on the Memphis campus, and available space on the Searcy campus makes it hard for a school like Harding University to invest in Memphis. Further, a sizable group has wanted to move HST back to Searcy for at least the last 35 years.

On Friday, August 4, 2023 the Harding Board approved the recommendation of President Mike Williams to move HST to the main campus in Searcy starting in fall 2024. Williams also announced a new tuition model where students will pay only $100 per credit hour, and a new organizational structure that places HST under the College of Bible and Ministry and the theological library under the Brackett Library.

At the time of the decision, fourteen employees served at HST: Administrators include Dr. Jim Martin (Vice President, served 10

---

[28] The HST seal, which includes the logo, is in the appendices of this book. Unfortunately, the logo will be retired when HST moves to Searcy and adopts the University's branding.

years), Dr. Mark Powell (Dean and Professor, 22 years), and Dr. Steve McLeod (Associate Dean, 30 years); faculty include Dr. Steve Cloer (Assistant Professor and DMin Director, 3 years), Dr. Lance Hawley (Associate Professor, 8 years), and Dr. Richard Oster (Professor, 46 years); librarians include Jessica Holland (Library Director, 3 years) and Sheila Owen (Associate Librarian, 24 years); and staff include Jeannie Alexander (Assistant to the VP, 21 years), Susie Buford (Assistant for Admissions and Advancement, 3 years), Brenda Curtis (Assistant to the Dean, 22 years), Greg Muse (Director of Advancement, 6 years), Tina Rogers (Library Assistant, 8 years), and Cecil Tomlinson (Maintenance, 27 years).

The most famous story from HST in Memphis dates back to July 29, 1993, when the mansion caught on fire in the middle of the night. Jack and Annie May Lewis got out of bed, drove to campus, and stood in front of the mansion as the top floor was engulfed in flames. Dr. Lewis lamented, "My life's work is in that building." But Annie May corrected him: "Your life's work is in the students, it's not in the building."[29] As HST transitions from Memphis to Searcy, we too need to be reminded that the school's mission is not about buildings and a physical location, but the training of Christian leaders and the proclamation of the gospel. May God continue to work in and through HST in Searcy, just as he's so clearly done in Memphis for the last 66 years.

> Now to him who is able to do immeasurably more than all we ask or imagine, according to his power that is at work within us, to him be glory in the church and in Christ Jesus throughout all generations, for ever and ever! Amen. (Ephesians 3:20-21, NIV)

---

[29] There are different renditions of Annie May's response, but I went with how Jack "remembered it" since he was there. Lewis, *As I Remember It*, 203-04.

CHAPTER TWO

Biblical Studies: Old Testament

Nathan Bills

It was near the end of a required senior course at Harding University entitled Advanced Introduction to the Old Testament.[1] The professor challenged my entire class of Bible majors to jointly produce a detailed timeline of OT events, dates, and people. His charge was surprising but not out of place because he had spent the better part of the semester teaching the content to us. He allotted to us fifteen minutes, instructed us to record it on the white board, and exited the room. One of our classmates seized the marker and hurriedly began to jot out a sequence while the rest of the class shouted facts and figures to be included. When our teacher returned, he slowly and sequentially studied our hastily compiled but nonetheless extensive timeline, occasionally registering his satisfaction with our offering. That is, until he reached the end. He yelped and threw his hands over his head in jesting exasperation. Our class had concluded the timeline with the entry "A.D. 33" above which we cheekily scrawled "OT is nailed to the cross."

Of course, my class's teasing postscript went against the grain of all that we had been learning. But the anecdote illustrates the (somewhat) peculiar challenge of reflecting on the study of the OT at Harding School of Theology. To put it bluntly—and to paint admittedly with a broad brush—the tradition of the Churches of Christ has functionally neglected if not outrightly spurned the OT as a serious theological resource.[2] As one preacher counseled me after I

---

[1] For simplicity I abbreviate wherever I can Old Testament as OT and New Testament as NT.
[2] Alexander Campbell's 1816 "Sermon on the Law" launched the perspective that would crystalize later into the tradition's distinctive disregard of the OT. Campbell reprinted the sermon in *The Millennial Harbinger* 3.3 (Sept 1846): 493-521. It is available

expressed my growing enchantment with the OT in my undergraduate classes: "Sure, but isn't the New Testament where the real action is?" After all, as he had been taught and had taught the church, the shadowy OT was a providential victim of Jesus's sacrifice that ushered NT Christians into a better covenant. Our Scripture usage was telling: we needed the stage setting of Genesis 1—3; we took comfort in the pastoral palliatives of (select) Psalms and took inspiration from the wise aphorisms of Proverbs; a collection of the grander stories provided fodder for VBS skits. But aside from these selections, we approached the OT as, well, *old* ... passé, archival, superseded. Maybe we were never so explicit. We would not deny its divine inspiration. But in my experience the OT was (and still is) effectively treated as a battle-scarred veteran long discharged of duty in a march toward NT Christianity.

The Churches of Christ are by no means alone in ignoring the

---

online at https://webfiles.acu.edu/departments/Library/HR/ restmov_nov11/ www.mun.ca/rels/restmov/texts/acampbell/mh1846/SOTL.HTM. Leroy Garrett, "Campbell, Alexander (1788-1866)," in *The Encyclopedia of the Stone-Campbell Movement*, edited by Douglas Foster, et al. (Grand Rapids, MI: Eerdmans, 2004), 120, records that "[s]ome historians have named this occasion the beginning of the Movement, and Campbell himself said thirty years later that had it not been for that sermon and the opposition it generated he might never have launched his reformation."

In the sermon Campbell asserted the superiority of the NT to guide and unite Christian believers in opposition to those who, assenting to the creeds of classic Reformed theology, accepted an authoritative role of the OT for the NT believer. Campbell's logic rested most significantly on making a sharp break between the dispensations of the Mosaic and new covenants. His hermeneutical severing of the ages meant for Campbell that the restoration of the ancient order of things began with the Acts of the Apostles and not Abraham. And unfortunately, his advocacy of a sharp break *between covenants* metamorphosed into a presumption of a sharp break *between testaments* in the movement's succeeding generations.

Campbell's sermon by itself, however, must not be given an oversized influence. Rather, as Everett Ferguson, "Alexander Campbell's 'Sermon on the Law': A Historical and Theological Examination," *ResQ* 29 (1987): 83, notes, the sermon was an early but paradigmatic expression of what became Campbell's weighty legacy of interpretation. For more analysis of the Campbell's sermon and the movement's relationship to the OT, see in addition to Ferguson's piece Ronald E. Heine, "Alexander Campbell and the OT," *S-CJ* 5 (2002):163-81; and Gary Hall, "A Critique of the Place of the Old Testament in the Early Historical Perspective of the Stone-Campbell Movement: Campbell through Lipscomb," *S-CJ* 5 (2002): 25-47.

OT. Whether it is indifferent disregard or a more aggressive "unhitching" of the Old from the New, the heretical ghost of Marcion haunts many churches' pulpits and classrooms.[3] In a recent book OT scholar Brent Strawn scours hard data from the U.S. Religious Knowledge Survey, hymns, sermons, and lectionary selections to determine the vitality of the OT in North American congregations.[4] He delivers a sobering diagnosis in the book's title: *The Old Testament is Dying*. He makes the penetrating point, especially apropos for Campbellites who have historically prided ourselves on Bible knowledge, that it is not just *if* the OT is present in preaching or teaching but *how* it is present.[5] Strawn shows that the task to revive, or in good Restorationist speak, *restore* the OT as a vital, constructive asset for Christian thinking and living is at present as daunting as it is necessary. But restore we must if we want to "do justice, love mercy, and walk humbly" with what amounts to 75% of our Holy Scriptures. We may be a new-*covenant* people, but we have been gifted a two-*testament* canon.

In what follows I assume the import of the study of the OT as a key focus in theological education.[6] My task here is to reflect, albeit briefly, on the engagement of the OT at HST. I will review a handful of strengths, note a couple of potential problems, and then offer a few humble suggestions on *how* the OT should be present at HST as the

---

[3] I use "unhitching" as a reference to the popular evangelical pastor Andy Stanley's lamentable counsel for the church to disregard the "worldview, value system, and regulations of the Jewish scriptures" (Michale Gryboski, "Christians Must 'Unhitch' Old Testament from their Faith, says Andy Stanley," May 9, 2018, https://www.christianpost.com/news/christians-must-unhitch-old-testament-from-their-faith-says-andy-stanley-223818/). Marcion of Sinope was a second-century theologian excommunicated by the church for his rejection of the OT and parts of the NT he deemed incompatible with the gospel of Jesus Christ.

[4] Brent A. Strawn, *The Old Testament is Dying: A Diagnosis and Recommended Treatment* (Grand Rapids, MI: Baker Academic, 2017). He recognizes that he speaks within the North American context (4).

[5] Ibid., 6, 215, 293.

[6] Others have done defended this ably: in addition to Strawn, see inter alia Ellen F. Davis, "Losing a Friend: The Loss of the Old Testament to the Church," *ProEccl* 9.1 (2000): 73-84; John Goldingay, *Do We Need the New Testament: Letting the Old Testament Speak For Itself* (Downers Grove, IL: IVP Academic, 2015); Katharine J. Dell, *Who Needs the Old Testament* (Eugene, OR: Wipf and Stock, 2017).

institution transitions into its next chapter.[7] In so doing I hope to honor my alma mater's legacy that has left its imprint on me and so many others for good.

Reviewing Strengths

The old joke that seminary is more like a cemetery has more than a hint of truth. The historical-critical methodology that has dominated academic study has not, on balance, contributed positively to a robust engagement of Scripture, let alone the Old Testament, in and for the church. It is, therefore, significant that HST's full-time faculty in Old Testament—Jack Lewis, John Scott, Paul Rotenbury, Jack Vancil, Phillip McMillion, and Lance Hawley—have all been committed, contributing members of local churches.[8] Their ecclesial fidelity has helped to form a context for students to learn how to interpret Scripture and faithfully wrestle with (what can be) some disorienting and deconstructing truths. A strength of HST continues to be virtuous instructors who can engage serious historical-critical scholarship on Scripture with empathetic hearts shaped by God's church and mission. In my experience, graduate training at HST was never study for study's sake alone; rather, HST has insisted upon a "ministry of study" that aims for scholarship in service to the church.[9]

The ecclesial commitment of faculty, however, has not meant that high academic standards were relaxed. *Quality* academic work has always been an expectation at HST. But quality academics takes *work*.

---

[7] In preparation of writing this article I solicited feedback from several HST associates who went on from HST to work on higher degrees in Old Testament. I want to thank Harold Shank, John Fortner, Lance Hawley, Clay Smith, Paavo Tucker, and Ryan Replogle for their replies which spurred my own thoughts.

[8] Current OT professor Lance Hawley's former career as a church planter in Madison, WI, well illustrates the point. I do not assume I have a complete list of regular adjuncts, but the same ecclesial commitment goes for those that I can list: Harold Shank, John Fortner, Kevin Youngblood, and Daniel Oden.

[9] See Jack P. Lewis, "The Ministry of Study," in *Leadership Questions Confronting the Church* (Nashville: Christian Communications, 1985), 101-06. Lewis's article is firstly concerned to defend "study" as a legitimate ministry in its own right. I would hasten to add that the commitment to the church did not translate into interpretation that towed doctrinal lines. In my experience HST's OT program did well to expose students to critical perspectives without an apologetic overlay.

One of my class colleagues once asked Dr. Lewis how to perform better in his graduate coursework. "Find a chair in the library," he replied wryly, "and apply the seat of your pants to it for long stretches of time." The advice was not the learning "hack" for which the student was hoping. Rather, the reply bespoke an assumption about the serious, exacting task of scholarship that I remember discerning when I first looked into HST. The prime contributor in this regard, apart from the faculty's demanding expectations, has been the library and its staff. The required and terribly useful course Advanced Theological Research ensured that all students near the beginning of their program not only engaged the library's wealth of resources but were oriented to an earnest disposition of rigorous study and research. The library in conjunction with the campus and classroom exuded an aura of focused reflection that catalyzed the vocation of scholarly inquiry on Scripture and otherwise.[10]

The strengths noted above apply generally across board at HST. Specific to OT studies HST has been appreciated, especially in the first half of its existence, for its strength in the exegesis of the text, historical backgrounds of the text, and translation of the text—likely unsurprising to anyone who is aware of the towering influence of Dr. Jack Lewis. Drs. Phil McMillion and Lance Hawley have deepened the legacy centered on interpretation of the text with added nuance of their own specialties. In recent decades I can personally attest that a boon to the study of the OT at HST has been, paradoxically, the contributions of the NT and theology faculty. In numerous classes professors Rick Oster and Allen Black raised students' awareness of the

---

[10] In this way HST had a spirit different from sister seminaries that were part of a larger, undergraduate campus. On occasion I heard others criticize HST for feeling like a monastery, but I did not think such a description was derisive. Anyone who knows a bit of Christian history cannot deny the significance of quiet abbeys for the gains made by church and Christian scholarship. But to characterize HST as monastic can ignore the fact that it was located in the midst of a metropolis. One of the great benefits of schooling on location at HST for me was the synergistic opportunities to study and minister *in the city*. My weekly "ping-ponging" between a church plant in a poor community (as part of an apprenticeship with Memphis Urban Ministry) and reflective study at HST's campus shaped my educational journey profoundly for the better. I cannot help but mourn the loss of this dynamic as the school moves to Searcy.

continuity between the testaments. Dr. Oster's injunction "to read the Bible forwards and not just backwards" prodded students to approach the Scriptures looking for exegetical and narrative integrity flowing from the OT into the NT. This is a posture that has been downplayed in the Restorationist tradition. In a similar vein, Dr. John Mark Hick's Theological Hermeneutics helped connect the dots for understanding the tradition's historical neglect of the Old Testament. His class also helpfully sketched possible avenues for its recovery. Thus, the faculty's collective handling of Old Testament texts—both inside and outside the field—encouraged students toward a two-testament, theocentric interpretation of Scripture.

Considering Impediments

Notwithstanding the strengths noted above, study of the OT at HST has not been immune from the aforementioned struggle to engage the "Elder" Testament as a full canonical partner to the NT.[11] At HST the knowledge of text and historical backgrounds has received the accent. But this has not always been accompanied by a corresponding diligence in grappling with the text's integration into life and ministry. I suggest two realities—one empirical and one hermeneutical—have contributed to this deficit. On the empirical hand, the sweep of study in many Old Testament courses is wide. Curricular objectives that focus on "coverage of content" in Old Testament courses —as laudable, even necessary, as that goal is—too easily marginalize space devoted to refiguring the content's contemporary, theological relevance.[12] On the hermeneutical hand, the challenge of situating the

---

[11] The designation "Old Testament" has been challenged in recent decades, especially in light of renewed Jewish-Christian dialogue. Christopher Seitz, *The Elder Testament: Canon, Theology, Trinity* (Waco, TX: Baylor University Press, 2015), advocates the name "Elder" Testament as a way to signal the literature's venerable, connected status vis á vis the New Testament that avoids disparaging connotations of "Old."

[12] Consider the difference in terms of possible coverage in a survey class on the OT (75% of the Bible) versus a class on the NT (25%), or a class on "Wisdom Literature" versus "Galatians and Romans." Of course, all professors are selective in their teaching whatever the subject. My point is that an OT class, especially one that sees coverage of content and "Bible knowledge" as the chief objective, can much more readily adopt a strategy that gives short shrift to theological appropriation.

OT's discrete voice vis à vis the NT finds little recourse in the traditional Restorationist interpretation. The movement's stark break between the old and new covenants/testaments has left its hermeneutical heirs poorly equipped to receive the OT as an indispensable gift for theological and ethical reflection. Those formed in this tradition often must first dismantle faulty, or at the very least inadequate, categories of thought about the OT before working to construct a more appropriate hermeneutic. These two realities pose barriers that must be navigated wisely if OT studies is to flourish in HST's future educational formation.

Going Forward

As HST enters a new chapter, Karl Barth's oft-repeated parting counsel to his students before his exile from Nazi Germany in 1935 is apropos: "And now the end has come. So listen to my piece of advice: exegesis, exegesis, and yet more exegesis! Keep to the Word, to the scripture that has been given to us."[13] Amen. Let the OT dwell richly at the heart of the HST experience, and not just in the textual division but also as a genuine dialogue partner in courses on history, homiletics, systematics, ministry, spiritual formation, and more. With regard to coursework specific to the OT, let HST continue to train students to grasp the OT *on its own contextual terms*, deploying as best it can historical and literary tools for a close reading of the text. Critical exegesis promotes a necessary awareness of the OT's diachronic depth and synchronic sophistication. I wish to recall, however, Strawn's shrewd observation that it is important to consider how—not just if—the OT is present in the endeavor of exegesis. And here HST would do well to find avenues to implement Ellen Davis's eloquent counsel on the exegete's disposition in "critical" reading.[14] Davis entreats interpreters to cultivate a friendship of intimacy with the OT. Friendship first entails a willingness to submit ourselves to the OT's own strange world, to listen with sincere generosity to its multivocal—at times tensive—testimony of Israel's

---

[13] Eberhard Busch, *Karl Barth: His Life from Letters and Autobiographical Texts* (Philadelphia: Fortress Press, 1976), 259.

[14] Cf. Davis, "Losing a Friend." Davis is addressing preachers, but I find her recommendation to apply no less to those doing scholarship for the church.

intimacy with its God. Furthermore, friendship suggests readers come ready to be changed (repent) in the course of reading and wrangling with the text. Finally, intimate friendship with the OT requires the patient work of attending to the register of its language. Davis means by this not only the linguistics of the Hebrew but the text's characteristic, poetic propensity to provoke imaginative construal and conversation. Developing these (spiritual) dispositions toward the OT will move readers toward a constructive "how" of exegesis that bends toward faithfully performing the world imagined by the text.

The critical interpretative task must attend well to the context of the OT, but it should not conclude there. The OT is given to be useful; it is God-breathed to make us "wise for salvation through faith in Christ Jesus." The pivotal concern on how one transitions from exegesis to living practice, especially with regard to the OT and the attendant issue of its canonical relationship with the NT, merits a much more involved discussion.[15] Along these lines I note that the recent rise of interest in the academy in the theological interpretation of Scripture is a propitious development.[16] As a part of this interpretative movement, OT scholars are freshly probing what it means to read Israel's Scriptures as *Christian* Scripture in full view of, but beyond a historical-critical approach.[17] These readings take seriously the Bible as an authoritative and unified canonical witness for the church. It does so without

---

[15] Indeed, it merits more than one discussion. During my time at HST I encountered this question in the course Theological Hermeneutics. This was the only course on offer on hermeneutics, and I never understood why this course was not required. Nonetheless, the relationship of the OT to the NT was somewhat tangential to the main thrust of that course (perhaps the issue received attention in Advanced Introduction to the OT but I did not have this class at HST). All in all, I would recommend HST pursue within the already required coursework additional means to deepen students' hermeneutical toolset and to broaden students' ability to "apply" OT texts.

[16] For a recent historical overview of the trend of theological interpretation in the academy, see the comments and cited literature in Daniel J. Treier, "From Adolescence to Early Adulthood: The Maturation of Theological Interpretation in the Work of R. W. L. Moberly and Darren Sarisky," *JTI* 17 (2023): 23-41.

[17] For background and suggestive descriptions of theological interpretation with regard to the OT, see R. W. L. Moberly, "Theological Interpretation, Second Naiveté, and the Rediscovery of the Old Testament," *ATR* 99 (2021): 651-55.

denying a place at the hermeneutical table to traditional criticisms while also welcoming groups historically marginalized by critical scholarship, especially Jewish and pre-modern interpreters. OT studies at HST would do well to help students think along with the categories and concerns highlighted by this stream of interpretation. Listening to and learning from its OT interlocuters can lead to a richer embodiment, more faithful and fitting both to the text and to the larger theological witness to God's work in Christ in the contemporary world.

No doubt there are many other methodological perspectives that can supplement, hone, and/or challenge the critical interpretation of the OT.[18] I have singled out the theological interpretation of Scripture because I think this academic current can propel OT studies at HST in ways that build on the school's interests and further develop much-needed competencies of its constituency.[19] A much broader arena within biblical studies that deserves more deliberate consideration at HST is global interpretation. It is no secret that the twentieth century saw a dramatic shift of Christian population from North to South. In 2024 Christians in Africa, Asia, and Latin America outnumber by more than two-to-one those in Europe, Russia, and Northern America (1.795 billion versus 836 million).[20] This reality has been progressively manifesting itself in the biblical academy through the blossoming of

---

[18] See the nice presentation of various exegetical methods in Michael J. Gorman, *Elements of Biblical Exegesis: A Basic Guide for Students and Ministers*, 3rd ed. (Grand Rapids, MI: Baker Academic, 2020), 259-66.

[19] In a similar vein, the trend of "missional hermeneutics" also offers a complementary track to the study of the OT at HST insofar as this trend incorporates the interpretation of the whole Bible as a grand narrative of God's redemptive mission. In fact, the intersection of a "missional hermeneutic" with the concerns of the theological interpretation of Scripture with specific regard to the critical interpretation of the Old Testament as *Christian* scripture is an arena ripe for contribution (a place to begin would be with the work of HST alumnus Greg McKinzie, "Missional Hermeneutics as Theological Interpretation," *JTI* 11 (2017): 157-79.)

[20] These numbers come from the Center for the Study of Global Christianity available at https://www.gordonconwell.edu/center-for-global-christianity/resources/status-of-global-christianity/. If current trends hold the population of Christians in the Global South will be more than triple those in the Global North by 2050!

theological hermeneutics from various cultures and subcultures.[21] Taken as a whole, these readings provide a much-needed corrective to, inter alia, modernism's presumed neutrality of the exegete, illustrating how the situatedness of the biblical interpreter always tilts interpretation and—perhaps more importantly—contextualization.[22] Furthermore, they are (broadly) characterized by an overriding concern to connect the Bible to the ordinary believers' local context. In many cases these interpretative contexts have a much closer kinship with the worldview and practice of Scripture than their Western counterparts. This kinship, especially with the world of the OT, means that these voices are strategically equipped to generate insight on a whole host of biblical texts and concepts (for example, creation, sin, family, blessing, marriage, priesthood, ecology, migration, poverty) that are far more removed in "enlightened" Western frameworks.[23] To state the obvious, then, HST

---

[21] Indeed, although it will not be as rapid a change, it is only a matter of time before the demographics of academic biblical studies corresponds to the demography of World Christianity. For a recent survey of global hermeneutics, see Michael J. Gorman, ed. *Scripture and Its Interpretation: A Global, Ecumenical Introduction to the Bible* (Grand Rapids, MI: Baker Academic, 2017).

[22] Postmodern approaches have successfully challenged the hegemony of historical critical methodologies even as they have opened up space for an array of other hermeneutical viewpoints, global voices among them. However, aside from providing different interpretative contexts, a significant difference between postmodern approaches and global interpretations is that the latter approach the text (in general) from postures of trust more so than the former. Hence, I suggest it is in the area of contextualization of the OT that global voices have greater gifts to give. See further Jerry Hwang, *Contextualization and the Old Testament* (Carlisle, UK: Langham, 2022).

[23] For example, my institution in Accra, Ghana, Heritage Christian University College, hosted a public lecture last year entitled "Witchcraft and the Christian Witness." It is a pressing topic addressed by the OT in multiple places, but it is not a topic I remember covering in any of my OT classes! It was serendipitous that shortly after composing this essay I finished reading the late Dr. Andrew F. Walls (doyen of World Christianity) posthumously published *The Missionary Movement from the West: A Biography from Birth to Old Age*, ed. Brian Stanley, Studies in the History of Christian Mission (Grand Rapids: Eerdmans, 2023), who is worth quoting at length on this point: "The trouble is that Enlightenment theology, conservative just as much as liberal, is theology for a small-scale universe, and most people in most of the world live in a larger, more populated universe than the Enlightenment allows for, with a permanently open frontier between the empirical world and the world of spirit, constantly being crossed in either direction. In other words, Western theology, Enlightenment theology,

professors and students stand to benefit in all sorts of ways by becoming more conversant with a diversity of global voices, especially as it pertains to OT interpretation and embodiment.

Finally, one urgent contribution that OT studies at HST can make in the coming years is to facilitate the creation of resources for Christians to engage the OT in more judicious ways.[24] A reason for the practical neglect of the OT in churches is the lack of high-quality material prepared appealingly for the pew. I am not in the first instance suggesting more books or commentaries written on a popular level. Rather, I think faculty and students could work to produce studies enlisting OT themes and texts that are packaged in even more digestible formats—videos, devotionals, children books, material for church or small group curriculum of all ages, and other popular online media. What if every OT class included one assignment or project that requires students to craft some aspect of their learning into a medium palatable for congregations or individuals? I want especially to recommend that HST harness the creativity of students to innovate around spaces of interchange outside of Sunday morning gatherings—where and when people walk, sit, lie down, and rise up (Deut 6:7).[25]

---

is too small for Africa and Asia. It has nothing to say on witchcraft or sorcery: in an Enlightenment universe, witchcraft and sorcery do not exist. It has nothing useful to say about ancestors, for in an Enlightenment universe, we do not have ancestors other than in a historical sense. In so many areas, Western theology, coming out of its little universe, is disabled, lame, limping in the face of the problems of those who live in a larger universe. It has no answers, because it has no questions" (362). His final chapter entitled "The Theological Challenge of World Christianity: New Questions and New Possibilities" is as winsome as it is wise on the opportunities global voices bring to the table.

[24] Strawn, *The Old Testament is Dying*, proposes a number of ways to recover or reintroduce the OT in churches. Unfortunately, nearly all his prescriptions think within the confines of Sunday gatherings (preaching, teaching, worship). While I commend his multiple suggestions, I do not think they go nearly far enough.

[25] I think the fine work of the Center for Christian Studies (www.Christian-studies.org) is a good example of my point, though I would push this initiative even further to explore ways to close the distance between the biblical material and contemporary use and theological appropriation. One potential advantage of the school relocating to Searcy is that the faculty can enjoy a greater pool of professional personnel and media resources on which to draw.

Conclusion

It is an irony of history that a bibliocentric movement that has stressed restoring the early church's doctrine and practice has functionally neglected the Scriptures from which the early church read and theologized. As Chris Wright sanguinely observes:

> [O]ur tendency to ask the puzzled question, Is the Old Testament really *Christian?* is actually the reverse of the question the earliest Christians, before the New Testament existed, felt they had to answer satisfactorily. *Their* question was, Is the Christian church *scriptural?* That is, can we justify our ecclesial and missional theology and practice from the authoritative (Old Testament) Scriptures? [26]

"Restoration" is a deeply biblical category, but the theme in the biblical imagination is rooted unapologetically in the "sacramental disclosure" of Israel's witness.[27] Biblical restoration draws upon the whole sweep of the story from creation to new creation, confessing that in Jesus of Nazareth God has declared a definitive "yes" to the people, purposes, and promises of God. To understand Jesus as a climax of God's grand narrative (and the church, which is his body, as the outworking of his fullness) does not dismiss or make the former revelation of God less important. It is, in fact, just the opposite. It is through inhabiting Israel's Scriptures alongside of and in continuity with their reconfiguration in the NT that we will learn what it means

---

[26] Christopher J. H. Wright, *The Great Story and the Great Commission: Participating in the Biblical Drama of Mission*, Acadia Studies in Bible and Theology (Grand Rapids, MI: Baker Academic, 2023), 57.

[27] I borrow "sacramental disclosure" from Christopher R. Seitz, "Between Athens and Antioch: Literal and Extended-Sense Reading," *ProEccl* 29.3 (2020): 286, who makes the further comment: "One form of Marcionism isn't just cutting away or downplaying the first witness, but rather a failure to understand the role of God's electing of a people whose identity is fundamentally that "much-in-every-way, they are trustees of the oracles of God" (Rom 3:2). The empty tomb is an explosive, apocalyptic event, but alongside this is the explosion of an elder testimony breaking forth and bearing witness to a reality whose sense is given in relationship to it, and without which it cannot deliver its fully divine truth."

to truly say "Jesus is the Christ" as we wait for the glorious unity of all things in heaven and earth.

In my undergraduate days a professor made a passing comment that those who were trained in OT studies "thought better" about biblical matters than their academic counterparts. At the time it was a shocking observation to me. While I (still) would not endorse the statement, I do think there is something true the professor had noticed: those who learn to think with both testaments, think better. When we become more perceptive readers of the OT, we become more astute readers of Scripture, church ministry, and life in general. As readers of the Old Testament, we know that the people of God have persevered through disruption, displacement, and even death (let the reader understand) not because they were clairvoyant, prepared, and determined. Rather, Israel's God was and is and forever will be tenaciously faithful in the face of Jesus Christ through the sustaining power of the Spirit. Let HST's next chapter be a testimony to this God.

CHAPTER THREE

Biblical Studies: New Testament

Garrett Best

As the final chapter of Harding School of Theology (HST) in Memphis is completed, it is impossible not to reflect back on the impact of this storied institution on the lives of countless individuals. Nestled within the heart of the city of Memphis since 1958, HST has been a beacon of academic study and spiritual transformation. The remarkable history of this hallowed institution clings to every brick of the Mansion (E. H. Ijams Administration Building), every pew in the chapel, every book of the L. M. Graves Memorial Library, and every classroom seat in the Dr. W. B. West Jr. Center. However, the impact of HST extends well beyond the physical campus and has transformed the lives of men and women for the kingdom of God. In the nurturing educational environment offered in Memphis at HST, numerous ministers and shepherds have been equipped, missionaries have been sent to evangelize, chaplains have been readied for the field, counselors have been trained, and scholars have discovered the thrill of study. As we bid farewell to HST in the city of Memphis, it is important to give God gratitude for the indelible mark this institution has left on the city of Memphis, churches in West Tennessee, the landscape of theological education, the global kingdom of God, faculty and staff, and on the hearts of those fortunate enough to be alumni of HST.

I began my journey at HST in Memphis in 2010 marking the beginning of one of the most intellectually stimulating and spiritually transformative chapters in my life. Over the four years of pursuing the Master of Divinity, I took numerous challenging courses that stretched my academic abilities and allowed me to form relationships with faculty, staff, and peers that inspired me to pursue the "ministry of study" for the sake of the church.[1] I am deeply grateful for every friendship formed with classmates, every worship gathering in the chapel, every conversation with professors, every discussion and theological debate in classes, every required reading, and every research paper. These experiences combined to shape me in profound ways. However, the impact of my time at HST went beyond my experiences on the campus. The vibrant diversity of the city of Memphis provided a rich backdrop to my educational experience, exposing me to a tapestry of cultures and perspectives that enhanced my worldview. Moreover, my involvement in ministry at the Oliver Creek Church of Christ became an integral part of my journey, offering me a supportive ministry context in which to put into practice all of the theological and theoretical concepts I was learning from professors and in books. As I walked across the stage in 2014 to receive the MDiv, I left not only with an academic accomplishment but also with a profound sense of spiritual growth and a storehouse of memories that will forever shape my life and my ministry.

HST has proven to be an important center for the study of the New Testament (NT). Beginning with Advanced Theological Research, students learned the best practices and critical resources for studying the biblical text. Accomplished and competent biblical scholars such as W. B. West Jr., Jack P. Lewis, Carroll Osburn, Richard Oster, and Allen Black taught students the exegetical method, but more importantly modeled academic rigor in their teaching and scholarship. The areas of study of the NT at HST have been comprehensive, focusing on Greek language proficiency and delving into every section of the NT. The commitment to scholarly excellence at HST was always coupled with the goal of building the kingdom of God, which created an academic experience that transcended mere intellectual pursuit. The profound influence of HST's dedicated focus on the NT resonates every time a graduate teaches a class or delivers a sermon, drawing upon the deep reservoir of insights and methodologies

---

[1] The phrase "The Ministry of Study" is taken from an article by that title written by Jack P. Lewis in *Leadership Questions Confronting the Church* (Nashville: Christian Communications, 1985), 101-06.

acquired during their tenure at HST. It is equally evident in the impressive number of alumni that have made scholarly contributions at conferences, written academic books and articles, pursued PhDs in NT, and assumed teaching roles in the area of NT studies at Christian universities and seminaries.

This project marks a pivotal moment for HST characterized by significant transition as the school adjusts to align with a changing landscape happening within higher education. In addition to institutional shifts, the field of biblical studies is constantly evolving. In the midst of so much change, this brief essay aims to highlight some current trends in NT studies as well as identify some key areas that theological education must address. My hope is that HST, in its next iteration, will continue to be a beacon of rigorous academic study, combining steadfast commitment to Christian faith with an openness to dialogue and interaction with diverse perspectives in the pursuit of knowledge.

Trends in Biblical Studies: New Testament

In *The State of New Testament Studies: A Survey of Recent Research* (2019), Scot McKnight and Nijay Gupta trace six general trends in NT scholarship:[2]

1. Proliferation of Tools and Methods

In the last century, many academic methods have been added to the dominant historical-critical method (literary criticism, social-scientific criticism, rhetorical criticism, sociopragmatics, empire criticism, etc.). While the addition of other disciplines into biblical studies is laudable, it can lead to microspecialization and fragmentation for scholars.

2. Global and Diverse Perspectives

The rationalist goal of "objective reading" has largely been abandoned. Marginalized and global voices have been prioritized in reading and interpreting the biblical text. The emphasis on diverse perspectives has led to the proliferation of socially located and explicitly

---

[2] The following is taken from Nijay Gupta and Scot McKnight, "Introduction," in *The State of New Testament Studies: A Survey of Recent Research*, edited by Scot McKnight and Nijay Gupta (Grand Rapids: Baker Academic, 2019), 1–8.

ideological readings (African American, African, Asian American, Asian, Latinx, womanist, feminist, postcolonial, LGBTQ, etc.).

3. **Tending to Neglected NT Texts**

There has been an increase in attention given to historically neglected NT texts. In the NT, Paul and the Gospels have received the most attention, but studies on Acts, Revelation, Hebrews, and the Catholic Epistles have grown in recent years.

4. **Sophisticated Historical Contextualization**

Biblical scholars have become increasingly interested in locating the NT documents within their ancient contexts (Jewish, Greek, and Roman). Beginning in the latter half of the twentieth century and continuing to the present in earnest, scholarship on Second Temple Judaism bourgeoned and scholars emphasized understanding Jesus, Paul, and the earliest believers as Jews. Similarly, scholars have continued to stress the background of the Roman Empire on early Christianity. Drawing on diverse disciplines such as archaeology, scholars have attempted to understand the daily life of ordinary men, women, and children in the ancient world.

5. **Theological Interpretation of Scripture**

In recent years, there has been a growing number of scholars within the academy reading biblical texts for their theological messages and meanings. While these readings are diverse, they fall under the umbrella of "theological interpretation of Scripture." There has been a growing interest in "precritical" readings and readings of Catholic, Orthodox, Reformation, and Anabaptist theologians.

6. **Looking to the Past**

Two quickly growing areas in biblical studies are reception history and history of interpretation of Scripture. These readings help modern scholars see our own cultural biases. These studies also highlight the impact of biblical texts on culture, media, art, music, and politics.

In addition to these general trends which characterize scholarship in every discipline of NT studies, I will now attempt to summarize some of the specific trends in NT studies.

Empire Studies (Postcolonial Criticism)

Against the backdrop of the twentieth century's numerous wars, the post-9/11 war on terrorism, sustained military engagements by Western nations, and the rise of Christian Nationalism, scholars are increasingly drawn to examining early Christianity in relationship to empire.[3] Early Christian communities, spread out throughout the Roman Empire in diverse contexts, faced unique challenges addressed by NT documents, which do not speak about empire with a singular voice.[4] Scholars attempt to explore how each author in the NT documents negotiates power dynamics and engages with the concept of empire. Empire studies have gained prominence, particularly in research on Jesus and the Gospels,[5] Pauline literature,[6] and Revelation.[7] Notably, the examination of slavery in the Roman Empire and its portrayal in NT

---

[3] See Greg Carey, "Early Christianity and the Roman Empire," in *The State of New Testament Studies: A Survey of Recent Research*, edited by Scot McKnight and Nijay Gupta (Grand Rapids: Baker Academic, 2019), 9–34; *An Introduction to Empire in the New Testament*, edited by Adam Winn (Atlanta: SBL Press, 2016); *Empire in the New Testament*, edited by Stanley Porter and Cynthia Long Westfall, McMaster New Testament Studies (Eugene: Pickwick, 2011); Warren Carter, *The Roman Empire and the New Testament: An Essential Guide* (Nashville; Abingdon, 2006).

[4] For example, see Cynthia Long Westfall, "Running the Gamut: The Varied Responses to Empire in Jewish Christianity," in *Empire in the New Testament*, edited by Stanley E. Porter and Cynthia Long Westfall (Eugene: Pickwick, 2011), 230-58.

[5] For example, see Thomas Thatcher, *Greater than Caesar: Christology and Empire in the Fourth Gospel* (Minneapolis: Fortress, 2009); Seyoon Kim, *Christ and Caesar: The Gospel and the Roman Empire in the Writings of Paul and Luke* (Grand Rapids: Eerdmans, 2008); *Luke-Acts and Empire: Essay in Honor of Robert L. Brawley*, edited by David Rhoads, David Esterline, and Jae Won Lee (Eugene: Pickwick, 2011).

[6] For example, see Richard Horsley, *Paul and Empire: Religion and Power in Roman Imperial Society* (Harrisburg: Trinity Press International, 1997); *Paul and the Roman Imperial Order* (London: Trinity Press International, 2004); Christoph Heilig, *Hidden Criticism? The Methodology and Plausibility of the Search for a Counter-Imperial Subtext in Paul*, WUNT 2/392 (Tübingen: Mohr Siebeck, 2015); *The Apostle and the Empire: Paul's Implicit and Explicit Criticism of Rome* (Grand Rapids: Eerdmans, 2022); Najeeb T. Haddad, *Paul and Empire Criticism: Why and How?* (Eugene: Cascade, 2023).

[7] Shane J. Wood, *The Alter-Imperial Paradigm: Empire Studies & The Book of Revelation*, BINS 140 (Leiden: Brill, 2015); Anathea E. Portier-Young, *Apocalypse Against Empire: Theologies of Resistance in Early Judaism* (Grand Rapids: Eerdmans, 2014); Wes Howard-Brook and Anthony Gwyther, *Unveiling Empire: Reading Revelation Then and Now* (Maryknoll, NY: Orbis, 2005).

texts has become a focal point.[8] As the field of empire studies continues to grow, scholars will continue to engage the sociopolitical dynamics embedded within and behind the texts of the NT.

Gospels

Scholarship on the Gospels involves several contentious issues, including debates on the genre of the Gospels, the so-called Synoptic Problem, the relation of the Fourth Gospel to the Synoptics, and Historical Jesus studies, among other contested elements in the interpretation of individual Gospels. Following Richard Burridge's influential 2004 monograph *What Are the Gospels?*, a semblance of consensus emerged, characterizing the Gospels as examples of the Greco-Roman genre of *bioi* (biographies).[9] Since then, several studies have expanded on this identification while others have challenged it, proposing alternative genre categories.[10] Given the critical interpretive role of genre identification in biblical studies, this remains a topic of interest for Gospel research.

Another focal point of debate has revolved around the so-called Synoptic Problem which addresses the literary relationship between

---

[8] For a summary, see Jonathan J. Hatter, "Currents in Biblical Research Slavery and the Enslaved in the Roman World, the Jewish world, and the Synoptic Gospels," *CBR* 20.1 (2021): 97–127; Jennifer Glancy, *Slavery as a Moral Problem: In the Early Church and Today* (Minneapolis: Fortress, 2011); S. Scott Bartchy, "Slaves and Slavery in the Roman World," in *The World of the New Testament: Cultural, Social, and Historical Contexts*, edited by Joel B. Green and Lee Martin McDonald (Grand Rapids: Baker Academic, 2013), 169–78.

[9] Richard A Burridge, *What Are the Gospels? A Comparison with Graeco-Roman Biography*, SNTSMS (Cambridge: Cambridge University Press, 1992; 2nd ed., Grand Rapids: Eerdmans, 2004).

[10] For research building on the Gospels as biography, see Michael R. Licona, *Why Are There Differences in the Gospels? What We Can Learn from Ancient Biography* (Oxford: Oxford University Press, 2017); Craig S. Keener, *Christobiography: Memory, History, and the Reliability of the Gospels* (Grand Rapids: Eerdmans, 2019); Helen K. Bond, *The First Biography of Jesus: Genre and Meaning in Mark's Gospel* (Grand Rapids: Eerdmans, 2020). For research criticizing the identification of the Gospels as biography, see Adela Yarbro Collins, "Genre and the Gospels," *JR* 75, no. 2 (1995): 238–46; Ryder Wishart, *Gospels or Biographies? The Gospels as Folk Literature*, LBS 25 (Leiden: Brill, 2024).

Matthew, Mark, and Luke.[11] Christian Hermann Weisse was the first to posit the two-source hypothesis which argues that both Matthew and Luke used Mark (referred to as Markan priority), and when Matthew and Luke share non-Markan material, they both drew from another written source referred to as Q (from the German word *Quelle* meaning "source").[12] The identification of Q prompted debates about the existence of the hypothetical source, leading scholars to explore more complex models incorporating social history, oral tradition, memory studies, and other factors to elucidate the relationships between the Gospels.[13]

A perennial issue in scholarship on the Fourth Gospel concerns John's relationship to the Synoptics. While a dominant strand of scholarship since the 1930s viewed John as independent of the Synoptics, recent works have challenged this consensus, giving rise to more complex models for understanding John's relationship to the Synoptics.[14] Additionally, a lively debate has emerged regarding the re-

---

[11] Robert H. Stein, *The Synoptic Problem: An Introduction* (Grand Rapids: Baker, 1987); *Rethinking the Synoptic Problem*, edited by David Alan Black and David R. Beck (Grand Rapids: Baker Academic, 2001); *The Synoptic Problem: Four Views*, edited by Stanley E. Porter and Bryan R. Dyer (Grand Rapids: Baker Academic, 2016).

[12] Christian Hermann Weisse, *Die evangelische Geschichte kritisch und philosophisch bearbeitet*, 2 vols. (Leipzig: Breitkopf & Härtel, 1838); The two-source hypothesis was then popularized by H. J. Holtzmann (*Die synoptischen Evangelien: Ihr Ursprung und geschichtlicher Charakter* [Leipzig: Engelmann, 1863]) and in the English-speaking world by B.H. Streeter (*The Four Gospels: A Study in Origins* [London: Macmillan, 1924], 151–98). Streeter further argued that Matthew and Luke used other sources which he referred to as M and L.

[13] For a defense of Q, see Joseph A. Fitzmyer, "The Priority of Mark and the 'Q' Source in Luke," in *To Advance the Gospel: New Testament Studies*, 2nd ed. (Grand Rapids: Eerdmans, 1998), 3–40; John Kloppenborg, *Excavating Q: The History and Setting of the Sayings Gospel* (Minneapolis: Fortress, 2000). For arguments against Q, see Austin Farrer, "On Dispensing with Q," in *Studies in the Gospels*, edited by D.E. Nineham (Oxford: Blackwell, 1955), 55–88; Mark Goodacre, *The Case Against Q: Studies in Markan Priority and the Synoptic Problem* (Edinburgh: T&T Clark, 2002); *Marcan Priority Without Q: Explorations in the Farrer Hypothesis*, edited by John C. Poirier and Jeffrey Peterson, LNTS 455 (London: Bloomsbury T&T Clark, 2015); Francis Watson, *Gospel Writing: A Canonical Perspective* (Grand Rapids: Eerdmans, 2013), 117–216.

[14] For arguments that John wrote independent of the Synoptics, see P. Gardner-Smith, *Saint John and the Synoptics* (Cambridge: Cambridge University Press, 1938); D.

liability of the Fourth Gospel as a source for knowledge about the historical Jesus.[15] In a post-Holocaust context, scholars continue to grapple with the troubling fact that the Fourth Gospel has been historically employed to promote anti-Semitism, prompting critical analysis of John's alleged anti-Semitic presentation of "the Jews."[16]

Historical Jesus

The extensive literature on the Quest for the Historical Jesus is one of the most vast in NT scholarship, delving into the core of the Christian faith–the identity of Jesus of Nazareth.[17] The so-called Third Quest for the Historical Jesus, characterized by the application of certain methodological criteria to determine authentic Jesus traditions,

---

M. Smith, *John Among the Synoptics: The Relationship in Twentieth-Century Scholarship* (Minneapolis: Fortress, 1992); Stanley E. Porter, *John, His Gospel and Jesus: In Pursuit of the Johannine Voice* (Grand Rapids: Eerdmans, 2015. For arguments that John knew the Synoptic Gospels or the Synoptic tradition, see Richard Bauckham, "John for Readers of Mark," in *The Gospels for All Christians: Rethinking the Gospel Audiences*, edited by Richard Bauckham (Edinburgh: T&T Clark, 1998), 147–71; James W. Barker, *John's Use of Matthew* (Minneapolis: Fortress, 2015); Wendy E. S. North, *What John Knew and What John Wrote: A Study in John and the Synoptics* (Lanham: Lexington Books, 2020).

[15] For arguments that John's Gospel is not a credible source for the historical Jesus, see Maurice Casey, *Is John's Gospel True?* (New York: Routledge, 1996). For arguments that John's Gospel is a useful source for history, see Richard Bauckham, *The Testimony of the Beloved Disciple: Narrative, History, and Theology in the Gospel of John* (Grand Rapids: Baker Academic, 2007), 73–123; Craig Blomberg, *The Historical Reliability of John's Gospel* (Downers Grove: IVP, 2011); *Jesus the Purifier: John's Gospel and the Fourth Quest for the Historical Jesus* (Grand Rapids: Baker Academic, 2023); *John, Jesus, and History*, edited by Paul Anderson, Felix Just, and Tom Thatcher, 3 vols. (Atlanta: SBL Press, 2007, 2009, 2016).

[16] Adele Reinhartz, *Befriending the Beloved Disciple: A Jewish Reading of the Gospel of John* (London: Continuum, 2002); *John and Judaism: A Contested Relationship in Context*, edited by R. Alan Culpepper and Paul Anderson, RBS 87 (Atlanta: SBL Press, 2017); Miroslaw Stanislaw Wróbel, *Anti-Judaism and the Gospel of John: A New Look at the Fourth Gospel's Relationship with Judaism*, Lublin Theological Studies 7 (Göttingen: Vandenhoeck & Ruprecht, 2023).

[17] For a summary of the Quest for the Historical Jesus, see Rebekah Eklund, "Jesus of Nazareth," in *The State of New Testament Studies: A Survey of Recent Research*, edited by Scot McKnight and Nijay Gupta (Grand Rapids: Baker Academic, 2019), 139–60; Helen Bond, *The Historical Jesus: A Guide for the Perplexed* (London: T&T Clark, 2012); *Handbook for the Study of the Historical Jesus*, edited by Tom Holmén and Stanley E Porter, 4 vols. (Leiden: Brill, 2011); Craig Keener, *The Historical Jesus of the Gospels* (Grand Rapids: Eerdmans, 2009).

witnessed a notable achievement in renewing emphasis on understanding Jesus as a Jew within the context of Second Temple Judaism. In *Jesus, Criteria, and the Demise of Authenticity* (2012), several scholars signaled the end of the Third Quest, known for its criteria-based approach to historical Jesus study.[18] James Crossley, in 2021, heralded the start of the Next Quest in the *Journal for the Study of the Historical Jesus*. He outlines ten primary concerns to align historical Jesus study with broader trends in the humanities: 1. Social History of Scholarship; 2. Study of (Human) Religion; 3. Historical Method; 4. Jewishness; 5. Comparison; 6. Class; 7. Slavery; 8. Race and Ethnicity; 9. Gender and Sexuality; 10. Reception History.[19] The Next Quest anticipates a more interdisciplinary, postmodern, and global approach, promising new avenues for understanding Jesus.

Paul and the Law

A parallel trend in scholarly study, alongside the rediscovery of the Jewish Jesus, is the reevaluation of the Jewish Paul, encapsulated in a movement known as the New Perspective on Paul (NPP).[20] The NPP challenged the Lutheran (Reformational or Old Perspective) interpretation of Paul which emphasized justification by faith as opposed to salvation by merit-based Jewish legalism. While the NPP encompasses diverse perspectives, scholars writing in the NPP generally contended that Paul, as a Jew, did not oppose the Torah or good works per se. Instead, Paul's objection was against the notion that Gentiles were required to obey Torah for inclusion in the people of God. Amid the waning of the NPP, other perspectives on Paul have emerged, with two noteworthy developments.[21] First, the publication

---

[18] *Jesus, Criteria, and the Demise of Authenticity*, edited by Chris Keith and Anthony Le Donne (New York: T&T Clark, 2012).

[19] James Crossley, "The Next Quest for the Historical Jesus," *JSHJ* 19 (2021): 261–64.

[20] The book which launched the NPP was E. P. Sanders, *Paul and Palestinian Judaism: A Comparison of Patterns of Religion* (Philadelphia: Fortress, 1977). For summaries of the New Perspective on Paul, see Kent L. Yinger, *The New Perspective on Paul: An Introduction* (Eugene: Cascade, 2011); James D. G. Dunn, *The New Perspective on Paul* (Grand Rapids: Eerdmans, 2008).

[21] For a summary of the perspectives on Paul, see Michael J. Gorman, "Pauline Theology: Perspectives, Perennial Topics, and Prospects," in *The State of New Testament*

of John Barclay's *Paul and the Gift* in 2015 has been heralded as one of the most important books on Paul in the last 100 years.[22] Barclay examines Paul's use of grace language (Gk: *charis*) in Galatians and Romans within the context of ancient gift-giving, offering a nuanced contrast between ancient and modern conceptions. Barclay's conclusions navigate the scholarly impasse of the NPP, asserting that, for Paul, the divine gift of Christ's life, death, and resurrection is an unconditioned and unconditional gift, though the grace gift necessitates obedient faith.[23]

Second, in recent years, much scholarly vigor has focused on the Paul Within Judaism (PwJ) perspective.[24] Comprising Jewish and Christian scholars, this group seeks to understand Paul as a Torah-observant Jew who did not oppose Jews, the Law, or Jewish practice of the Law but rather contended that Gentiles were not obligated to adhere to the Law to follow Messiah Jesus. Within certain versions of PwJ, proponents argue that Paul believed Jews did not need to put faith in Christ for salvation, being already justified as Jews. Paul's gospel, according to this perspective, preached a distinct pathway for non-Jews to be saved, often termed the *Sonderweg* ("special path") hypothesis.[25] The PwJ camp rejects any interpretation hinting at supersessionism. Despite the explosion of PwJ's influence, some

---

Studies: A Survey of Recent Research, edited by Scot McKnight and Nijay Gupta (Grand Rapids: Baker Academic, 2019), 197–223; *Perspectives on Paul: Five Views*, edited by Scot McKnight and B.J. Oropeza (Grand Rapids: Baker Academic, 2020).

[22] John M. G. Barclay, *Paul and the Gift* (Grand Rapids: Eerdmans, 2015); See the essays in *The New Perspective on Grace: Paul and the Gospel after Paul and the Gift*, edited by Edward Adams, Dorothea H. Bertschmann, et. al (Grand Rapisd: Eerdmans, 2023).

[23] For a summary of Barclay's argument, see *Paul and the Gift*, 562–74.

[24] For examples of this perspective, see *Paul within Judaism: Restoring the First-Century Context to the Apostle*, edited by Mark D. Nanos and Magnus Zetterholm (Minneapolis: Fortress, 2015); Pamela Eisenbaum, *Paul Was Not a Christian: The Original Message of a Misunderstood Apostle* (New York: HarperOne, 2009); Matthew Thiessen, *Paul and the Gentile Problem* (New York: Oxford University Press, 2016); *Jewish Paul: The Messiah's Herald to the Gentiles* (Grand Rapids: Baker Academic, 2023); Paula Fredriksen, *Paul: The Pagans' Apostle* (New Haven: Yale University Press, 2018).

[25] For example, see Mark D. Nanos, *The Mystery of Romans: The Jewish Context of Paul's Letters* (Minneapolis: Fortress, 1996), 239–88; John G. Gager, Reinventing Paul (Oxford: Oxford University Press, 2000), 59; Eisenbaum, *Paul Was Not a Christian*, 59.

scholars have raised critiques.[26] The "Within Judaism" perspective is being applied to nearly all other texts in the NT and is poised to continue impacting NT studies.[27]

Key Areas Biblical Studies Must Address

Christian theological education is facing unprecedented challenges demanding a steadfast commitment to God, His kingdom, and the local church. Within the realm of NT studies, there is a vital need for capable individuals to address the contemporary needs of the world and the church with clarity, conviction, and competence. It is imperative that HST embrace its role as a leader, diligently training students in biblical studies and equipping them to navigate these challenges with a profound understanding of Scripture. In doing so, HST can play a pivotal role in shaping individuals who, trained in the interpretation of Scripture and empowered by the Holy Spirit, will be able to navigate the complexities of our time and lead churches deeper into the life of God. The following highlights key areas and challenges that biblical studies must address for the flourishing of the world and the church to the glory of God.

1. Women in Early Christianity and the Contemporary Church

The debate surrounding NT passages regarding women continues to be both controversial and consequential. Scholars continue to discuss the meaning of these texts in their original contexts, applying new methods and research to better understand their relevance for the contemporary church.[28] This multifaceted

---

[26] See Michael Bird, "An Introduction to the Paul within Judaism Debate," in *Paul within Judaism*, edited by Michael Bird, Ruben A. Bühner, et. al., WUNT 507 (Tübingen: Mohr Siebeck, 2023), 1–28; Brant Pitre, Michael P. Barber, and John A. Kincaid, *Paul, A New Covenant Jew: Rethinking Pauline Theology* (Grand Rapids: Eerdmans, 2019), 11–63; A. Andrew Das, *Solving the Romans Debate* (Minneapolis: Fortress, 2007), 115–48; *Paul and the Jews*, LPS (Peabody, Hendrickson, 2003), 96–106.

[27] See the essays in *Within Judaism? Interpretive Trajectories in Judaism, Christianity, and Islam from the First to the Twenty-First Century*, edited by Karin Hedner Zetterholm and Anders Runesson (Lanham: Lexington Books, 2023).

[28] The literature is vast. For representative complementarian arguments, see *Recovering Biblical Manhood and Womanhood: A Response to Evangelical Feminism*, edited by John Piper and Wayne Grudem (Wheaton: Crossway, 1991); *Women in the*

discussion encompasses the interpretation of individual texts, theological considerations, hermeneutics, and the ongoing application of new methods.[29]

2. The NT and Sexual Ethics

Sexual ethics, particularly the affirmation or non-affirmation of same-sex relationships and discussions around transgender, non-binary, and queer persons, stands out as one of the most divisive issues in the global church.[30] A vast literature has emerged, engaging in debates over how to understand and apply key passages in the OT and NT regarding sexuality.[31]

3. Ecology and Eschatology

In the face of ecological crises such as the climate crises, loss of biodiversity, pollution, and food insecurity, Christians much reclaim Scripture's vision for caring for God's creation. Biblical scholars have

---

Church: An Analysis and Application of 1 Timothy 2:9-15, edited by Andreas Köstenberger and Thomas R. Schreiner (Grand Rapids: Baker, 2005). For representative egalitarian arguments, see *Discovering Biblical Equality: Biblical, Theological, Cultural, and Practical Perspectives*, edited by Ronald W. Pierce and Cynthia Long Westfall, 3rd ed. (Downers Grove: IVP Academic, 2021); Cynthia Long Westfall, *Paul and Gender: Reclaiming the Apostle's Vision for Men and Women in Christ* (Grand Rapids: Baker Academic, 2016). For hermeneutical questions, see William J. Webb, *Slaves, Women, and Homosexuals: Exploring the Hermeneutics of Cultural Analysis* (Downers Grove: IVP, 2001). For an argument that attempts to bring fresh perspective to the complementarian/egalitarian impasse, see Michelle Lee-Barnewall, *Neither Complementarian nor Egalitarian: A Kingdom Corrective to the Evangelical Gender Debate* (Grand Rapids: Baker Academic, 2016). For essays written by biblical scholars in the Stone-Campbell Movement, see *Essays on Women in Earliest Christianity*, edited by Carroll D. Osburn, vols. 1–2 (Eugene: Wipf & Stock, 1993, 1995, 2007).

[29] For a recent work applying historical research, see Sandra Glahn, *Nobody's Mother: Artemis of the Ephesians in Antiquity and the New Testament* (Downers Grove: IVP Academic, 2023).

[30] As I write this, the Global Anglican Communion is fracturing over same-sex blessings, the United Methodist Church has officially split creating the Global Methodist Church, and the Roman Catholic Church has had to clarify the controversy surrounding the release of *Fiducia supplicans*, which permitted blessing same-sex couples in some cases.

[31] For studies on male and female homosexuality in the ancient world, see Bernadette Brooten, *Love Between Women: Early Christian Responses to Female Homoeroticism*

begun addressing these unprecedented challenges, with a need for more scholarship in this area.[32] An over-spiritualized eschatology has contributed to Christian neglect of the material creation, and scholars must address these concerns, especially given the severity of the crises affecting our world.[33]

4. The Role of Postmodern Biblical Interpretation in NT Studies

The decline of historical criticism has given way to a proliferation of postmodern interpretive strategies.[34] Postmodern interpreters reject neutral or objective readings of the text, emphasizing the social and

---

(Chicago: University of Chicago Press, 1996); William Loader, *The New Testament on Sexuality*, Attitudes Towards Sexuality in Judaism and Christianity in the Hellenistic Greco-Roman Era (Grand Rapids: Eerdmans, 2012); For representative non-affirming interpretations of biblical texts, see Preston Sprinkle, *Does the Bible Support Same-Sex Marriage? 21 Conversations from a Historically Christian View* (Colorado Springs: David C. Cook, 2023); Robert A. J. Gagnon, *The Bible and Homosexual Practice: Texts and Hermeneutics* (Nashville: Abingdon, 2002). For representative affirming interpretations of biblical texts, see Matthew Vines, *God and the Gay Christian: The Biblical Case in Support of Sam-Sex Relationships* (Colorado Springs: Convergent Books, 2015); Karen Keen, *Scripture, Ethics, and the Possibility of Same-Sex Relationships* (Grand Rapids: Eerdmans, 2018).

[32] Richard Bauckham, *The Bible and Ecology: Rediscovering the Community of Creation* (Waco: Baylor University Press, 2010); *Living with Other Creatures: Green Exegesis and Theology* (Waco: Baylor University Press, 2011); Steven Bouma-Prediger, *Creation Care Discipleship: Why Earthkeeping Is an Essential Christian Practice* (Grand Rapids: Baker Academic, 2023); Daniel Bruner, Jennifer Butler, and A.J. Swoboda, *Introducing Evangelical Ecotheology: Foundations in Scripture, Theology, History, and Praxis* (Grand Rapids: Baker Academic, 2014); David Horrell, Cherryl Hunt, and Christopher Southgate, *Greening Paul: Rereading the Apostle in a Time of Ecological Crisis* (Waco: Baylor University Press, 2010).

[33] Richard J. Middleton, *A New Heaven and a New Earth: Reclaiming Biblical Eschatology* (Grand Rapids: Baker Academic, 2014); Jonathan Moo and Robert White, *Let Creation Rejoice: Biblical Hope and Ecological Crisis* (Downers Grove: IVP Academic, 2014); N.T. Wright, *Surprised by Hope: Rethinking Heaven, the Resurrection, and the Mission of the Church* (New York: HarperOne, 2008).

[34] For a discussion, see Joel B. Green, "Modern and Postmodern Methods of Biblical Interpretation," in *Scripture and Its Interpretation: A Global and Ecumenical Introduction to the Bible*, edited by Michael Gorman (Grand Rapids: Baker Academic, 2017), 187–204; N. Clayton Croy, *Prima Scriptura: An Introduction to New Testament Interpretation* (Grand Rapids: Baker Academic, 2011), xx–xli; Dennis R. Edwards, "Hermeneutics and Exegesis," in *The State of New Testament Studies: A Survey of Recent Research*, edited by Scot McKnight and Nijay Gupta (Grand Rapids: Baker Academic, 2019), 63–82.

cultural location of every interpreter. This has led to diverse ideological approaches to biblical interpretation such as African American, African, Asian, Latinx, indigenous peoples, womanist, feminist, LGBTQ, postcolonial, liberationist, ecological, disability, and more. Postmodern interpreters differ in their commitment to the authority of Scripture and their disposition toward the text.[35] These approaches contribute to a more ecumenical and global biblical studies landscape and many socially located readings have shed new light on the biblical text.[36] These and other postmodern approaches are likely to be part of the biblical studies landscape for years to come, but care must be taken that these approaches do not abandon the study of the cultural, social, and political context of the author and original audiences.

5. Theological Interpretation of Scripture

The Enlightenment's positivist rationalism excluded ecclesial and confessional concerns from historical investigation. The rise of postmodern ideological readings has opened the door for explicitly confessional readings. Theological Interpretation of Scripture, encompassing subdisciplines of canonical criticism, premodern interpretation, *lectio divina*, missional hermeneutics, and exegesis from specific theological traditions (Roman Catholic, Orthodox, Pentecostal, evangelical, Wesleyan, etc.), recognizes that the NT texts were written with theological motives for audiences with theological interests which were collected, preserved, and canonized because these documents were believed to communicate divine revelation.[37] Reading NT texts with theological reflection is integral to hermeneutics.

---

[35] Interpreters might approach the text with a hermeneutic of suspicion or trust. For discussion of these two dispositions, see Richard Hays, "Salvation by Trust? Reading the Bible Faithfully," *Christian Century* 114 (1997): 218–23.

[36] See for example, the essays in *Scripture and Its Interpretation: A Global and Ecumenical Introduction to the Bible*, edited by Michael Gorman (Grand Rapids: Baker Academic, 2017).

[37] For a discussion, see Stephen E. Fowl, *Theological Interpretation of Scripture*, Cascade Companions (Eugene: Cascade Books, 2009); Daniel J. Treier, *Introducing Theological Interpretation of Scripture: Recovering a Christian Practice* (Grand Rapids: Baker Academic, 2008); *Dictionary for Theological Interpretation of the Bible*, edited by Kevin J. Vanhoozer (Grand Rapids: Baker Academic, 2005); Joel B. Green, *Practicing*

6. The Role of Technology in Biblical Studies

New technologies affect NT studies in at least four crucial ways. First, as seminaries transition to largely online models, scholars must consider how online platforms effect learning and adjust pedagogical methods appropriately.[38] Second, new technologies are being employed in various areas of biblical studies. Computer-generated models are illuminating the relationship of manuscripts in textual criticism.[39] Biblical scholars and archaeologists have embraced 3D modeling allowing scholars and students to experience ancient cities, temples, synagogues, and other structures through the use of virtual reality (VR).[40] Scholars use computer-generated data modeling to study the authorship of NT documents.[41] Third, the rise of Artificial Intelligence (AI) raises new possibilities for biblical research. Fourth, more collections and resources for the study of biblical texts are being digitized.[42] The availability of digital resources and the rise of new technologies will continue to impact biblical studies in numerous ways.

Theological Interpretation: Engaging Biblical Texts for Faith and Formation, Theological Explorations for the Church Catholic (Grand Rapids: Baker Academic, 2011); For an example of theological interpretation in the commentary genre, see David F. Ford, *The Gospel of John: A Theological Commentary* (Grand Rapids: Baker Academic, 2021).

[38] Timothy Luckritz Marquis, "The Course Site, Interpretation, and Community in Online Biblical Studies," in *Teaching the Bible with Undergraduates*, Resources for Biblical Study 99, edited by Jocelyn McWhirter and Sylvie Raquel (Atlanta: SBL Press, 2022), 251-60.

[39] A new branch of textual criticism called "Coherence-Based Genealogical Method" (CBGM) uses computer-based tools to study relationships between texts. See Tommy Wasserman, "The Coherence-Based Genealogical Method as a Tool for Explaining Textual Changes in the Greek New Testament," *NovT* 57 (2015): 206–18.

[40] Bradley C. Erickson, "Synagogue Modeling Project Report: a Multi-faceted Approach to 3D, Academic Modeling," in *Ancient Manuscripts in Digital Culture: Visualisation, Data Mining, Communication*, edited by David Manidović, Claire Clivaz, and Sarah Bowen Savant, Digital Biblical Studies 3 (Leiden: Brill, 2019), 261–75.

[41] For example, Patrick Juola, "Authorship Attribution," *Foundations and Trends in Information Retrieval* 1 (2006): 233-334; Ashley Roy and Paul Robertson, "Applying Cosine Similarity to Paul's Letters: Mathematically Modeling Formal and Stylistic Similarities," in *New Approaches to Textual and Image Analysis in Early Jewish and Christian Studies*, edited Garrick V. Allen, Sara Schulthess, et. al., Digital Biblical Studies 5 (Leiden: Brill, 2022), 88-117.

[42] For example, *The Dead Sea Scroll Electronic Library* has made all the biblical and

Conclusion

As HST bids farewell to the vibrant city of Memphis, its legacy is marked by rigorous academic study, spiritual transformation, and a commitment to the kingdom of God. This legacy significantly impacted the lives of numerous ministers, missionaries, chaplains, counselors, churches, and scholars. While acknowledging the challenges posed by the evolving landscape of higher education and the dynamic field of biblical studies, there is a hopeful anticipation for the next chapter of HST's history. May HST continue to be a beacon of academic excellence, blending unwavering commitment to the highest standards of scholarship with a profound love for the church. My hope is that as the academy and church grapples with contemporary issues, HST will stand as a guiding force, equipping individuals who are deeply rooted in Scripture and empowered by the Holy Spirit to courageously lead churches deeper into the life of God. May the future of HST be to the glory of God.

---

non-biblical texts available. The Thesaurus Linguae Graecae (TLG) contains the digitized version of most literary texts written in Greek from Homer to the fall of Byzantium. The Perseus library and online Loeb Classical Library allow for searches of digitized Greek and Latin literature. High resolution images of Greek manuscripts are available through *Institut für Neutestamentliche Textforschung* (INTF) (https://ntvmr.uni-muenster.de, accessed 22 January 2024) and at the Center for the Study of New Testament Manuscripts (csntm.org, accessed 22 January 2024). The 10-volume publication of *Roman Provincial Coinage* is now available in a searchable database (rpc.ashmus.ox.ac.uk, accessed 22 January 2024). The *Supplementum Epigraphicum Graecum* (SEG) database of Greek inscriptions from the archaic period to the 8th century is available online.

CHAPTER FOUR

Theological Studies

C. Leonard Allen

All through my upbringing and years of education, the word *theology* was not a readily acceptable word. It's why, I surmise, Harding School of Theology, at that time, was called Harding University Graduate School of Religion. I don't know all the reasons for the name change, but I'm pretty sure one of them was the new acceptability of the word theology.

The first graduate-level course I taught as a young professor was a course titled Introduction to Doctrinal Studies. It would normally have been called Introduction to Theology, but that word hadn't quite reached—it was 1982—the level of acceptability. Within a few years it did. That acceptance came as we realized more and more that we were actually doing theology, and had been all along. That is to say, those who pioneered the restoration plea of modern Churches of Christ were making basic interpretive choices, responding to their place and time and to the things they were trying to correct. We might say that they were doing a fresh theological construal—they called it reading the Bible straight without human creeds; they were determining, in light of their own cultural context, which parts of Scripture to make pivotal and how these more central parts relate to and shape the meaning of the whole.

That is what theologians do. As the faith passes from generation to generation, people constantly make such judgments, sometimes in big and influential ways (John Calvin in the sixteenth century, for one example, and Alexander Campbell in a somewhat lesser way in the nineteenth, for another), but most often in smaller ways—theological judgments about what is most basic and most needed for the church's teaching and preaching at that time. Making creed-like summaries of the Bible's basic message is a necessary task that the church undertakes in every generation. This is so because churches face three basic and necessary tasks as they seek to carry out God's mission; we can call them exegesis, catechesis, and polemics: interpreting and ordering the content of Scripture, grounding children and new believers in the faith, and setting boundaries on what constitutes acceptable or "orthodox" teaching. Emil Brunner called these practices the three roots of Christian theology—three basic requirements of Christian churches that call forth the work of theology.[1]

So church leaders prepare manuals for instructing new believers, craft doctrinal summaries (most traditions call them creeds, confessions, and catechisms), and set boundaries for acceptable belief. They attempt to formulate what it means to be "orthodox" and how that plays out in specific times and settings. Their best judgments are always open to critique and adjustment—unless, of course, the tradition has become so fixed and doctrinaire that little honest and lively engagement can ensue.

We can say that theology is "faith seeking understanding." But let me expand that simple classic statement by drawing from James McClendon (1924-2000), a theologian in the anabaptist/baptist tradition. Theology, he says, involves the discovery, interpretation, and transformation of the convictions of a Christian community, including the discovery and critical revision of disciples' relation to one another, to the Triune God, and to the rest of creation.[2] Note several characteristics of the task implied in this statement. First, theology is contextual: it is done in different historical and cultural contexts and in separated Christian communities. Second, it is done in relation to a historical narrative: it takes into account the story or tradition of actual communities. Third, it is rational: it deals with the logical relations of the community's convictions to one another and to the ideas swirling around it. Fourth, theology involves convictions that are held deeply and form

---

[1] Emil Brunner, *The Divine–Human Encounter*, trans. Amandus W. Loos (London: SCM, 1944), 11.

[2] James W. McClendon, *Ethics: Systematic Theology, Volume 1*, rev. ed. (Nashville: Abingdon, 2002), 22-23. I have reworded his definition for brevity and clarity.

who we are, not simply opinions or ideas, which change easily, even day by day. Convictions are deep and strong, and changing them changes the character of a community. And fifth, theology is doxological, that is, framed by worship; an early Christian guideline declared that "the rule of praying is the rule of believing," so theology functions properly within a praying, worshiping community.

Three Doors That Opened

During my years at Harding School of Theology, I began to learn about theology's essential role as a basic practice of the church on mission. I can say that a number of important doors were opened for me. Let me describe three of them.

1. A Door into the Christian Tradition

It was at Harding School of Theology that a door opened for me into the long and rich Christian tradition, and I walked through it with a sense of wonder and fascination and not a little puzzlement. I glimpsed its richness and breadth, its complexity and conundrums. It drew me in. It seemed to hold the promise of helping me answer the pressing questions about my faith that emerged for me as a very young teenager. The door that opened during my years at Harding launched me on six years of doctoral work in the history of Christian theology, and then on a life project: to make sense of that rich history in light of my own particular Christian heritage.

Especially important in this regard were the courses I had with Earl West and Harold Hazelip. Dr. West, over the course of two semesters, ushered us into the story of the Stone-Campbell Movement/Churches of Christ. From Barton Stone and the Springfield Presbytery, to Thomas and Alexander Campbell and the Christian Association of Washington, to Walter Scott and John Smith, then into later generations with Tolbert Fanning, Moses Lard, Daniel Sommer, David Lipscomb, and James Harding. And many more. Dr. West lectured on this history as if many of its central actors were his good friends with whom he had regular conversations. His classes threw beams of light onto the pathway I had been traveling—without really knowing it—since I was a child.

Harold Hazelip's courses on the history of Christian theology opened the horizon out much further. With him as my tour guide over three semesters, I was inducted into the rich theological trajectory of the faith over two millennia. It seemed overwhelming at first. I was impeded by the deep bias I had grown up with against the relevance of any of this. (We were only New Testament Christians.) But it didn't take long for the wheels to begin turning. There was Athanasius, the three Cappadocians, Augustine of Hippo, and Aquinas; then Luther and Calvin and the Reformation; then Wesley, Jonathan Edwards, and the Great Awakenings; then the Catholic tradition, with the turning points of Vatican I and II; and Barth, the Niebuhrs, Pannenberg, and more. We saw how the classic creeds and confessions sought to preserve and carry forward through time the basic doctrines of the faith.

2. A Door into the Doctrine of the Trinity

In my classes with Dr. Hazelip I found a door opened to the doctrine of the Trinity. In his robust overview of Christian theology across the ages, it became unmistakably clear that the doctrine of the Trinity loomed large; indeed, that it was the centering doctrine of the faith. Up to that point in my theological journey I had scarcely heard of it. In Dr. Hazelip's classes I learned that Christian faith has a grammar, a proper way of speaking, and that learning to speak Christian involves, among other basics, a careful and strong orientation to the doctrine of the Trinity.

The New Testament writers have a deep, almost unreflective recognition of the diversity and unity of God. As Gordon Fee put it, "Paul affirms, asserts, and presupposes the Trinity in every way; and those affirmations . . . are precisely the reason the later church took up the question of how."[3] The explicit doctrine of the Trinity that steadily emerged in the first three centuries was the result of the necessary work of filling out the New Testament's pervasive triadic language

---

[3] Gordon Fee, *Paul, the Spirit, and the People of God* (Peabody, MA: Hendrickson, 1996), 38. For in-depth documentation of Fee's point, see *The Trinity in the Canon: A Biblical, Theological, Historical, and Practical Proposal*, ed. Brandon D. Smith (Brentwood, TN: B&H, 2023), 61-365.

about God as the gospel mission encountered paganism. As evangelists proclaimed Jesus, they were faced with the question, "But who is Jesus?" To answer that question, the church "very soon found itself compelled to articulate a fully Trinitarian doctrine of the God whom it proclaimed."[4]

I began to become aware that, among Churches of Christ and the other Stone-Campbell traditions, the doctrine had receded to the background. Trinitarian language was optional at best. So over the years I've attempted to address this theological challenge.[5] I saw that we didn't have a tradition of valuing and embracing a Trinitarian-based orthodoxy; indeed, we had a tradition of rejecting the creedal tradition that maintained it—and have tended to think we could function just fine without any "rule of faith" to guide us. This remains an ongoing challenge.

3. A Door into the Church's Embeddedness in Culture

Beginning with my graduate studies at Harding and in the doctoral work that followed, I learned to place Christian movements in the context of their time and place. This kind of historical work, which I first glimpsed at Harding, was what I was after in my doctoral training, and I sought to apply it to my own heritage. I wanted to understand Alexander Campbell's nineteenth-century "restoration movement" as a function of its time and place—the way it was shaped (and limited) by its cultural context in profound ways. So it became clear that, though Mr. Campbell made an heroic effort to throw off all tradition, he remained shaped profoundly by it: by the Presbyterian tradition in which he was reared, by the Scottish intellectual tradition in which he was schooled, and by the young American tradition of democratic individualism in which he lived.

One key part of the work of theology is to recognize and engage the tradition and the times in which one finds oneself. The Stone-

---

[4] Lesslie Newbigin, *Trinitarian Doctrine for Today's Mission* (1963; Eugene, OR: Wipf & Stock, 2006), 34.
[5] Leonard Allen and Danny Swick, *Participating in God's Life: Two Crossroads for Churches of Christ* (Orange, CA: New Leaf, 2001).

Campbell Movement/Churches of Christ tended to assume that tradition could be leaped over or swept away. It didn't want the burden of it. It wanted only the untraditioned Bible. But the reality is that the Bible is always traditioned to us. Its message is always handed on through ongoing communities (traditions) of believers. It has slowly dawned on us that, as Alasdair McIntyre insisted, we are all "tradition constituted."[6] We are embedded in a time and place and it always forms us at a deep level. Our theologies are shaped more than we often know, by our traditions. That is to say, by where we have come from and who has influenced us. That certainly doesn't mean we are fixed or completely stuck in that place, but it does mean that we best attend to it, that we seek to become conscious of the traditions that have formed us.[7]

The strength of the restoration vision is that it enables us to shine fresh light upon Scripture and thus to keep testing—in light of our pervasive human finitude—the faithfulness of our theological construals, our interpretive decisions, and our discipleship practices. It is constantly putting burrs under the seats of the comfortable, the doctrinaire, and the culturally accommodated. It works from the conviction that accommodation and compromise are easier than most suppose, and that the call of Christ is more demanding than many wish to entertain.

Catechesis Old and New

The work of theology engages, inevitably, with the practice of catechesis. In the first four centuries a rigorous process of catechetical instruction and formation emerged and was fully in place by the early third century. Its outlines appear in the *Didache*, Justin's *First Apology*, Hippolytus' *Apostolic Tradition*, and other early writings. Its basic structure included three features: (1) enrollment (which entailed extensive examination), (2) instruction in Bible, doctrine, and discipleship (guided by teachers and sponsors who oversaw a kind of spiritual apprenticeship),

---

[6] Alasdair MacIntyre, *After Virtue: A Study in Moral Theory*, 3rd ed. (Notre Dame: University of Notre Dame, 2017), 9.

[7] See Leonard Allen, "The Burden and Blessing of Tradition," in *In the Great Stream: Imagining Churches of Christ in the Christian Tradition* (Abilene: ACU Press, 2021), 13-30.

culminating in (3) rites of initiation during Holy Week (focusing on exorcism, baptism, and eucharist). Throughout these early centuries, the Christian movement grew steadily, even dramatically, in face of strong cultural pressure and often persecution.

But as Christendom took shape over the centuries, the rigorous catechumenate of the early Christian movement faded until it was mostly forgotten. In Christendom most everybody was already a "Christian" and the rigors of the catechumenate found fewer and fewer takers. The rite of confirmation took its place as a completion of the baptism of infants. Some instruction was involved, but not always.

We no longer live in the world of Christendom or in a "Christian" America where church membership—often nominal—was normal. In the West today, nominal church membership is becoming less attractive and unbelief more compelling. According to recent research, thirty million people in North America who used to call themselves Christian have now deconverted—become "nonverts."[8] And as Christian Smith has famously shown, the dominant faith of emerging adults in our time is Moralistic Therapeutic Deism (MTD for short).[9] Its *summum bonum* is maximizing the opportunities for individuals to express and satisfy their desires—a belief that orthodox Christianity opposes but that Christianized MTD embraces and baptizes.

For this reason, the early Christian movement, where discipleship was inherently costly and rigorous training needed to become a disciple of Jesus, has something to teach us in a time when the church is finding itself pressed to function more and more as an outsider institution. What might we learn from early Christian catechesis for our formation of Christian leaders in a university and seminary context?

Daniel Aelshire, long-time and now retired president of the

---

[8] Stephen Bullivent, *Nonverts: The Making of Ex-Christian America* (New York: Oxford University Press, 2022).

[9] Christian Smith and Melina Lundquist Denton, *Soul Searching: The Religious and Spiritual Lives of American Teenagers* (New York: Oxford University Press, 2005), 163-71.

Association of Theological Schools, argues that we are currently in a third wave of change in modern seminary education: he calls it *formational theological education*. The first wave was an *apprenticeship* model (colonial period and beyond); the second was *professional theological education* (throughout most of the twentieth century and beyond). Aelshire argues that the professional model will continue to recede and focus will fall more on formational education, with growing attention to "authentic humanity, relational ability, and spiritual maturity." This approach "makes Christian character and spirituality central rather than co-curricular as has been the tendency in the professional model of theological education."[10]

In this new context, Fuller Seminary has refocused its formational goals for church leaders in a recent mission statement (2018), which says, in part: "The classic seminary is an institution that forms pastors for the *church in Christendom*; we're trying to move from that to being a seminary that forms leaders for a *church in exile*."

A church in exile—that's more and more where we are finding ourselves in this era. Theologian Ephraim Radnor recently opined that the West is facing a new Dark Age. "In this new era," he insisted, "theology will need to be sparer, stripped of speculative distractions, courageously at home with death and the 'other world,' and, most importantly, deeply engrossed in Scripture. Otherwise, the public face of the Christian faith will be washed away by the storm surge of our destructive culture." Churches in the West seem unprepared for this rising era, so "theological work in the Dark Ages ahead will need to learn from the Dark Ages behind. It must be stripped down and focused on the Scriptures' invitation to bring the apostolic world into the present, and not be 'updated' but rather 'backdate' our spiritual imaginations."[11] Radnor is a conservative Anglican but here sounds like an unbowed restorationist. I would say that Churches of Christ, in

---

[10] Daniel Aelshire, "The Emerging Model of Formational Theological Education," *Theological Education* 52, No. 2 (2018), 25-37; Aelshire, *Beyond Profession: The Next Future of Theological Education* (Grand Rapids: Eerdmans, 2021).

[11] Ephraim Radnor, "Dark Age Theology," *First Things* (November 2021).

their best impulses, have sought to "backdate"—rather than "update"—the Christian imagination. And in the modern era, where updating has been the name of the game, backdating is always a challenging theological undertaking, easily appearing retrograde, unenlightened, and out of touch.

A Theological Typology of Churches of Christ

Churches of Christ may have eschewed theology—all the while immersed in theology's three essential tasks, exegesis, catechesis, and polemics; but in our time Churches of Christ are becoming, in fact, much more theologically diverse. Let me propose a typology of five distinctive theologies that I believe can be discerned among Churches of Christ in this time.

1. Traditional Theology

It is oriented around a precise New Testament pattern or blueprint of the church. One must follow that pattern exactly to be considered a New Testament church. The Bible is the only acceptable creed. It is fully inspired and authoritative, God's infallible Word. All denominations have departed from that one and only creed and are thus out of favor with God. A cappella singing in worship is a vital part of that pattern and thus a salvation issue.

2. Nonsectarian Theology

This theology has moved beyond the strict patternism of the tradition, focusing instead on the overarching story of Scripture as the means of centering God's people and defining what the church in mission looks like. It takes a softer and nonsectarian approach to the denominations. The Bible is the only acceptable creed and is fully inspired and authoritative, God's infallible Word. Worshipping a cappella remains a strong and important practice but not a salvation issue.

3. Evangelical Theology

Evangelicalism is often defined by four features: biblicism (Scripture alone), crucicentrism (Jesus' saving death on the cross), conversionism (emphasis on being "born again"), and activism (a call to share one's faith and do good works). The Bible is viewed as fully inspired and authoritative, God's infallible Word. Churches of Christ have generally shared these commitments. But Evangelicals are shaped by another key influence: the eighteenth- and nineteenth-century revival movements and the pietism that accompanied them. Churches of Christ, shaped by Alexander Campbell, sharply rejected this revivalist theology, especially its experiential view of conversion. They remained separate and critical (though of course forming their own take on revivals: the gospel meeting). In recent decades a growing number of people in Churches of Christ have been drawn to Evangelicalism, attracted, it seems, by its somewhat more ecumenical spirit, its focus on a personal relationship with Jesus, and its warmer spirituality.

4. Post-Church of Christ Theology

I'm using this label as somewhat parallel to the term Post-Evangelical since both are reacting against some of the same things. Post-*Evangelicals* have been disturbed by Evangelicalism's grasping at political power, its harboring of racism, its embrace of nationalism, its limiting of women, and its lack of sufficient concern for social justice. Some have gone further, critiquing not only Evangelicalism but also basic doctrines of the historic orthodox faith. The Post-*Church of Christ* type is similar but reacting against traditional Church of Christ conservatism rather than the Evangelical form of it.

5. Progressive Theology

This term covers a range of views. Some versions appear somewhat more traditional and evangelical, others closer to classic liberal theology. It sometimes seems like an unsettled halfway house between traditional orthodoxy and classical liberalism. It tends to downplay the atoning sacrifice of Christ for sin and to focus heavily on social justice. It sometimes speaks of Jesus not so much as having a fully divine and fully human nature but rather a fully human nature that was strongly transparent to the divine. It often challenges the complete truthfulness of Scripture and usually affirms that the church's historic position on sexual ethics needs to be updated for late modern Western culture.

This is a typology, not a detailed map. Adjust some of the descriptions a bit and it could apply to other conservative Christian traditions. The typology points to a growing theological diversity in Churches of Christ—the reality that, despite the bias against theology, its members have been the recipients of lots of it. This growing diversity reflects, not surprisingly, the cultural pressures of our time. Modern Western culture, with its scientific and rationalistic canons of truth—and now its extreme individualistic canons—has long put Christian faith steadily on the defensive, pressuring it to adapt its doctrines, temper its claims, and accommodate the rising (post)modern outlook. It has made the practice of telling "subtraction stories" more and more common (cf. the discussion of Charles Taylor below).

The fragmenting pressures creating this diversity will continue. And mount.

Resistance and Retrieval

We now face new and strong challenges. A key challenge is a new kind of secularism pressing on Christian faith in the West. Charles Taylor calls it life in the "immanent frame." In the immanent frame the very awareness of and openness to divine transcendence—to an unseen spiritual realm—diminishes. In the immanent frame firm and settled Christian beliefs are steadily buffeted by fierce "cross pressures" that make truth seem flimsy and unstable.[12]

This spirit blows through our culture affecting all of us. People of faith are now pressed hard to privatize their beliefs and practices. The result is highly individualistic and experience-oriented articulations of what "feels authentic to me." In 1993 John Paul II well captured this spirit of the age in his powerful encyclical "The Splendor of Truth." With transcendence diminished, he wrote, "the individual conscience is afforded the status of a supreme tribunal of moral judgment which hands down categorical and infallible decisions about good and evil."

---

[12] Charles Taylor, *A Secular Age* (Cambridge: Harvard University, 2007), 542-56.

The result is that "the inescapable claims of truth disappear, yielding their place to a criterion of sincerity, authenticity, and 'being at peace with oneself.'"[13] The result is a constant undermining of firm, settled, and fulsome beliefs.

So we face an unavoidable theological question: To what degree will we accommodate the new secular order and to what degree resist? In a time like this, many of us who were formed in isolated, separated Christian traditions and have moved toward a broader perspective will likely be drawn (as James K. A. Smith noted) in one of two directions. Some will seek to play catch-up to the dominant culture, to get in step with the modern moral order, and to pursue a path toward some variety of "progressive" faith. That is, to update. And some will attempt to push back against the accommodationist posture and seek a faith anchored solidly in classic Christianity—the Great Tradition.[14] That is, to backdate.

I've cast my vote for the second option: the retrieval of the classic Christian tradition. I remember Flannery O'Conner's advice to "Push back against the age as hard as it pushes against you." The age has its own deep-seated, often hidden assumptions about reality, its own shifting and faddish orthodoxies. C. S. Lewis once said, "The most dangerous ideas in a society are not the ones being argued, but the ones that are assumed." We want to clarify and push back against some of those deep assumptions, against the spirit of the age and its reigning ideologies. This is part of the work of theology in any age.

And regarding the Bible itself, we want to embrace the classic doctrine of Scripture, not a modern reconstructed version (sometimes called liberal) and not a modern rationally enhanced version (sometimes called fundamentalism). That is, we want to embrace a view of Scripture's origin, nature, and function that most Christian theologians and pastors over the last two thousand years would recognize and embrace.

---

[13] Pope John Paul II, "*Veritatis Splendor*," Encyclical Letter (1993).
[14] James K. A. Smith, *How (Not) to Be Secular: Reading Charles Taylor* (Grand Rapids: Eerdmans, 2014), 138-39.

We do not mean thereby to reject the gains of modern historical study—the strong insights into the cultural and historical contexts of the Bible's authors and texts. We do mean, however, to reject the ideological strictures of the so-called higher criticism, with its methodological skepticism, its high-flown speculations, the tendency toward philosophical naturalism, the distancing from the life of the church, and the narrowed sense of what Scripture is, what it means, and what it is for. With the classic doctrine, we embrace the layered richness of Scripture, the claim that it is the living voice of God, that it bears trustworthy witness to the true and living God, and that it is primarily the church's book (not the academy's).

This is the theological foundation we want to give our students. We can call it indoctrination. Or maybe catechesis sounds a little better. William J. Abraham liked to call what we do in seminary "university level catechesis." We want to give our students strong tools for studying the text and a broad horizon against which to see the possibilities. But we also want to to catechize, to ground them in the core tenets of the faith—and make that a basic goal of theological study.

We shouldn't fear this task. Those of us who teach are, in fact, already doing that in some fashion, whether we call it indoctrination or not. We are already setting students on the path we believe they should go. So Stan Hauerwas says: "Any education that is worthy is obviously indoctrination. Our inability to acknowledge it as such in the name of respect for the student is but a sign of our corruption."[15] Hauerwas, of course, has a way of putting things bluntly.

In view of the lightness of truth in our time, this task of catechesis takes on a new urgency. It is one important aspect of the work of theology on behalf of the church. This should not be catechesis in your or my own theology, in your or my own considered conclusions and preferences (with the quirks and hobbies that usually go along with it)—though we certainly can't avoid a measure of that. Rather we want to make our best effort to ground and fortify students—and

---

[15] Stanley Hauerwas, *Dispatches from the Front: Theological Engagements with the Secular* (Durham: Duke University, 1994), 169.

church members—in the basics of the historic faith. What those basics are is not a deep mystery, though they are, of course, full of deep riches and plenty of mystery. As Flannery O'Connor put it, "Dogma is the guardian of mystery. The doctrines are spiritually significant in ways that we cannot fathom."[16] So we want to guard the mystery. We want to get the big rocks in place. We want our students to step into the "full wealth of conviction" (Col. 2:2, NEB). The weakening and steady receding of the Christian faith in the contemporary West demands it. In a culture where Christian belief gets steadily destabilized by rival and domineering accounts of reality, students need to be grounded and formed into a more substantial, more sound, and more vibrant Christian faith. This is the goal of theological study at its heart.

Believing, Teaching, and Confessing

This challenge means a basic grounding in Christian orthodoxy. The very word "orthodoxy" has fallen on hard times. Many today appear to have little idea what it means, and some who think they do are finding it quaint or maybe even oppressive. It's a notable sign of the times.

In one sense we can say that grounding in the classic faith is a fairly simple task: learn the Apostle's Creed or the Nicene Creed. But at another level, it is a profound challenge, involving a strong grasp of the Trinitarian vision that began in the earliest days of the Christian movement, a more robust classic doctrine of Scripture, the vital role of the early "rule of faith," the anchoring role of the apostolic tradition, and some sense of how modernity has challenged and compromised this classic foundation.

I have found it helpful to compare learning Christian theology to learning a language. Both involve a disciplined submission to a set of rules (a grammar), a new vocabulary, and a long tradition which carries forward a body of knowledge. In theology we begin learning the common language of faith. We learn Scripture and the history of its interpretation, the contours of the tradition as shaped by the creeds,

---

[16] Sally Fitzgerald, editor, *The Habit of Being: Letters of Flannery O'Connor* (New York: Farrar, Strauss and Giroux, 1979), 229.

catechisms, and classic doctrinal treatises, and at least an outline of how the Christian church made its way through history. We enter humbly into worlds and ways of speaking not our own, and this long perspective shapes how we make it our own in our own time. If the goal of language learning is to speak confidently and effectively in that language, then the goal of theology learning is to speak and live out the way of Christ in the church and before the world.[17]

As part of the framework for this, I have pointed students over the years to the work of Jaroslav Pelikan, the greatest historian of Christian doctrine in the twentieth century. In a magisterial five-volume work entitled *The Christian Tradition*, he sought to trace what the church "believed, taught, and confessed on the basis of the Word of God" over the centuries. He defined what is "believed" as the form of doctrine found in the literature of devotion and worship. What is "taught" was the content of Scripture extracted by exegesis and communicated through sermons and catechisms. And what is "confessed" was the church's testimony against false teaching and set forth in confessions and polemical writings.

I have long stressed that the form Christian doctrine has taken over the centuries is tradition. Tradition designates the handing down of Christian teaching. And dealing with tradition is inescapable. It is simply unavoidable that humans receive the witness of Scripture through a process of traditioning or handing down. Along the way, the church always faces the pull toward tradition*ism*—toward becoming, we might say, a fossil museum, where nothing ever changes; but with the wisdom of the tradition itself as a guide, it serves to anchor and help sustain our mission under God as we face new times and challenges.

The Ballast of Tradition

In our time Christian truth, normally passed on and weighted by tradition, has become lighter and more malleable. The ideological and social currents of our time have created an atmosphere where truth

---

[17] This paragraph and the next three are adapted from my book, *The Bookroom: Remembrance and Forgiveness—A Memoir* (Abilene: ACU Press, 2024).

seems to shift and float with the currents. Truth becomes mostly private and personal. You can pick and choose from the traditional package of Christian beliefs, guided by what seems personally preferable, by what speaks to you. You can make up your own orthodoxy—just you and your Bible, maybe aided by your favorite podcasters.

Churches of Christ have long been marked by a traditional disregard for tradition. But tradition is not an iron shackle to be cast off—as we have often presumed—but a weighty and living voice offering strong restraints when the winds howl and the swells rise. Tradition can be our ally, not our enemy. It can help us "stand fast." It can provide ballast, bearings, and wisdom as we seek to live out—and to hand on—the faith.

Some take this as a time for handwringing and dark pessimism. I don't. During my years at Harding, I first began to learn that, over its long history, Christian faith often remained vital when it lived outside the cultural mainstream. Though the church is always embedded in its particular culture and place, at the same time it is an outpost of another country, another kingdom. Its citizens are drawn from every tribe, nation, and tongue. And so it has its own distinct culture and politics. Not of the left or the right, the libertarian or the liberal. It is a politics of the cross, set up and exemplified in our baptism where the old gets put to death and the new is being birthed. In the power of the Spirit, the church is living—often haltingly—into the new.

The steady—and essential—work of theology is to monitor, focus, and support the church's mission through time as it witnesses to the lordship of Christ, tangles with the principalities and powers in the power of the Holy Spirit, and waits confidently for the fullness of God's coming kingdom.

CHAPTER FIVE

Library and Theological Scholarship

Carisse Mickey Berryhill

I'm honored to have been asked to write about the library and theological scholarship. In this chapter, I am concerned mainly to define the key points about the role of the library at HST so that those elements can be sustained as the school transitions to a new setting. I want to do this by developing the notion of *scholarly formation*.

The 2023 Mission Statement of HST says that it "challenges Christian leaders to develop deeper faith in God and higher standards of ministry *and scholarship*." It "challenges Christian leaders to integrate spiritual growth, ministry experience, and *rigorous scholarship*." Harding School of Theology "provides quality training for excellence in ministry and *scholarship*. We offer strong biblical and theological *scholarship* that is seasoned with a commitment to ministry."[1]

So, *HST sees itself as a community that intends to form students by a system of discipline as scholars for service to the churches.*

The notion of *formation* is rooted in the authority of a community to guide its members toward maturity. It commonly is organized around doctrine and discipline in community. In Churches of Christ, we are most familiar with this terminology in the New Testament epistles. For example, James W. Thompson asserts in *The Church According to Paul: Rediscovering the Community Conformed to Christ* that "formation is a uniquely Pauline word."[2] Thompson's focus in Chapter 4, titled "Spiritual Formation is Corporate Formation," is

---

[1] *School of Theology 2023-2024 Academic Catalog*, Harding University, accessed February 16, 2024, https://catalog.harding.edu/content.php?catoid=1&navoid=29.

[2] James W. Thompson, *The Church According to Paul: Rediscovering the Community Conformed to Christ* (Grand Rapids, MI: Baker Academic, 2014): 103.

not on individual perfection but on the "community conformed to Christ."[3] In *Moral Formation According to Paul*, Thompson asserts that Paul establishes "a group ethos for his communities, a collective identity as the basis for the 'ought.'"[4]

The language of spiritual formation has lately become familiar to us, as exemplified in HST's year of Spiritual Formation in 2002, inaugurating curricular opportunities for spiritual formation of ministers in HST degree programs. As Dave Bland and Keith Mask wrote then, "All of us in the various academic departments are committed to one common goal: the spiritual formation of ministers and counselors. We believe that it is the one goal of spiritual formation that unites all disciplines in the task of theological education."[5]

Theological education, in the case of HST, is carried out by an accredited institution of education which is church-related but not church-owned. That is, the *authority* of the school comes not from the church proper, but resides in accreditation, or academic credentialing according to standards. HST voluntarily participates in the Association of Theological Schools in the United States and Canada, an association of similar institutions who develop standards and mutually hold one another accountable to these standards of best practice.

In *scholarly formation*, maturity is called scholarship. *Scholarship* is participation in intellectual discourse in a disciplinary community which has conventions of inquiry and standards of authority, namely advancement of knowledge, governed by peer review. In order to advance knowledge, a person must have wide and deep knowledge in their discipline, so that they can see where work needs to be done to expand the field. To begin achieving this expertise, aspiring scholars go to graduate school and submit to the academic *disciplines* of course work, research papers, and dissertations. To develop expertise, they read, attend conferences, and reflect on what they are learning. To

---

[3] Thompson, *Church According to Paul*, 104.

[4] James W. Thompson, *Moral Formation According to Paul: The Context and Coherence of Pauline Ethics* (Grand Rapids, MI: Baker Academic, 2011): 44.

[5] Dave Bland and Keith Mask, "The Year of Spiritual Formation," *The Bridge* 43.5 (September 2002), 1.

contribute to their field, they write articles and books, and speak. A scholar is someone whose contributions to the advancement of their discipline have been recognized by peers in the field. A scholar becomes an authority by an outstanding record of achievement that has been received by disciplinary peers.

Scholarly formation, like spiritual formation, is an intentional process carried out in community. As we just saw, HST intends to develop students in an atmosphere of rigorous scholarship. In this effort, I assert that the librarians and the professors are symmetrical partners. My remarks will explore four symmetries in their partnership: faculty status, teaching, spaces, and community.

The first point of symmetrical partnership is that both the professional librarians and classroom professors have *faculty status*. Faculty have advanced training in various academic disciplines. Professors at HST hold doctorates in their respective disciplinary fields, such as biblical studies, ministry, or counseling. Librarians hold masters-level degrees in library science and in a theological discipline. Professional librarians are not support staff. They are faculty. The academic activities of faculty, including librarians, have been routinely reported in the *Bulletin* or *Bridge* in a "Faculty Highlights" section. Because the faculty are scholars in their own fields, they track new developments in fields of study and in educational standards. They serve on accrediting teams. And because of their respective academic qualifications, the faculty work together as partners to determine the degrees offered and the requirements of the curriculum. The curriculum itself is owned by the faculty. Each one has a vote.

The second point of symmetrical partnership is that they work side-by-side as partners *to realize the curriculum* they have devised. The professors develop and teach their courses; the librarians collect the resources for all the professors and students to use for teaching and research in all the courses. Both help each other. Annie May Alston once wrote, "The library ... is the one place where all of the disciplines of the classroom find a home."[6] Professors' syllabi are scoured by the librarians every year. Every new book on the syllabus is ordered. Suggestions for resources are always welcomed from the professors, while librarians reciprocate by generating notices of new books received. From September 1969 until her retirement in 1983, Annie May Alston Lewis sent faculty—in her inimitable conversational style—a monthly one-page update about new resources and occasional tidbits from the latest library annual report. When I worked with Don Meredith, he distributed bundles of newly filled library order slips to faculty boxes. The suggestion box for new titles was open to students and local readers as well. Don would get a very determined look on his face if someone asked for a book we didn't own. Of course, he would order it immediately if it was in scope. (Usually we had the book and he knew the call number by heart.) When I interviewed for the assistant librarian position in 1992, I met with Phil McMillion and Allen Black and asked them what role the faculty played in determining the books the library acquired. They may have mentioned the syllabi. Phil may have mentioned the suggestion box. Allen looked at me with a bemused smile and said, "Well, I just assume that everything I need will be here."

Building the collection is the constant work of the librarian for all the disciplinary fields taught. A new course or new degree field means retrospective collections must be added to the constant flow of new books. To find books, the selector relies on bibliographies, indexes, periodicals, catalogs, and now electronic services as well. Early on, Annie May decided to routinely buy books published in major monographic series. Before we had electronic means of tracking these titles, the assistant librarian scoured the pages of scholarly journals received to identify new titles in scholarly series, typing them onto sheets in a set of three-ring binders. Don pounced on catalogs from publishers and used book dealers. If you were a student worker in the library, you checked to see if the library owned a book which Don had marked in a sale catalog. If not, Don typed an order card. One of my

---

[6] Annie May Alston, "Place of the Library in the Minister's Education," *Graduate School Bulletin* 12.5 (Aug 1973): 1.

most familiar audible memories of working with Don was hearing him hammering on an IBM Selectric typewriter, typing out 3x5 order cards to be filed in the To-Be-Ordered file drawers in the work room. If a book went out of print before it could be ordered, it was moved to the Out-of-Print file drawers. He had five 1,000-card drawers ready when money was available. I asked him once how long it would take him to spend a million dollars. He said, "I could spend it as fast as Miss Billie could type the orders. Two weeks." We laughed. But I believed him.

Gifts of books or dollars from the professors have been a significant source of library growth. Of course, we all know that if you use the library to research your book, you owe a copy of that book to the library! Professors have been generous and reliable donors to the library. The most significant financial gift from a professor, of course, is Dr. Jack Lewis's gift of the P. G. and Anna Lewis Endowment fund, begun in 1983, which provided interest income of upwards of $15,000 a year to augment the book budget for more than 30 years. When Dr. Jack died in 2018, his bequest of $1 million went to the Lewis endowment and tripled its principal.

When Annie May came to Memphis in 1962-63, her first annual report showed that the library had 7,317 volumes. The library grew by about 2,800 volumes every year, reaching 50,000 volumes in 1975, 75,000 volumes in 1985, 100,000 volumes in 1994, 125,000 volumes in 2001, and 150,000 volumes in 2013. Sixty years and $5 million dollars after Annie May began, the 2023 annual report lists 171,299 volumes, including e-books.

The library, of course, is not a one-person shop. Since 1962, the library has had four head librarians (HST has had twice that number of deans): Annie May Lewis (21 years), Don Meredith (35 years), Bob Turner (3.5 years), and Jessica Holland (now in her third year). The head librarian manages the library, selects the resources, teaches Advanced Theological Research, and assists readers with their questions. Since 1968 one or more professional librarians have served alongside the head. The assistant librarian makes the library's resources visible by cataloging them and managing electronic and access services. After Don, only five other professionals have held this role: Bonnie Baker Barnes (twice for a total of 7 years), Melanie Pennington (2 years), Carisse Berryhill (12 years), Sheila Owen (23 years) and Bob Turner (8 years). There have been 14 library staff serving one or two at a time, who manage circulation, interlibrary loans, periodical subscriptions, purchasing, and the student workers. Longest serving among them were Evelyn Meredith (40 years), Billie Thomason (27 years) and Pat Hughes (11 years). There have been at least 155 different student workers.

Realizing the curriculum, of course, means teaching the students. Here again, the librarians and the professors are partners in scholarly formation. In 1968 Annie May co-taught a newly-required course called Introduction to Graduate Study (now Advanced Theological Research) that was required for the MA. By 1970 she was solely responsible for the course. In 1973 it was required for all students before they could advance beyond 9 credit hours. During the peak on-campus enrollment years, it was taught several times a year. Each student worked through 15 sets of exercises on general library tools and on resources for each area of study, updated annually. The exercises were accompanied by a requirement to compose a bibliographic essay on a biblical text, which was graded meticulously for writing and documentation. "No one on our faculty reads papers like Don does," Dr. Black commented when Don Meredith retired in 2017 after having taught the course 177 times. "[H]is hard work is a foundation for every paper each student writes in later courses."[7] When I worked at HST, I remember seeing Don take a cart up into the stacks with one student paper in hand, retrieve all the sources used, and then look up each citation to see if it was not only formatted correctly but also if the paper represented the source fairly. This method of instruction had two great benefits: it prepared students to succeed in courses by learning how to treat sources responsibly; and it imprinted the students with confidence in using the library's resources and in calling on the librarian's ability to help them in scholarly work. The bibliographic expertise of the librarians is awesome.

The professors not only teach their courses and give exams, but

---

[7] Allen Black, "Reflections from the Dean," *The Bridge* 58.1 (Fall 2017): 3.

they supervise research assistants; they direct and scrutinize student research for guided research papers, theses, and dissertations; and they model the life of scholarship by publishing articles and books, by presenting at professional conferences, and by teaching in the churches. I said earlier that HST intends to form students by a system of disciplines as scholars for service to the churches. The professors' scholarship provides a wide range of materials for study by ministers, Bible teachers, church leaders, and counselors. They not only help these people; they *are* these people, serving as elders, ministers, teachers, and counselors.

The third point of symmetrical partnership in scholarly formation is that both professors and librarians function in *spaces* designed to encourage scholarship. I think we are accustomed to thinking of the classroom or the seminar room, or even the professor's study, as the place where students are taught and tutored as they develop as scholars. Here I'd like to point out how the library's physical spaces are also formative for scholarship.

There is, of course, the obvious truth that if you have thousands of print volumes, you need a place to make them available for use. The library in its first year was in the former bookstore. Then it moved to the basement of the mansion until 1974, when the 9,300 square-foot library building was completed. Besides stack space for 65,000 volumes, the new building included an office for the librarian, a large seminar and rare books room, a main lobby with the card catalog and consulting tables, a front circulation desk, a large staff workroom, restrooms, a coat rack, a reference room with reading tables, tables for print indexes, a current-periodical display area, and several small study rooms suitable for one person.

In 1978, a 6,344 square-foot two-story addition on the west side expanded the capacity to 95,000 volumes. It included an elevator, a restroom, a classroom, a group study room, a storeroom, and 50 downstairs carrels.

In 2006, an eastside addition of 6,100 square-feet increased the capacity to 125,000 volumes. It also included a new front entrance and lobby with easy chairs, an exhibit area, tables, main-floor periodical and reference shelving, revamped offices and workroom areas, two restrooms, a larger classroom/computer lab, an interior ramp to the upper level, and an area for archives.

As I consider these iterations of the library spaces, I see three trends besides more room for materials. The first is space for scholarly work, such as consulting indexes, reading, and writing. As methods of research access change, the spaces include technological interfaces. The second trend is teaching space, most recently including a large classroom designed for hybrid teaching. The third trend is more space for discussion and conversation. I remember thinking in 2000 or so that almost the only place not for quiet study was the lobby, where people leaned on the consulting tables by the card catalog to chat about courses, churches, and football. There wasn't a coffee pot for readers. No easy chairs. Although there were a fridge, a coffee pot, and social space in the classroom building on the other side of campus, the library didn't really feel socially hospitable. It was designed as a service point, not a social setting. The library addition in 2006 accomplished real progress in that direction. Bob Turner even added a pour-over coffee station fashioned from a decommissioned card catalog. As Bob observed in 2017, "The library will continue not only as a collection but also a commons—to foster disciplines of research, study, conversation, fellowship, celebration and renewal."[8]

Of course, not all scholarly work takes place in a campus classroom or in the library. Even in the 1950s, extension classes took place in churches in Memphis and other cities so far away that some of the faculty bought a plane and flew it themselves! Hardwired network internet access arrived about 1998, and eventually Wi-Fi. I taught my first web-based asynchronous course for HST in Spring 2002. It was called Writing in Ministry and there were five students; I still have the HTML files. In Fall 2004, Dr. Black pioneered teaching NT Greek online. Like most veteran online instructors, we have seen migrations through several online course management systems as Harding University geared up for online teaching. The COVID-19 pandemic

---

[8] Bob Turner, "The Final Chapter," *The Bridge* 58.1 (Fall 2017): 4.

accelerated the shift to remote work and remote teaching, even if some of us were dragged kicking and screaming into it. I was grateful that HST had asked me to start using Zoom in Fall 2019 to teach LIVE (live interactive video education) sessions in History of the Stone-Campbell Movement, so I knew how to help my church Bible class go online.

Meanwhile, the library's reference tools vendors necessarily gradually shifted to online access. When desktop computers arrived before the internet did, researchers could come to the library to use reference tools on CD-ROM or to request database searches carried out by the assistant librarian by dial-up. The first time I saw an electronic TLG (Thesaurus Linguae Graecae) search, it took all night on a dedicated dial-up computer and was marvelous! Now that same search online takes nanoseconds. Now the Atla Religion Bibliographies that used to occupy a twelve-foot index table have turned into databases which students may log into remotely. Online tools, of course, can be used anywhere an authorized researcher has access to a computer. Let it be understood that such opportunities are made possible by the subscriptions paid by the library. These subscriptions are part of the library's partnership with the professors to support their research and the scholarly formation of their students.

The fourth point of symmetrical partnership in scholarly formation is that both professors and librarians participate in *community life* with students on-campus and in ever-broadening circles. Chapel in the mansion is first. I will never forget a 15-minute chapel talk by Allen Black on the structure of Mark. Not to mention how the singing sounds when the men outnumber the women by such a huge margin! One of my great privileges of working on campus for twelve years was worship together.

Community starts very locally, and for decades that local spot has been 1000 Cherry Road, where student housing even had to be expanded in 1964 and again in 1998. Because she lived on campus until she married Dr. Lewis, Annie May often wrote in the *Bulletin/Bridge* affectionately about student life on campus, and especially about women whose husbands were students or who were students themselves. She felt especially attached to the young men, all of whom she taught in Introduction to Graduate Study. She told me one time with a wink, "I hug the students, and shake hands with their wives." She wrote in the *Bulletin* in 1996,

> I thought I was the most blessed of all the faculty members because I lived with the students day in and day out. I wept with them, and I rejoiced with them.... We were in and out of each other's apartments for numerous cups of tea, for supper and for late-night snacks. I think they considered me as one of their own, though they kept their respect when we were in the classroom and I was the teacher and they were the students. However, I shared the student status with them when we took courses together.[9]

Three members of her family died during the years she lived in the apartments. She wrote, "I do not believe I could have borne those losses without the comfort the students brought to me. I realized that the God of all comfort was my ultimate comforter, but the students were his hands and feet to help me through those dark days."[10]

Both professors and librarians participate in national and international scholarly communities. Since its beginning the *Bulletin/ Bridge* has been filled with reports from both about faculty publications and presentations at conferences, about alumni who are faculty at other colleges and universities, about speeches at lectureships and forums. There is a quilt of scholars whose scholarship is rooted at HST. Alumni know they have lifetime borrowing privileges at the library. The library subscribes to Atla for alumni, so that they can continue to use the Atla databases.

Then, think about the hundreds of library student workers and professors' graduate assistants who have worked beside and shared a coffee or a meal with the scholars who are teaching them and who write them recommendations to churches and to nonprofits and to

---

[9] Annie May Lewis, "Campus Housing: More Than Bricks and Mortar," *The Bulletin* 37.3 (May 1996): 1.
[10] Ibid.

PhD programs. I have loved for years the local churchmanship of our administrators, professors, and librarians as they serve congregations as elders, ministers, and teachers. Think about how the life of the professors and alumni are interwoven in congregations in Memphis and all over the world. They are scholars whose scholarship serves the churches. And the churches have loved the school back—think about all the dinners, pie auctions, and fundraisers that church folk have cooked for, attended, and generously supported. Consider how generously alumni and their families have donated year-after-year.

I'd like to mention one very-focused way that HST librarians have facilitated past and future scholarship about the churches, and that is by collecting and preserving archives, such as thousands of small-press publications, periodicals, pamphlets, church directories, curricula, sound recordings, missionary reports, oral histories, and personal papers of leaders in the Churches of Christ specifically and the Restoration Movement broadly. I vividly remember taking a prospective student to the mission reports cabinets—twelve of them at the time—and finding the newsletters his parents had published when he was a child. There he was, a seventh grader. That young man found his story at HST and he enrolled. I have taught the History of the Stone-Campbell Movement online for HST for ten years, all the while administering the Stone-Campbell archive at ACU, so I admit a special bias here. But I think some of the most fruitful research in the future will mine these resources. I tell my HST students when I assign them to collect an oral history interview that it is one thing to read history and another thing to *do* history. None of them will ever read a history book the same way again.

Persistent Partnership in Scholarly Formation

I've described and illustrated the partnership between the library and the professors in scholarly formation of the students at HST. I think this formational partnership is crucial to HST's identity. The following key elements of the library's role need to be sustained if HST's mission to prepare scholars to serve the churches is to be sustained:

- Librarians qualified in library science and theology must be appointed as faculty and participate in curricular decision-making.
- Advanced Theological Research is the keystone of scholarly formation and must be taught by library faculty.
- Funding for acquisition of scholarly materials must continue to grow.
- The library's physical collections must be professionally packed, transported, and reshelved.
- The library's rare books and archival collections must be properly preserved and made accessible in the new space.
- The library's physical space must have a freight elevator and ample space for the current collections and for annual growth for twenty years.
- The library's physical space must have ample space and appropriate furnishings for librarians, staff, student workers, and users, including offices, a workroom, a classroom, exhibits, and workspaces for individuals and groups. All spaces must be handicap accessible.
- The library must have excellent electrical supply, electronic networks, computers, and scanners for responding to offsite user requests and for onsite user access.
- The library must have increased staff funding to process and deliver offsite requests for materials from faculty, students, and alumni.
- Careful attention must be given to developing community on campus in Searcy and online.

Many of us remember when the Mansion was severely damaged in a fire on July 29, 1993. We may also remember that when Jack and Annie May Lewis arrived and saw the smoke and the fire fighters, he remarked, "Well, there goes my life's work." Annie May answered, "No, Jack. Your life's work is in the students you taught working all over the world."[11] Dr. Bill Flatt remembered his anxiety that day as a newly appointed dean. How, he wondered through heartsick tears, could he operate the school without an administrative building? Annie May told him, "Bill, this is a time for faith."[12] It is such a time for HST today.

---

[11] Allen Black, "Reflections from the Dean," *The Bridge* 59.1 (2018): 3.
[12] Bill Flatt, "Fire Severely Damages Old Mansion," *The Bulletin* 34.5 (Sept 1993): 1.

CHAPTER SIX

Preaching

Matthew D. Love

"Others have labored, and you have entered into their labor."

(John 4:38, NRSV)[1]

Some time ago, Devin Swindle, HST alumnus and professor of Preaching at Harding University, introduced me to a piece of artwork: "The Legacy" by Ron DiCianni. The painting shows a preacher dressed in his Sunday attire, standing behind a pulpit, and holding an opened Bible. He is preaching. To the eyes of the congregation this man stands alone. But, the painting depicts something unseen. Surrounding the preacher—in bleached out color indicating a spiritual reality—stands a great cloud of witnesses: angels and biblical heroes gathered around this preacher, strengthening him, and praying for him. We, the viewers of the painting, understand the intended message: *no one who preaches stands alone.*

This truth resonates with me personally. After nearly a decade preaching, I have come to rely more fully on the promise of Christ: "Behold, I am with you always" (Matt 28:20). Yes, some Sundays I feel unsure about preaching: I feel too tired or too sinful or too unprepared. Yet, I am coming to trust the words of Scripture, that, even when my heart condemns me, God is greater than my heart (1 John 3:20). *Christ is with me*, and he is with me when I preach. I believe the truth portrayed in "The Legacy," that a spiritual host stands at my back and at the backs of all persons who are called to preach.

Yet, there is a more (how to put it?) *earthly* sense in which this is also true. Not only does the preacher stand in the company of a

---

[1] All scripture quotations in this chapter are taken from the New Revised Standard Version Updated Edition.

heavenly host, the preacher also stands in the company of another host, in the midst of Christian men and women who have come before us and helped create the world into which we were born. Some of these are still alive, while others have "fallen asleep." They are the humble servants, the spiritual giants on whose shoulders we stand.

Some in the congregation marvel that a preacher has a gift for public speaking, the nerves to address large audiences, such recall of the Scriptures, and the ability to bring a fresh sermonic word every week. Some may give preachers a lot of credit and acclaim for their preaching. Perhaps they see the preacher standing behind the pulpit alone but fail to perceive what we preachers do: that had it not been for a great host of men and women investing in us, supporting us, bearing with us, and praying for us, we could not stand where we stand. Our work is only possible because of those who came before us. Here, the words of Jesus come to mind: "Others have labored, and you have entered into their labor" (John 4:38).

As I reflect upon these truths, names and faces come to my mind—those who have had a hand in leading me to the pulpit. I think of my childhood preacher from back home in rural Ohio: Jim Mitchell, a preacher unknown to most the world, but cherished in my memory. I cannot remember a single sermon he preached, but I remember his faithfulness and humble presence as he appeared before the church each Sunday and opened God's word to us. Then, I think of my Christian grandparents, and specifically my grandfather Franklin Love, who preached in small, country churches in tiny towns in western Pennsylvania and southern Ohio. I think of how his sincere faith which dwelt first in his own children now dwells in me. Many still besides these who come to mind: family, friends, church camp counselors, undergraduate professors, missionaries—the list goes on. But, as I recall these names and faces of the persons and communities who have made me the Christian I am today, I cannot do so without remembering the people who taught and served me while I was a student at Harding School of Theology.

I share these personal reminiscences not merely to highlight myself, but because they reflect what many preachers who have attended HST would surely say: that this school has left an indelible imprint on our lives. We have been deeply formed by this school, and we are forever grateful. We perceive this truth even if others do not: that, on any given Sunday when we stand up to preach, we sense, in some spiritual and real way, the HST community standing with us.

Memories of Harding School of Theology

The well-known Methodist preacher and homiletician Will Willimon entitled his 2019 memoir *Accidental Preacher*. That title strikes a chord with me. I began preaching full-time in 2015, nearly a decade ago, and started work on a PhD in Preaching at Baylor University in 2019. That is to say, around the year 2015 I jumped into the deep end of the preaching pool with both feet. *I am a preacher.* And yet, looking back over the course of my life, this fact is an amazement to me. Some preachers knew very early in life that there were preachers and that preaching was what they wanted to do—not me. Many days I find myself amazed that *I am a preacher.*

There were many moments when my life could have taken another turn: I was almost a Buckeye but became a Bison, and I wonder what my life would have been had I gone to Columbus as a freshman rather than Searcy. I shudder to think about it. I began Harding as a Theater major, and switched to Bible after one semester. But even then, I thought I would go to the mission field. I never wanted to preach—at least not full-time. The Lord had other plans. He led me to the Beebe Church of Christ and surrounded me with a congregation that has loved on me and "helped raise me," as one member has been fond of putting it.

I began work on an MDiv at HST in 2012. Some of my fondest memories of these days are of piling into a car with my good friend Harrison Dell at 5:00 AM and driving two hours to campus, spending the day in Memphis, and driving home to be back for dinner. There are many ways to "do grad school." I worked full-time in ministry while taking classes and so had the benefit of ministry and education cross-pollinating. It took me seven years to graduate: a perfect number for a wonderful season of my life.

When I think about HST, I think first of the library. *How could one not?* I never felt like I was "on campus" until I had gone inside to see and smell the books. I remember Don Meredith and his quad-color pen, and how one of those colors was all but spent correcting the research paper I wrote for him. Beyond that sacred space of books and quiet, I think also of the many wonderful classes I took. I recall reading portions of Barth's *Dogmatics* for Dr. Powell, and watching Dr. Black pour out his wisdom on the "Synoptic Problem" as he enjoyed an afternoon can of Diet Coke.

By 2015, I had transitioned into the role of Preaching Minister at Beebe, and so I had a brand-new use for classes which explicitly dealt with the task of preaching. I had three. First, I took Exposition of Luke with Drs. Black and Martin; second, Creative Practices and Resources for Preaching with Dr. Bland; and third, Biblical Preaching" also with Dr. Bland. The books we read and the conversations we had in these classes were invaluable, and the materials I collocated through these classes are ones I still consult.

In describing campus life, one part that might be overlooked or underappreciated is chapel. Some may suppose that chapel is a nod toward sentimentality or an afterthought in the presence of such serious academics; maybe a theological nicety that outside eyes (like donors) like to see on campus. Some may find it merely a brief occasion for collegiality or a necessary time for sharing announcements. Yet, for me (and I think truly), chapel represents the heart of Harding School of Theology. After all, HST is foremost a place of faith. I looked forward to chapel whenever I was on campus. It was a holy time, a place of rest and spiritual refreshment. It was a sacred (though, too brief) respite from the stresses of personal life, the trials of ministry, and the demands of serious study.

Chapel was also a time of preaching. Seminaries, of course, offer classes *on preaching*, but chapel is a time of actual preaching, a moment when the word was told. I still remember several talks, and that I came to chapel (divinity student as I was) as a mere Christian yearning to hear the voice of Christ. Chapel captures the heart of the school. What I learned in chapel was as valuable to me as anything I learned in class, that world-class Christian intellectualism need not abandon simple and earnest faith. In chapel I leaned that HST was not merely a place to earn a degree: it was a community in which one could come find God.

The Impact of Harding School of Theology on Preaching

There are many ways in which one could chronicle the 66-year impact of Harding School of Theology. One might number the students who have passed through the school, enumerate the publications of graduates and faculty, or list those who have gone on to do doctoral work or to teach. But, no chronicle of this school's impact could suffice which does not feature HST's impact in and through preaching. In fact, one could argue that the greatest impact of HST on the church has come *via* the pulpit.

The list of preacher-graduates is stunning for those familiar with Stone-Campbell heritage; names that (without hyperbole) have defined preaching in this movement over the last half-century or more. Jimmy Allen and Jerry Jones are two, both of whom have preached all over the world and led hundreds of individuals to Christ in baptism. Tim Sensing writes that Jerry Jones was "the first person [from our heritage] formally trained in homiletics to teach at a Christian college."[2] Another prominent graduate and preacher, Lynn Anderson, was a preacher and the founder of HOPE Network Ministries. Lynn is said to have influenced the preaching of several others, including Max Lucado. The list continues with names like Leon Sanderson, Rubel Shelly, Mike Cope, Harold Shank, Randy Harris, and Harold Redd. For those familiar with these individuals and their influence, even this brief list of names is quite impressive. Equally impressive are the dozens and dozens of other graduates who are less known but equally faithful, who have preached in countless churches all over the globe. It makes little difference that many of these preacher-graduates have not achieved any sort of fame, even among Churches of Christ; they are known to their churches and communities, as well as to God. Their impact is real and significant.

---

[2] Mary Alice Mulligan, ed., *The Living Pulpit* (St. Louis: Chalice, 2018), 14.

Besides practitioners of preaching, there have been several graduates who have gone on to teach Preaching. For instance, Tim Sensing is an HST graduate who has taught preaching at Abilene Christian for some twenty-five years. Most of those graduates who have gone on to teach Preaching have done so at Harding University, including Tom Alexander, Eddie Cloer, Mike Ireland, Ken Neller, Phil Thompson, and Devin Swindle.

This incredible impact of graduates who have come *through* the school is due, in great part, to what has taken place *in* the school. Certainly, all courses impact students who go on to preach or teach. But the teaching of Preaching at HST deserves special attention here. In the 66 years that HST has existed, there have not been many to teach Preaching. Phil Slate did so for a spell, but mostly out of necessity, as I understand. One professor, however, has devoted his career to studying and teaching Preaching, as well as directing the DMin program and teaching various ministry-related courses.

Dave Bland began teaching in 1993. Spring of 2024 is his final semester, which puts him at 30 years of service. During this time, he has taught several courses and influenced many students. His direct impact on preaching in our movement is profound. As I have known him—and those with whom I have spoken about him concur—Dr. Bland is an extremely humble man. In fact, when I was a student at HST, I had little awareness of the broad and impressive career in homiletics that Dr. Bland has had. I knew him as a gracious and good teacher whose classes I enjoyed, yet I never fathomed his larger impact on the communities of faith and scholarship around the world.

Dave has published several journal articles and book essays, including articles contributing to *Baker Illustrated Bible Dictionary* (2013), *Feasting on the Word* commentaries (2008, 2010, 2011, 2013), and the *New Interpreter's Bible Handbook of Preaching*. Many in Restoration fellowships will be familiar with his co-edited volumes with David Fleer published by Chalice Press and ACU Press, some eleven volumes altogether. He helped edit *The Living Pulpit* (2018) and contributed a volume in the College Press commentary series, *Proverbs, Ecclesiastes, Song of Songs* (2002). Perhaps, most noteworthy are two monographs he has written: *Creation, Character, and Wisdom: Rethinking the Roots of Environmental Ethics* with Wipf & Stock in 2016, and *Proverbs and the Formation of Character* with Cascade in 2015, which was reviewed some 15 times in various journals.

Beyond these publications, Dave has also served as a book review editor for the journal *Homiletic* (2007–2020). He has spoken and led workshops around the country and world, from Abilene to Malibu, and from Scotland to Germany. Recently, he was invited to participate in a gathering in Oxford, England with Old Testament scholar John Goldingay where he will present a lecture about aphorisms in spiritual formation.

As I student, I failed to appreciate the scope and impact of Dr. Bland's work beyond the classroom. But others have noted and appreciated it. He was an "Outstanding Alumnus of the Year" for Harding in 2010, and Distinguished Teacher of the Year in 2016–2017. Beyond this institution, he is a member of the "Chrysostom Club" of the Evangelical Homiletics Society, and in 2021 he received the prestigious "Lifetime Achievement Award" from the Academy of Homiletics. His papers are being archived at Baylor University.

Any conversation about the impact of Harding School of Theology must include its impact on preachers and through preaching. After 30 years of teaching service, that conversation must also include the name Dave Bland.

What Is Next for Preaching?

With the transition of the school from Memphis to Searcy, one's mind goes toward the future of the school and (in conversation with this essay) the future of preaching. For more than sixty years, Harding School of Theology has been—among other things—a place for the formation of preachers. One prays that this same legacy continues, so that this new chapter beginning in the Fall of 2024 redoubles the already impressive impact that the school has had in and through the pulpit. In imagining this future, questions concerning the future of preaching arise, and a few more critical questions, which concern both the church and the academy, come to mind as well.

Whether We Value Preaching

It is a blunt question, but one that needs asking. *Do we value preaching?* In my experience, the answer is often *yes, preaching is tremendously valued.* Listen closely to the opening and closing prayers in our assemblies and one will occasionally hear the sermon given unique import: "Be with the preacher as he brings us a word today" or "Help us to take this morning's sermon to heart and live it out." Prayers like these are evidence that the unique importance of the preaching is deeply embedded in our ecclesial subconscious. The sermon is still seen as the central or climatic moment of the worship service.

But there is also evidence that the sermon has fallen on hard times. The sentiment is expressed ever and anon that "anyone can preach." When a new minister is hired, someone might opine that the church does not need someone who "only preaches," as if the "real work" of ministry took place everywhere but Sunday morning. Even though we read that the apostles devoted themselves to the ministry of the word and to prayer (Acts 6:4), how many elderships would be content to allow their preacher to do only that? It is little wonder that Christian news outlets continue to report shortages of ministers. Ministers often do not receive the support they need, financially or otherwise. But, what is more, preachers are not always taken seriously. How many of our young people do we talk to about becoming preachers and intentionally work with to put them on that path? Perhaps for someone else's child. As for me and my house, I would feel better about a career in medicine, law, or engineering.

One could wish that such devaluation of preaching was only visible in congregations among laypersons who have not been to Bible college or seminary, and so, who do not know any better; but this devaluation is also observable in the academy. At most institutions, an MDiv approaches 80 credit hours, comprising more than 20 classes. Yet, often, only one required course directly concerns preaching. The attitude toward courses in Preaching is just as striking. When Fred Craddock took the Bandy Chair of Preaching at Emory University, he remarked how, when he first began teaching preaching in the sixties, "you couldn't sell a course in preaching," and (with typical Craddockian wit) "those seminaries that tried to make it required had petitions from the students signed by most of the faculty." Preaching is like a "soft science" in the midst of "hard sciences"—think of courses in backgrounds, languages, and exegesis, which are sometimes treated as the real courses in seminary. Preaching is more of an afterthought, a "just in case" you are so unfortunate as to be asked to preach. Preaching has been caricatured as a Christian class in communication, and probably a poor-man's version at that. It is a class about *how* to say something, granting that we have already learned *what* to say elsewhere. We like Cato's advice: *Tene rem, verba sequentur*: "Grasp the subject, the words will follow."

But the problem is, knowing a subject does not make one competent to teach it or preach it. A brilliant mathematician is far from pre-qualified to teach fourteen-year-olds Pre-Algebra. In the same way—and as many parishioners painfully know—the ability to parse Greek words or know the difference between *homoousios* and *homoiousios* may not pass muster on Sunday morning. But, even these playful jests are misleading, as if the task of preaching were to take what is learned elsewhere and find a way to communicate it. The longer I am in preaching, the more clearly I find deficiencies in the content of my coursework in backgrounds, languages, and texts. Preaching brings its own questions to these disciplines, putting them on trial, and asking—if nothing else—*So what?*

Whether We Will Give the Preached-Word Authority

The second question is related to the first, for if we do not value preaching, then we will not yield to its authority or continue to grant preachers the space to speak for God. *Will Christians yield to the authority of a faithfully preached word?*

Many of our churches are in a precarious position regarding this question, whether we are aware of the forces which have shaped us or not. We float downstream of the Protestant Reformation and the Enlightenment. We have rejected traditionalism in favor of rationalism, and embraced liberalism which assumes the sovereignty of the individual. We have commandeered verbiage like "kingdom of priests" to our own benefit, for the purpose of safeguarding our right to live by our own religious opinions. We do not want anyone telling us what to do, or "preaching at us." In the words of Stanley Hauerwas,

> The Bible [has become] the possession not of the Church but now of the citizen, who has every right to determine its meaning. Ironically, by freeing the Bible from the Church and putting it in the possession of the individual conscience, the Bible becomes, in the process, the possession of nationalistic ideologies.[3]

In such an environment, preaching becomes a cartoon. No one ultimately cares what the preacher says because we have made up our minds that we alone will make up our minds.

When the issue of authority in preaching arises, an immediate retort surfaces concerning its abuse. It is lamentable that abuses do occur in ministry and preaching, and far too regularly. Preachers have uttered "thus saith the Lord" on their *own* authority and to bully their parishioners, intimidating and manipulating the vulnerable, serving their own ends. To be sure, misuses of authority ought not be, especially in Christian circles. Nevertheless, abuses in proclamation and leadership are as old as the Bible, and the list of false prophets and preachers who spoke twisted things is too long to rehearse here. Sadly, we must admit that the pulpit is susceptible to abuses. This susceptibility ought not make abuse tolerable; but neither ought it warrant a prohibition of vigorous preaching or encourage ministers to preach more tepidly. The answer to hushing bad spokepersons might not be to silence the good ones. Even into this world so allergic to authority, Christ sends us out: "Go into all the world and proclaim the good news to the whole creation" (Mark 16:15). He gives his authority away to his disciples, "Whoever listens to you listens to me" (Luke 10:16).

It is no mystery how relativism and post-modernity might undermine preaching. Truth with a capital T has become lowercase,

---

[3] Stanley Hauerwas, *Unleashing the Scriptures: Freeing the Bible from Captivity to America* (Nashville: Abingdon, 1993), 32.

and society agrees that a lone individual monologuing 52 weeks a year is not spiritually healthy for anyone. What the church needs, it might be said, are not answers but questions, not speaking but listening, not a pulpit but a panel.

Yet, good preachers understand that their work is always conversational: between them and God, the word, their own lives—including their struggles, doubts, and experiences—and certainly, the lives of their congregants. Churches do well to grapple with which voices—men and women—ought to be heard for the nourishment of the body, and how they might be heard. This may mean equipping and empowering the laity to preach, or finding ways to incorporate the perspectives of voices in the church. Yet, this does not mean that congregations must cede authority and accept a democratic process, where everyone's theological vote weighs the same, and the word of God is only heard if we have a consensus. Peter calls the Lord's spokespersons to more: "Whoever speaks must do so as one speaking the very words of God" (1 Pet 4:11).

Authority in the sermon, I believe, also raises the question of *what the sermon is for*. That is to ask, *What end does the sermon serve?* Preaching within the Stone-Campbell heritage has tended toward *instruction*. Richard Voelz describes the provenance of preaching in our movement; having been influenced by the "Puritan Plain Style" (which eschewed all that smacked of rhetoric), it was characterized by "rational or logical exposition of biblical texts or topics."[4] Thus, preaching has often been reduced (whether in theory or in practice) to *teaching* the Bible, or something like catechesis. Apart from teaching, another option is to turn the sermon into a time of spiritual therapy, which aims at an emotional experience or catharsis with hopes that, Sunday after Sunday, people walk away feeling "better." Still another option is to leverage the sermon toward some missional purpose, such as making disciples or using the time slot as a dress rehearsal for the "real work" of the church which premiers each Monday morning.

---

[4] Richard W. Voelz, "Preaching in the Stone-Campbell Theological Family," in *Preaching the Manifold Grace of God, Volume I: Theologies of Preaching in Historical Theological Families*, ed. Ronald J. Allen (Eugene, OR: Cascade, 2022), 244.

How we conceive of the *telos* of preaching is telling. This is not to suggest that some of the above *teloi* are completely fraudulent. There is room for teaching and empowering the church to be the church not only on Sundays but every day of the week. Nevertheless, certain of these purposes have a way of robbing the sermon of its inherent value: whether by casting the sermon as another opportunity for biblical explanation (for which there are other occasions), therapeuticizing the sermon in hopes that everyone feels uplifted afterwards, or depicting the Christian life as taking place everywhere but Sunday morning. One's answer to *what the sermon is for* belies claims concerning the sermon's importance.

What is the sermon for? In short, the sermon is for the proclamation of the gospel. Paul tells Timothy to preach the word (2 Tim 4:2) which is not Scripture as such, but the gospel which is "God's saving power" (Rom 1:16). In preaching, the church hears the word by which it is saved. In preaching, the church is confronted with the gospel and the God of that gospel. Through preaching, the church is reconstituted as the church, and become again *those who hear*.

Conclusion: Growth in a Warm Climate

In his seminal work *Design for Preaching*, homiletician H. Grady Davis compares the sermon to a tree. Like a tree, the sermon ought to be "a living organism" with depth ("as much unseen as above the surface") and possessing the force of an "inner life." At the close of this comparison, Davis writes that "to be all this [the sermon] must grow in a warm climate"; it must grow "in love" as in the warmth and brilliance of the sun.[5]

The sermon *must grow in a warm climate*. I love that phrase and that image. It points to the truth that no worthwhile sermon can ever be produced merely mechanistically, by stapling together so many verses or anecdotes or illustrations—pounding blocks of wood together to build a dogbox, to borrow another image Davis offers. No, a sermon must *grow*, like all good and natural things. After all, a sermon is part

---

[5] H. Grady Davis, *Design for Preaching* (Minneapolis: Fortress, 1958), 16.

of a *person*, arising out of lived experience, a *mind* and *heart*, articulated from listening and mediating on the word of God.

What is true of the sermon is true of the preacher. *The person of the preacher must grow in a warm climate.* Preaching, at its best, is not merely about applying the right techniques—pulling the right levers, learning the buttons to push—to "communicate more effectively." Only to the danger of the church can preaching be conceived as this sort of task. Good preaching is intimately tied to the life of the preacher ("truth through personality," à la Phillips Brooks). Thus, if *preaching* will thrive in the future, I believe it will depend on *preachers* thriving. And if *preachers* are to thrive, it will depend, in large part, on the existence of *warm climates*.

It makes one ask where such *warm climates* can be found. Is the church, the local congregation, such a climate which might yield lives worthy of the calling to preach? One surely hopes. I can testify that my church growing up was that for me, as well as the one of which I am now a part. The above narration of my path to the pulpit shows, or so I intended, that many who preach had not planned to. Many who will preach in the future have no idea of that fact in the present. The trouble is if we think linearly about our work and our lives. Life does not grow linearly. We might imagine that all we need to see that preaching flourishes is to ensure there are competent professors teaching the subject for those few persons who plan to go into preaching. But this sort of strategy will only work for a few. I contest that in order for preaching to thrive we need more than a good class on preaching or that sort of thing. We need *warm climates*.

Harding School of Theology has been such a climate for me. More than a seminary in which I took a preaching course or two, HST was a community of faith that nurtured my life toward God and the church. It prepared me to be the sort of man, Christian, and minister who was ready to stand before the Lord's assembly on any given Sunday and preach the word. I am forever grateful for this, and I pray that, in the future, HST continues to provide such a climate for others. And, if it does, God will give the growth.

CHAPTER SEVEN

Congregational Ministry

Carson E. Reed

An essay to reflect on the ways that Harding School of Theology has personally impacted me and influenced the church while considering the discipline of congregational ministry begins not in a discipline at all. Rather, such an essay begins with people who had and have a love for God and for God's work in the world. They devoted their lives in faithful pursuit of God's calling. Seminaries, good seminaries, are learning communities committed to the formation of ministers, church leaders, missionaries, and scholars that serve the church. Such learning communities need scholarship, deep reflection, excellent teaching, and a web of relationships with congregations. Yet at the heart of such learning communities are people whose scholarship, teaching, and faith are given over to the work of forming new generations of learning and passing on the Christian tradition. That is what I received as a student at HST in the early 1980s. Let me note three groups of people and the corresponding ways in which these people shaped me—and in some way, influenced communities of faith more broadly.

First, I would name Jack Lewis, Richard Oster, Carroll Osburn, and Allen Black. As biblical scholars their passion for excellence, close readings of texts, attention to the material artifacts of the ancient world as a key to attending to Scripture, and devotion to the Bible as Scripture invited me into the world of Scripture. These scholar-teachers, through their personal devotion to students and to their craft, drew me into a deeper respect for Scripture's authority and the witness of Scripture as God's revelatory Word. A second gift emerged for me later, as I found myself in congregational contexts. The skills I developed and the capacity for curiosity that came from these gifted scholar-teachers resourced the work of ministry. To pay attention to the world of Scripture shaped the way I sought to pay attention to the world of my congregation and to the larger community. The questions of history, textual criticism, and extant material and literary artifacts, and patient sitting with texts, informed the similar work of good pastoral leadership.

A second grouping of faculty that informed my work would be Mac Lynn, Phil Slate, and Bill Flatt. These professors, committed practitioners of congregational ministry, shared their passion for their arenas of expertise in congregational life, mission and preaching, and therapeutic care and counseling. Their witness declared that ministry matters, congregations matter, and the work of the minister is a high and sacred calling.

A third grouping of faculty invited me into a new way of being in the world. If the biblical faculty deepened my convictions about Scripture and the ministerial faculty offered a telos or aim for good ministry practice, the historical/theological faculty introduced me to new ways of understanding faith and spirituality by placing my journey and the Stone-Campbell tradition within the Great Tradition. Doug Brown and Harold Hazelip introduced me to the larger heritage of the Christian tradition. In so doing, I began to experience the wisdom in prayer life, the ongoing theological reflection of Christian people as they navigate their own times and cultures, and the diverse witness of the Holy Spirit's presence in communities of God's people from age to age. Placing my own limited congregational experience within the larger arena of Christian life past and present, along with the wisdom of seeing the church wrestle with hard questions posed by ancients like Marcion or by contemporary debates about nationalism fosters a mediated space for listening to God's Word for ministry and life today.

I offer these brief reflections to name three valuable gifts I received from the dynamic learning community that I knew in the 1980s, and I continue to be grateful for the many ways that HST extends its leavening impact in the kingdom of God today. These gifts—that the texts and the world of Scripture deserve attentiveness, that ministry and congregations matter, and that God is faithful and present from generation to generation—will surface again as this essay unfolds into the ways in which theological education resources congregational ministry in our present time.

Practical Theology

The three gifts I named above could be reframed slightly, and doing so sets the stage for a constructive conversation about practical theology and theological education. Practical theology, by definition, finds itself in interdisciplinary spaces that pays attention to contextual reality, interpretation, theological and biblical reflection, and ministerial action.[1] Practical theology finds its starting point in human contexts, ascertaining God's action and the vagaries of human existence.[2] These contexts call for close reading and attention to the congregation and its larger contexts. Such work attends to both theological and ethnographic imagination as ministers practice a contextual exegesis that leads to faithful ministry practice.[3] Faithful ministers are constantly asking what is going on in this context and then probing deeper to ask the interpretive question of why this is happening.[4] This descriptive and

---

[1] See Kathleen A. Cahalan and Gordon S. Mikoski, eds. *Opening the Field of Practical Theology: An Introduction* (Lanham, MD: Rowman & Littlefield, 2014): 1-10; Pete Ward, *Introducing Practical Theology: Mission, Ministry, and the Life of the Church* (Grand Rapids, MI: Baker Academic, 2017).

[2] Space does not permit unpacking the internal debate of practical theologians regarding lived experience. Some scholars simply assume that the examination of human experience is primarily a social science endeavor. Others scholars understand the work of the practical theologian/minister to be primarily about paying attention to God's presence in human experience. See Richard R. Osmer, "Toward a New Story of Practical Theology," *International Journal of Practical Theology* 16 (2012): 66-78, and Osmer's essay, "Empirical Practical Theology" in Kathleen A. Chalan and Gordon S. Mikoski, eds. *Opening the Field of Practical Theology: An* Introduction (Lanham, MD: Rowman & Littlefield, 2014) to see some delineation and contours of this debate. For a more critical appraisal and articulation of a confessional or God-centered focus for practical theology see Andrew Root, *Christopraxis: A Practical Theology of the Cross* (Fortress Press, 2014).

[3] See Robert J. Schreiter, *Constructing Local Theologies*, (Maryknoll, NY: Orbis Books, 1985/1999); Mary Clark Moschella, *Ethnography as a Pastoral Practice: An Introduction* Second Edition (London: SCM Press, 2023).

[4] Richard Osmer frames his *Practical Theology: An Introduction* (Grand Rapids, MI: Eerdmans, 2008) around four questions. The first two are "what" and "why."

interpretive work requires great exegetical skill of the minister on the text and context of the congregation. To do this work well, the minister attends to multiple streams of "data"—including personal and congregational narratives; congregational history; quantitative data about the congregation and the larger surrounding community; an awareness of the declared theology of the community and the underlying operant theology that informs practice; various congregational dynamics regarding leadership, power, decision-making processes, and communication; and a high level of personal emotional awareness of the leader.[5]

Thus, this descriptive work marks the first elements of practical theological engagement. Yet, as clarity about the *what* and *why* can begin to be named, the work of the minister within a ministry context then turns to theological reflection. What does this mean? What is God doing? Or, following Richard Osmer's third question in his introduction to practical theology, "What ought to be occurring?"[6] Such questions move the minister/practical theologian to the normative work of ministry. What is the witness of scripture, of the theological tradition, of the historical narrative that informs this present moment? Theological reflection is the capacity to observe and interpret human activity with more than informed sociological or psychological insight. Theological reflection engages in observation and interpretation informed by the reality of God's presence and action in human affairs in addition to the sociological or psychological dynamics in play. The minister uses Scripture, theology, and the witness of Christian tradition to interpret particular ministry contexts.

As clarity or possibility emerges in that hermeneutical task, a third move arises. After contextual attention and theological reflection comes ministerial action. What is the ministerial response to the theologically-informed interpretive work of reflection? Such action

---

[5] David Gortner's essay, "Congregational Studies and Ministry," offers an excellent summary of these various sources in *The Study of Ministry: A Comprehensive Survey of Theory and Practice*, edited by Martyn Percy (London: Society for Promoting Christian Knowledge, 2019): 70-88.

[6] Richard Osmer, *Practical Theology: An Introduction* (Grand Rapids, MI: Eerdmans, 2008).

requires ministerial skill in leadership, homiletics, spiritual formation, pastoral care, administration, social action, worship, prayer, and more.[7] Yet skill or technique is not all that is required. For good ministerial practice to emerge from good theological reflection, a certain kind of wisdom, practical wisdom, or *phronesis* is necessary. By *phronesis* I mean the wisdom that emerges from three factors coming together when a minister confronts a context: knowledge, skill, and the tempered experience that the minister brings to her work and life.[8]

By taking up the three key factors of my own experience as a student at HST and framing those factors with insights from practical theology, I want now to turn to questions about theological education and congregational ministry. How might contextual description and hermeneutical engagement that gives rise to informed theological reflection, which moves to wise ministerial action, shape conversations around theological education today?

Theological Education and Congregational Ministry

A recent series of ten books published by Eerdmans titled Theological Education Between the Times offers an excellent starting place to assess the state of theological education. The most recent of the series by Ted Smith, *The End of Theological Education*, may well signal the time of crisis that faces schools and institutions called to educate and form congregational leaders.[9] Smith presents a historical look at theological education and the many sociological and cultural factors that are in play. Those factors, including a significant decline in religious affiliation, individuality, a pursuit for meaning beyond traditional ecclesial forms, and the collapse of professions, locate theological education in a precarious place. Yet Smith is not a doomsday prophet; rather, he invites readers to engage imagination with an eschatological

---

[7] Consider Kathleen Cahalan's six forms of ministerial practice in *Introducing the Practice of Ministry* (Collegeville, MN: Liturgical Press, 2010).

[8] See my exploration of *phronesis* in Carson E. Reed, "The Ends of Leadership: Phronesis and the Leader as Guide" in *The End of Leadership?: Christian Perspectives and Social Ethics* (Brussels: Peeters Publishing, 2017).

[9] Ted A. Smith, *The End of Theological Education* (Grand Rapids, MI: Eerdmans, 2023).

perspective. Theological education matters because God matters. However, theological education will look different. Theological education will intentionally focus on its connection to congregations, and it will pay attention to God's work in the world as communities of faith live in the time between the times. As these two activities develop what will emerge will be a robust set of postures that will serve congregations and practical theologians. What follows is a brief exploration of connection to congregations and paying attention to God's work that will lead to a concluding set of postures or assumptions that inform healthy theological education for congregational ministry.

Connection to Congregations

Before speaking directly about connections to congregations, I wish to name an internal dynamic that has shaped theological education. Theological education has found itself in a divided world for perhaps two hundred years. One way to mark that division would be with the work of Frederick Schleiermacher. In the early nineteenth century at the University of Berlin, Schleiermacher was the principal in a three-person committee charged with developing a rationale for including the study of theology and the training of pastors into a university that was emerging as place for empirical research.[10] Schleiermacher's rationale, originally published in 1811 and due to the popularity of his approach enjoyed several revised editions, offered a justification for theological education in a research setting.[11]

Schleiermacher offered a series of three broad disciplines

---

[10] Gijsbert D. J. Dingemans, "Practical Theology in the Academy: A Contemporary Overview" *The Journal of Religion* 76 (January 1996): 82-96. John E. Paver recounts this story in *Theological Reflection and Education for Ministry: The Search for Integration in Theology* (Farnham, UK: Ashgate, 2006), 7-10; see also Bonnie Miller-McLemore, *Christian Theology in Practice: Discovering a Discipline* (Grand Rapids: Eerdmans, 2012), 2ff.

[11] Friedrich Schleiermacher, *Kurze Darstellung des theologischen Studiums zum Behuf einleitender Vorlesungen* (Berlin, 1811). Sociologically, Schleiermacher reminded his readers of the significant and pervasive role of religion in society. Philosophically, he declared that Christianity was rooted in experience and therefore was worthy of study. Thus the academic discipline of theology was justified and that in order to have professionally trained clergy it was necessary for universities to prepare competent ministers for the good of society.

necessary for theological education including philosophical theology, historical theology (which included biblical studies, systematic theology, historical theology, and church history), and then practical theology. In the first edition of his *Brief Outline* he took care to present the interconnectedness of these three disciplines through the use of an illustration of a tree.

The roots of the tree represented philosophical theology—which explore the foundational polemical and apologetic questions that undergird the Christian faith.[12] The trunk of the tree, what is visible to us in texts and what is observable to us by observation and correlation is the work of historical theology (and its attendant sub-disciplines of biblical studies, etc.). The crown of the tree—its branches, limbs, and leaves—is the place of practical theology.

However, this integrated focus was soon lost. In the subsequent edition of his *Brief Outline* published in 1830, the tree disappears. Authors Howard Stone and James Duke suggest that Schleiermacher "feared that readers would mistakenly believe that he intended to subordinate philosophical and historical theology to practical theology, when his true intention was to emphasize the equality of the three."[13] Yet subordination did occur. Even as Schleiermacher sought to show the integration of the three disciplines, the way in which practical theology was framed eventually led it to be, in the words of John Paver, "intellectually inert!"[14]

The enduring legacy of Schleiermacher's proposal was not the

---

[12] See Friedrich Schleiermacher, *Brief Outline of Theology as a Field of Study*, Revised translation of the 1811 and 1830 editions, translated and with notes by Terrence N. Tice (Louisville: Westminster John Knox Press, 2011), 7-14.

[13] Howard Stone and James O. Duke, editors of Friedrich Schleiermacher, *Christian Caring: Selections from Pastoral Theology* (Fortress, 1988), 22. Interestingly, Elaine Graham states: "He argued for the essential unity of theory and practice, by stating that the practical should be given preferential status in assessing the authenticity and validity of the truth-claims of theological discourse. Thus it is the congregational reality that serves as the validating norm for Christian theology, and not simply abstract or ideal philosophical principles." In *Transforming Practice: Pastoral Theology in an Age of Uncertainty* (Eugene, OR: Wipf and Stock, 2002), 60.

[14] Paver, 10.

integration of these various disciplines. Rather, the disciplines became separated, specialized silos of knowledge of which any pastor must be able to demonstrate competency. And perhaps most telling is that practical theology was distanced and sometimes divorced from work in biblical studies and theological studies.

As a result, practical theology gave way to skills to be developed and the management of congregations. And with that, any reciprocity between the leaves and branches with the trunk and the roots were cut off. Practical theology came to be known as the "helps and hints" department of theological institutions.[15] The real heavy lifting was taking place in the other departments, and what became neglected was practical theology's capacity to ask the really hard questions and work in the very context where theological inquiry begins.[16]

The focus on competency in a variety of disciplines and upon the trained individual who is supposed to be skilled at delivering religious goods and services, gave rise to the term "the clerical paradigm."[17] The goal of theological education was to prepare experts in various disciplines to dispense ministry in their respective congregations. But is this idea of competency, the skilled "technologian," sufficient to build our understanding of the practice of ministry? Is the knowledge of Hebrew, or for that matter the latest in homiletic theory, really the thing that is needful for congregations? Is the real end or *telos* of ministry to have a specially-trained person to do ministry for, among, or to other people?

So both the disconnect between the disciplines that often

---

[15] Seward Hiltner, a leading pastoral theologian who kicked off a path toward integration writes in 1958: "The notion of 'hints and helps', implying the right to dispense with structural and theoretical considerations, to set aside scholarship in this area, and to appeal to the more degraded forms of parallelism, helped to drive most systematic books out of this field by the turn of the century." In *Preface to Pastoral Theology* (Nashville: Abingdon Press, 1958), 48.

[16] For full critiques, see Browning, 1991, Farley, 1983.

[17] For a recent critique and exploration of the term see Bonnie J. Miller-McLenore, "The 'Clerical Paradigm' A Fallacy of Misplaced Concreteness," *International Journal of Practical Theology* 11(2007): 19-38. She presses and nuances her critique in the volume of essays, *The Practice of Theology?* (Grand Rapids: Eerdmans, 2012).

diminishes ministerial practice and the movement to make ministers "technical" experts contributes to barriers that are often present in congregations to theological education. One of my professors during my time as a student pointed out the limitations of the classic dimensions of the seminary education. Doug Brown articulated those limitations in an essay titled "Theological Training and Christian Ministry" in 1986.[18] He suggests that the work of theological education may pass on the "mind of scholarship" without passing along the "mind of Christ."[19] He posits that well-rounded ministers need more than the academic resources of the academy. He identifies two additional resources beyond the academy. Students need the challenge of the "desert" and the complexities of the "marketplace."[20] Brown uses the term "desert" to assert the necessity of experiencing doubt and the absence of God that has its own formative work in the way of faith. And Brown uses the term "marketplace" to describe the incongruities of human experience that push beyond easy answers. The formal study of theology, in Brown's day, becomes useful for ministry only when academic training is complemented and followed by seasoning experience in the marketplace and self-examining experience in the wilderness. Brown was correct in assessing the need for contextual complexity (marketplace) and spiritual and emotional maturity (desert) in addition to the intellectual work of the academy. However, theological educators today will reimagine their work to understand that the seminary needs to attend to all three aspects within their formative programs rather than assume that ministers will survive the marketplace and the desert on their own.

This wholistic approach is exactly what Daniel Aleshire articulates in his book on the future of theological education.[21] For Aleshire, like

---

[18] Douglas Brown, "Theological Training and Christian Ministry," *Restoration Quarterly* 28, no. 1 (1986): 1-10.

[19] Brown, 1-2.

[20] Landon Saunders also uses the metaphors of desert and marketplace in his noted lectures on preaching. Landon Saunders, *21st Annual Lectures on Preaching*, Abilene Christian University, Lectureship and Summit Collection (1971).

[21] Daniel O. Aleshire, *Beyond Profession: The Next Future of Theological Education* (Grand Rapids, MI: Eerdmans, 2021).

Brown, the singularity of theological education is its attention to formation. And formation concerns itself with three distinct aspects—intellectual, affective, and behavioral. For students to be formed into ministers they need the intellectual formation of traditional seminary work. However, students also require the spiritual and emotional development (affective) and the behavioral or skills formation that shapes their practices. Theological education has long focused on intellectual formation. However, intentional work in spiritual and emotional formation, along with the development of ministerial practices, will need to come alongside the intellectual work in such a way that *phronesis*—a practical wisdom—emerges. The past 200 years of division within the theological curriculum is subsiding, yet the work of integrating and forming ministers will continue to require intentionality.

When ministers are more wholistically formed, they will serve more wholistically in congregations. And one way that institutions can engage and learn from congregations is to be more fully engaged with congregational life and mission. One encouraging pragmatic approach, as reflected in Harding University's newly announced Center for Church and City Engagement or Abilene Christian University's Siburt Institute for Church Ministry, is the direct, sustained relationship with congregations. For example, the Siburt Institute engages in conversations with hundreds of churches, ministers, and other church leaders each year through listening groups, consultation, programming, publishing, and networking services. Those engagements inform theological education and give rise to research and scholarship that serves both the church and the academy.[22]

Sociological and Theological Themes in a Secular Age

A second arena to name at the intersection of theological education and congregations is the critical need to identify the sociological realities of a secular environment and the corresponding theological convictions needed for congregational life and mission. By secularity I am speaking of more than just declines in worship

---

[22] Consider the double blind, peer-reviewed journal that the Sibert Institute began publishing in 2015, *Discernment: Theology and the Practice of Ministry*.

attendance and the rise of younger adults who no longer affiliate with a religious tradition. To speak of secularity is to identify the extent of human experience fully in the material world.[23] Transcendence no longer is a necessary or needed category. As material beings in a material world, establishing trust or holding trust with institutions or authority figures is quickly reduced. Individualism dominates social engagements and the autonomous self gets to decide everything. Such an environment has little place for conversations about faith or God. Theological education seems superfluous and the historic place of congregations in society is fading quickly.

This secular frame calls for a robust Christian response. That response is especially needed in churches and in theological education. Simply put, as Andrew Root notes in his recent book, *When Church Stops Working*, the crisis is not secularity or shrinking churches.[24] The crisis is that the church has neglected to recognize the reality of a God who is present and active in human experience. Following the trajectory of Karl Barth, who as a minister in a congregation recognized the paucity of faith in God's action present within the community, Root develops a theological argument that claims that God is the God who is always arriving and doing the work that God claims to do.[25]

Related to the prior observations of the separation of church and academy, or the separation of the classical disciplines that reduced practical theology to helpful hints, the often-practiced posture of deconstruction in theological schools, combined with the realities of a secular age, often leave ministers and churches in a place of functional atheism. Communities of faith sing songs and hymns, offer prayers, and talk about the Bible. Yet do communities of faith listen for the living voice of a God who is present and has a preferred future for a congregation?

---

[23] I have written about secularity along with my colleague Shelby Coble in "Leadership in a Secular Age: Divine Action, the Early Church, and Relationship Leadership Theory in Conversation" *Journal of Religious Leadership* 22, no. 2 (2023): 118-43.

[24] Andrew Root, *When Church Stops Working: A Future for Your Congregation Beyond More Money, Programs, and Innovation* (Grand Rapids, MI: Brazos Press, 2023).

[25] Andrew Root, *Churches and the Crisis of Decline: A Hopeful, Practical Ecclesiology for a Secular Age* (Grand Rapids, MI: Baker Academic, 2022).

For schools of theology the open challenge is to introduce more fully the realities of Brown's marketplace and desert. Or perhaps, to see the work of theological education less as deconstruction and more fully as the constructive work of formation. Such work will find resource in a deepened commitment to a confessional stance toward both the historic Stone-Campbell commitment to relational orthodoxy and toward the *regula fidei* of the larger Christian tradition. By relational orthodoxy I am naming the posture present in early Stone-Campbell circles reflected in Robert Richardson who expressly drew this distinction against other traditions. He declared:

> In other words, [other traditions] suppose doctrines, or religious tenets, to be the subject-matter of this faith; we, on the contrary, conceive it to terminate on a person—the LORD JESUS CHRIST HIMSELF. While they, accordingly, require an elaborate confession from each convert—a confession mainly of a doctrinal and intellectual character, studiously elaborated into an extended formula—we demand only a simple confession of Christ—a heartfelt acknowledgement that Jesus is the Messiah, the Son of God.[26]

By the *regula fidei* I am naming a commitment to attending to Scripture and the tradition that honors the way that the Triune God was present and continues to be present in the ongoing life of the church. That honoring calls the church to listen closely to the ways that Christian people have responded to God's action and shapes our own present-day response.[27] These two foundational

---

[26] Robert Richardson, *Principles of the Reformation* (Abilene, TX: New Leaf Press, 2002): 44.

[27] This, in part, is part of the Canonical Theism project. Canonical Theism attends to the ways that the church's canons—creeds, councils, and more—reflect God's ongoing disclosure and bring people to salvation. William Abraham, the leading voice in Canonical Theism, remarks: "Canonical Theism is both a vision of church renewal for the twenty-first century and a long-haul, intergenerational theological project." In William J.Abraham, Jason E. Vickers, and Natalie Van Kirk, eds., *Canonical Theism: A Proposal for Theology and the Church* (Grand Rapids, Eerdmans, 2008), xii.

commitments will inform wholistic formation that attends to intellectual, spiritual, and behavioral formation.

Moving Toward Practical Theological Frames

Quickly reviewing, I have suggested that the various disciplines of theological education are necessarily intertwined. They need each other organically. Likewise, the church and the academy need each other as well. To attend to a wholistic connection, theological educators will find concrete ways of partnership with congregations and they will also attend to the fullness of formation—not merely engaging in intellectual acquisition for students. Additionally, I have briefly noted the post-Christendom reality that raises the prospects of secularity. These secular assumptions, held by Christian and non-Christian people, call for theological educators to attend to the constructive work of forming ministers who can articulate the faith and utilize the core of the faith in constructive projects for the life and mission of congregations. Such work centers around the claim that the God whom Christians confess is three-in-one and is active and present in the life of persons, communities of faith, and in the world.

These convictions then lead me to make some observations or postures that might guide theological educators, practical theologians, and ministerial leaders in the active work of their vocation. I offer seven of these observations.[28]

First, the triune God is at work in the world. That claim centers the life and work of leaders. It is the beginning point of listening, responding, and doing all theological reflection. The revelatory declaration in Genesis, "In the beginning God," is the foundational assumption of ministerial and congregational life. The reality of the triune God present in congregational life and in the world suggests that mutuality, relationality, mission, and much more are central to the ways in which ministers see their work.

---

[28] Consider Craig Van Gelder's list as another helpful set of frames as he reflects on ministry and the Spirit. Craig Van Gelder, *The Ministry of the Missional Church: A Community Led by the Spirit* (Grand Rapids, MI: Baker, 2007), 59-61.

Second, ministers assume the particularity of place, of context. Every community of faith is distinct and different. Each congregation has its own particular story and its own particular relationship with the larger context. Seeking both sociological and theological readings, congregational leaders recognize both that they are in a particular context and that they are framing a context for their communities. This leads to a related, third, claim.

Third, the first work of ministerial leaders is to pay attention—to God and to the context. Listening well and fully is a foundational ministerial practice. As I learned long ago from biblical scholars that good exegesis matters, so does good exegetical engagement with context. Yet the metaphor of exegesis has its limits here. A minister or scholar may exegete a text—a text is a thing. One does not exegete living persons. Living persons continue to shift, change, and surprise.[29] Nor does the idea of exegeting the mystery of God's divine presence seem constructive. The listening I name here is done through humility and with a tentativeness. It requires new ways of seeing and hearing—and it will give way to the work of the Spirit as leaders attempt to discern and interpret. This interpretive work seeks clarity—first and foremost—of God's action.[30]

Fourth, ministers will engage Scripture and tradition with curiosity and imagination. God's revelatory work in Scripture and the

---

[29] Ministerial students will benefit by learning intentional listening practices like appreciative inquiry and ethnography. See Mark Lau Branson, *Memories, Hopes, and Conversations: Appreciative Inquiry, Missional Engagement, and Congregational Change* (New York: Rowman & Littlefield Publishers, 2016); Mary Clark Moschella, *Ethnography as a Pastoral Practice*, Second Edition (London: SCM Press, 2023).

[30] Andrew Purves states this frankly: "As the risen and ascended Lord, Jesus does not now sit in heaven with his arms folded waiting for us to do something religious that he can affirm (an image from Karl Barth). Jesus is not our cheerleader from the heavens hoping we will get faith and ministry right. Neither does Jesus want to get more involved in our ministries. Why would he? Our ministries are not redemptive. We don't raise the dead, forgive the sinful, heal the sick or bring in the reign of God. Rather, Jesus has his own resurrected ministry to do—raising the dead, forgiving the sinful, healing the sick, bringing in God's reign (note the present tense!)—and he wants us in on it." Andrew Purves, *The Resurrection of Ministry* (Downers Grove, IL: IVP Press, 2010), 44.

great cloud of witnesses serve as authoritative guides to our present work. I use the term "authoritative" here intentionally. Since God is God, then God's present action will be resonant with God's past action. And since God is the author of our common life and salvation, attending to God's intent will fuel the work of ministerial practice by stirring imagination and fostering curiosity.

Fifth, the posture of ministerial leaders and congregations is to respond to God's action and ministry. God's ministry is what matters, not human activity and ministry. Yet God invites us to partner with God. So ministerial leaders look and develop practices for the communities of faith they serve that aligns with God's action.

Sixth, ministerial leaders understand that leadership is foundationally relational. God is both one and three. "God in three Persons, blessed Trinity" evokes the witness of Scripture and tradition and invites Christian leaders into a way of relationality, because God is relational. Living into this claim will shift and alter the way of leadership and once again give way to refreshing and energizing historic terms like elder, shepherd, minister, or steward. Recently, three elders from a vibrant church in Houston asked whether it was possible to find meaning in their service as elders. As we discussed leading through relationality the joy in their faces and in their words became palpable. What was missing in all their work was the reason for all their work—extending the presence of God through relationships.

Seventh, ministerial leaders rely not merely on the past witness of Scripture and tradition. They also claim the future witness of the *eschaton*. God will complete what God begins. So the one word that gives currency to ministerial leadership today is *hope*. Hope in God's faithful promise reorients all present contexts and dilemmas, and resources the reimagining necessary to see and hear God at work in congregations and in the world.

Moving Toward Practical Theological Frames

Practical theology, as it engages with congregational ministry, listens to the contexts of place, attends to the presence of God, and responds in faithful partnership with God to God's transforming ends for the sake of the world. As institutions that provide theological education move forward, the wholistic formative work that is necessary will sit in those same areas—contextual awareness, biblical and theological attention to God's present action, and skilled, loving practices that transform. It will look different in many ways in the days ahead—yet these three things were modeled well in the persons I encountered as a student at HST some forty years ago.

CHAPTER EIGHT

Global Missions

Craig Ford

This essay has two twin objectives. The first is to look back and tell a story of Harding School of Theology's (HST) impact on global missions. Ideally, if this story is told well, the reader will see ample reasons to give glory to God for all the ways he has been at work through the school. The second objective is to look ahead and speak to changes on the horizon that may impact global mission efforts. As HST seeks ways to prepare for these changes, she will continue to prepare and equip missionaries for many generations into the future.[1]

Looking Back: HST's Impact on My Life and Ministry

It is difficult to see her because the room is so dark. Only a small kerosene lamp contributes any light to the room. I scan her face looking for a subtle hint of a smile or anything that might indicate this was some kind of joke. I am wondering if this is a part of some type of initiation process for new missionaries. She had just asked me a question: "Is there anything wrong with rebuking rats in Jesus' name?" Despite my skepticism about her seriousness, her demeanor is clear. This is an authentic question.

Certain it is a genuine question, my mind starts scanning memories in hopes of finding an answer to a question I had never previously considered before. Within seconds, I am reviewing all my biblical and theological training. If recent memories are easier to retrieve, it would explain why my mind reviews class after class at HST.

---

[1] While there are important discussions about the limitations and connotations associated with the term *missionary*, I still use the term in this chapter. It will be used in a way that it has been commonly understood and historically defined: a Christian worker doing ministry in a country that is different from his or her home country.

Did one of my professors ever address the question? I consider the classes I took with Dr. Richard Oster, Revelation and Romans and Galatians. There were discussions about a beast, justification by faith, and a few references to the bed of Procrustes. There was not, however, any mention of rats. Rats may have come up in Dr. Phillip McMillion's Old Testament Survey class. If we discussed rats, they would have been the gold rats mentioned in 1 Samuel 6:18. I could not recall any one of those rats being rebuked. Did Dr. Mark Powell mention it in his Systematic Christian Doctrine class? What about Dr. Evertt W. Huffard's Spiritual Leadership course? Did the topic come up in Dr. Dave Bland's Sermon Design and Development class? No. No. No.

It is a disappointing moment when you realize how unprepared you are for something. At least a part of me must have assumed that the student and the seminary have some type of implicit yet binding agreement. I would regularly pay tuition bills. I would read assigned books. I would endure a few stress-filled and sleepless nights. In return for my investment, I would graduate fully prepared for Christian ministry. I would be prepared to answer any difficult question that came my way—questions like the one just posed: "Is there anything wrong with rebuking rats in Jesus' name?"

She was still looking at me and waiting for a response. What had been the point of those early morning classes? Had those long days of studying been meaningless? What did I have to show for thousands of dollars in tuition payments? Worst of all, my contribution to my education is minuscule when compared to the investment of others. HST teachers, staff, and faculty members give decades to training students. Librarians listen patiently and graciously assist in locating the resource in question. Professors circle back and try to address the topic in a way that might be understood. Generous donors give so individual students can afford an education that would otherwise be out of reach. After everyone's investment, I still do not know if it is or is not appropriate to curse rats in Jesus' name. Am I a disappointment to all those who taught me?

Eventually, a light pierces the dark clouds of my mind. Never once did anyone at HST indicate that they measured success by their ability to adequately disseminate information on every conceivable topic. Not once did anyone hint at the impossibility of being stumped by a question. The school never tried to hand over a proverbial academic fish. Instead, the school taught me how to think, how to study, and how to deal with difficult questions.

Perhaps just as important, I discovered that we learn, work, and minister in community. What HST does to equip students extends far beyond the classroom. While attending HST, Drs. Evertt and Ileene Huffard regularly hosted a monthly Missions Interest Group (MIG). Anthony Gleghorn summarizes the purpose of the MIG: "This group is a place of community for those who want to work for God in different fields. We know that we will probably end up in different corners of the earth, but we also know that we serve the same God."[2] As an HST student, Gleghorn anticipates something to come so he speaks in the future tense. What he hopes will come to pass is something I have experienced. For two years, my wife and I attended MIG meetings at the Huffard's home. During those meetings we developed relationships with other couples who were also heading to the mission field. Over the years those relationships provided much needed mutual encouragement during various challenging seasons of ministry.

After going to HST together and attending MIG meetings together, we have been blessed to connect with many of those friends again. Our family has fond memories of spending time with Jason and Nicole Whaley when they hosted us in their home in Wollongong, Australia. Drew and Jamie Custer were incredibly hospitable when we spent time together one furlough in Houston, Texas. We've shared long, healing conversations in Quito, Ecuador with Joshua and Julie Marcum. Even as we now work in Montana, we have various occasions to spend time with the Huffards and receive regular encouragement from them. Amazingly, the seeds of each of those relationships can be traced to those MIG meetings in the Huffards' home in Memphis, Tennessee. Not only does HST's impact extend beyond the classroom, but it also extends beyond the student's time in Memphis.

---

[2] Anthony Gleghorn, "Mission Interest Group," *The Bridge* 54, no. 4 (Spring 2014): 4, https://scholarworks.harding.edu/hst-bridge/55.

With the gift of time to study and research, along with the helpful insights of others, I was eventually able to give an answer to the question: "Is there anything wrong with rebuking rats in Jesus' name?" In case you are curious to know the answer, true to my HST education, all I can say is this: do not allow someone else's answer to get in the way of your discovery and investigation of the answer for yourself.

The savvy reader probably already realizes that my story is representative of a much greater whole. Every student has situations where lessons learned at HST influenced their approach to a ministry situation. No, it does not happen just once. It happens repeatedly. This story must be multiplied many times across my lifetime. Moreover, similar stories can be multiplied across the lives and ministries of thousands of HST students.

Looking Back: HST's Impact on Global Missions

How does one begin to measure and quantify HST's impact on global missions? As a starting point, imagine pulling out a large map of the world. On that map, place a pin on each location where a missionary from the Churches of Christ works or has worked as a missionary. Now ask those missionaries where they received some education or training for missions. Place a pin on those locations and tie a string from their present location to the location where they received some training. A hypothesis: there would be a few places where there would be large clusters of pins. The strings tied to the clustered pin would look like a spider web expanding outward from a geographic center. Those geographic clusters would align with the locations of Christian colleges and training programs affiliated with Churches of Christ. These clusters would illustrate the important role these institutions have played in educating, equipping, and training Christian missionaries.

HST would be one of those hubs responsible for training, equipping, and sending missionaries throughout world. HST's role in training missionaries is no accident. Instead, it is a byproduct of the school's intentional emphasis on the mission of God. In 2008, Evertt W. Huffard, a former dean at HST, wrote of HST's core values. One of those core values is: "The churches of Christ will always need well trained preachers, missionaries, scholars, teachers of the Word, counselors and leaders to transform lives, plant churches, and glorify God among the nations."[3] When the doors opened in 1958, until the present, HST has been training, equipping, and sending missionaries abroad. As proof of this claim, Matt Carter notes, "Some of [HST's] very first students went on to serve for decades on the mission field. Just a few examples include Maurice Hall ('59) in Vietnam, J.C. Choate ('61) in Pakistan and India, Doyle Kee ('62) in France and Switzerland, and Malcolm Parsely ('67) in Korea."[4] This is why Carter can assert, "Mission work is a part of our history. It's in our DNA; it's who we are."[5]

How then does one faithfully show the fruit that comes from 66 years of training men and women for the mission field? Again, you can imagine taking a map and this time, take a pin that represents every HST student who went on to serve in the mission field. For each of those students, place a pin at 1000 Cherry Road, Memphis, Tennessee (the current home of HST). Next, place a pin in each location where each missionary subsequently worked. Now tie a string between the two pins. The result: there would be hundreds pinned in Memphis connecting to all areas around the globe. Just consider this representative list of counties where former HST students have done mission work: England, Uganda, New Zealand, Kenya, Australia, Argentina, China, Papua New Guinea, Bolivia, Brazil, Peru, Ecuador, Angola, Cambodia, Mozambique, Italy, Thailand, Pakistan, Greece, France, Switzerland, Korea, Taiwan, and Tanzania.[6]

Nevertheless, tracking the movement of individuals does not

---

[3] Evertt W. Huffard, "Dean's Note: Core Values," *The Bridge* 49, no. 2&3 (Summer/Fall 2008): 2, https://scholarworks.harding.edu/hst-bridge/62.

[4] Matt Carter, "Still Global," *The Bridge* 53, no. 1 (Summer 2012): 3, https://scholarworks.harding.edu/hst-bridge/54.

[5] Carter, "Still Global," 3.

[6] The list is not in any way exhaustive. In fact, it is probably embarrassingly inadequate. Each country listed was gleaned from one of three sources: my personal knowledge, countries mentioned in the HST publication *The Bridge*, and responses to an email requesting when and where various graduates served.

adequately capture all that HST has done to contribute to global missions. There is a paradoxical way to help the reader grasp the depth of HST's contribution to missions: share all the possible pathways or vantage points one could use to highlight HST's involvement in missions. What is left out of this chapter may be as powerful a testimony to HST's missionary influence as what is included.

To highlight HST's contribution to missions, one could introduce the reader to students who came to Memphis from outside of the United State and then returned to do work in their country of origin. Taking this approach might involve introducing former students like Masa Nonogaki who came from Japan,[7] or Lenin Munguia who came from Nicaragua and taught in Honduras,[8] or Ananias Moses who returned to his home nation of Botswana. Today, HST has taken a further step in training leaders from outside the United States. HST uses video conferencing to offer synchronous online classes (HST LIVE), and leaders from throughout the world can study at HST while continuing to live and minister in their home countries.[9] HST currently has 23 students from 14 other countries (Australia, Bahamas, Bolivia, Canada, Columbia, Ghana, Honduras, India, Mexico, Nigeria, Russia, Singapore, Switzerland, and Ukraine). Sixteen of these students are sponsored by Global Christian Studies (GCS), an organization that partners with HST to recruit, fund, and support Christian leaders from other countries. GCS students pursue an advanced degree at HST while remaining in their current ministry context.[10]

Another possible angle on the HST story would track the ministries of the students from outside of North America who have received one of HST's sabbatical grants. HST offers a Latin American Missions Sabbatical grant so individuals like Selvin Monterroso of Guatemala could train in Memphis. Ong Chong Fatt of Malaysia is one

---

[7] Dwight A. Albright, "Masa and Mari Nonogaki Spread the Gospel in Japan," *The Bridge* 42, no. 6 (November 2001): 3, https://scholarworks.harding.edu/hst-bridge/13.

[8] "Student Profile: Walking by Faith, Not by Sight," *The Bridge* 53, no. 1 (Summer 2012): 6, https://scholarworks.harding.edu/hst-bridge/54.

[9] LIVE stands for "live interactive video education."

[10] For more information on Global Christian Studies, see https://www.gcspathway.org.

of the recipients of the Hogan-Cate Asian Missions Sabbatical grant. This chapter could focus on exploring the global impact HST professors have had through classes and lectures taught around the world. One single data point illustrates the scope of this impact. Speaking of a three year period between 2000-2003, Evertt W. Huffard shared, "Our faculty at [HST] has been involved in 16 mission trips since 2000, to Germany, Switzerland, Ukraine, Hungary, Scotland, Malaysia, Papua New Guinea and Israel."[11] Another possible point of view on the story of HST's impact on global missions would explore the good work accomplished by HST graduates who have served internationally as US Military Chaplains.[12] What each of these possible storylines have in common is that they trace the direct impact an HST student or faculty member had on other individuals across the world.

Apart from direct impact, HST's impact could be measured by its indirect contributions to missions. These contributions would be like ripples in a pond. Once again, the stories that cannot be told help tell the story about the school's influence on missions. One might choose to highlight impact by exploring the books, articles, and journals written, published, or edited by HST graduates. Through various publications, HST graduates continue to inform theological thought and practices associated with global missions.[13] HST's influence could be illustrated by exploring the ongoing work of HST graduates who are now training and equipping upcoming generations of missionaries. At a minimum, this includes graduates working with parachurch missionary organizations or professors who teach at Christian universities.

---

[11] Evertt W. Huffard, "From the Dean: Discovering Hope," *The Bridge* 44, no. 4 (July 2003): 2, https://scholarworks.harding.edu/hst-bridge/6.

[12] See Leanne Braddock and Michelle Mentzer, "Ministering to Our Military Families," *The Bridge* 44, no. 3 (May 2003): 1, 3, https://scholarworks.harding.edu/hst-bridge/11. Dorn Muscar discusses further HST's impact on military chaplaincy in the US in chapter 13 of this book.

[13] For a sample, see "Online Missions Journal Edited by Alumni," *The Bridge* 52, no. 1 (Summer 2011): 3, https://scholarworks.harding.edu/hst-bridge/53. This article lists the editors of *Missio Dei: A Journal of Missional Theology and Praxis*. The list includes: Greg McKinzie (Arequipa, Peru), Danny Reese (Huambo, Angola), Jason Whaley (Wollongong, Australia), Bob Turner, (Memphis, Tennessee), and Mark Clancy (Lima, Peru).

In terms of indirect influence, another possible avenue of exploration would be the influence graduates continue to have through their positions in American churches. Local ministers and teachers play a vital role in training Christians to see and imitate the missionary heart of God. In their survey of the status of missions in Churches of Christ, Gailyn Van Rheenen and Bob Waldron note, *"the church's missions involvement is directly related to the number of sermons preached about missions!"*[14] HST focuses on introducing all students to the mission of God. This teaches students that mission is not a subsection or specialty within Christian life and ministry. Instead, all Christians and all Christian workers are participants in the missionary work of God. Through this healthy theological foundation, HST contributes to global missions through students who use their positions to promote the missionary message.

At this point, I have introduced many of the possible perspectives one could take in telling the story of HST's part in world missions. This list alone illustrates the depth of influence the school has had in the past. Still, the most direct impact HST has on global missions is through the individuals and families who trained at HST and then served in various mission fields. Effective missionaries, according to Gailyn Van Rheenen and Bob Waldron, have the following five qualities: (1) emotional stability, (2) spiritual maturity, (3) skills as effective teachers of the Word of God, (4) effective interpersonal communicative skills, and (5) the aptitude and training to effectively plant churches, nurture new Christians to maturity, and equip natural church leaders for Christian service.[15] That is an intimidating list of qualities for anyone. Now consider that it is not unusual for people in their twenties and thirties to begin to serve as missionaries. For there to be any legitimate hope of success, institutions like HST must, in partnership with God's will, provide training for future missionaries. That is the very work that HST has been doing for 66 years.

---

[14] Gailyn Van Rheenen, and Bob Waldron, *The Status of Missions in Churches of Christ: A Nationwide Survey of Churches of Christ* (Abilene: ACU Press, 2002), 22. Italics in original.

[15] Van Rheenen and Waldron, *The Status of Missions*, 81-83.

At the start of this essay, I shared just one example of how HST contributed to my own ministry. I am one among thousands who are deeply indebted to HST for the ways that it equipped us for ministry. What follows is just a few brief vignettes of how other graduates say the school had a positive impact on their lives as global missionaries.

With insight beyond his years, twenty years ago Josh Marcum said, "I entered the Master of Divinity program because I knew that I needed the best education and training possible for the demanding task of missionary work."[16] Between their time in Bolivia and now Ecuador, Josh and his wife, Julie, have now worked for seventeen years doing mission work. How does Josh now feel about the training he received at HST? "Our four years at [HST]," Josh wrote in an email, "will always be some of my favorite memories."[17] Looking back on his time in Memphis, he recognizes now how much it positively transformed his life and philosophy of ministry. Moreover, HST allowed him to "develop close friendships with like-minded missional people that continue to this day."[18]

In 2010, *The Bridge* recorded some interviews with second generation HST students. Discussing his reasons for attending HST, Jeremy Daggett shared how much the school influenced another HST student, his dad Shawn Daggett. As Jeremy tells it, "Dad told me that the single greatest tool on the mission field was having attended [HST]. The education, ministry and community he experienced there, in the hands of God, produced fruit on the mission field."[19] After working sixteen years in Taiwan, Edward Short reflected on his HST experience saying, "At HST, I learned to study; I learned how to do research. I learned (from Annie Mae Alston Lewis) that 'Truth is truth, no matter who says it.' HST engendered a deep faith in God

---

[16] As quoted in Larry Arick, "Investing in Ministry," *The Bridge* 45, no. 1 (January 2004): 4, https://scholarworks.harding.edu/hst-bridge/4.
[17] Josh Marcum, e-mail message to author, January 23, 2024.
[18] Ibid.
[19] "Training the Next Generation," *The Bridge* 51, no. 4 (Winter 2010/Spring 2011): 4, https://scholarworks.harding.edu/hst-bridge/65.

and the Bible, and that faith enables me to teach others more confidently."[20]

Looking Forward: Challenges, Barriers, Possibilities

Theological educators play a crucial role in developing leaders for the next generation. Theological training schools are located upstream from local churches. Within a decade or two, much of what flows out of the academy will, in one form or another, flow into the life of the church.[21] Surely Dietrich Werner is on the right track when he states, "Theological education is the seedbed for the renewal of churches, their ministries and mission."[22] The academy must humbly recognize and accept her important role in partnering with the church for the glory of God. The challenges confronting missionaries in the future can be categorized into two segments: external challenges and internal preparation.

When speaking about upcoming external changes and challenges associated with global missions, it is not unusual to hear bold and declarative statements. Jared Looney provides one such example when he writes: "We do not know what else to call our current epoch except *post*—post-something, post-everything. We simply know that seismic shifts are taking place, and big changes spell new challenges (and opportunities) for the church and its mission."[23] What has changed? Those who have a better read on such matters point to the following issues.

---

[20] Edward Short, e-mail message to author, January 26, 2024.

[21] The timeframe of one or two decades come from Joint Information Service of ETE/WCC & WOCATI, "Challenges and Opportunities in Theological Education in the 21st Century: Pointers for a New International Debate on Theological Education," Edinburgh 2010 – International Study Group on Theological Education World Study Report 2009, October 2009, https://www.wocati.org/wp-content/uploads/2012/06/2009-nov-Theological-Education-in-World-Christianity.pdf, 31.

[22] Dietrich Werner, "Letter from ETE/WCC Staff," 5 in Joint Information Service of ETE/WCC & WOCATI, "Challenges and Opportunities in Theological Education," 5.

[23] Jared Looney, "Global Shifts and Practical Implications for Mission," *Missio Dei* 9, no.2 (Summer-Fall 2018): https://missiodeijournal.com/issues/md-9-2/authors/md-9-2-looney.

- **Pluralistic and relativistic mindsets** are increasing.[24] How do missionaries develop new ways of speaking the truth of the gospel to people who have a relativistic mindset?
- The worldwide **urban populations are exploding** while rural populations are decreasing. With a less-than-stellar track record, how will we meet the challenge of establishing faith communities in expansive global cities?[25]
- **People are increasingly mobile.**[26] What are some of the best practices for the forming of faith communities when so many are living transient lives?
- There has been dramatic **numerical growth of Christians in the Global South.** That shift has not resulted in a corresponding shift of influence.[27] Many churches in the Global North continue to think and speak of missions in terms of *our* going to *them*. In this way, the Global North continues to see themselves at the controlling center of the missionary movement. Instead, as Dana Roberts contends, Christian mission "is truly to and from all parts of the world."[28] The question we might ask ourselves is not just, *who should I teach?* but *who should I learn from?* How much theological training incorporates voices from the Global South to help shape or refine our thinking and approaches to global missions?
- What theological and missional question ought to guide our **thinking about digital technology?** Mark Woodward suggests churches are increasingly only interested in supporting *"successful* missions."[29] Woodard infers that most churches define a successful

---

[24] Monte Cox, "Missions in the Churches of Christ: Trends in Theology and Strategy" (paper presentation, Stone-Campbell Dialogue on Foreign Missions, St. Louis Christian College, June 9, 2008).

[25] Cox, "Missions in the Churches of Christ."

[26] Looney, "Global Shifts and Practical Implications."

[27] See Albert W. Hickman, "Christianity's Shift from the Global North to the Global South" *Review and Expositor* 111 (2014): 41-47.

[28] As quoted in Kapya J. Kaoma, "Post Edinburgh 2010 Christian Mission; Joys, Issues and Challenges," *Journal of Theology for Southern Africa* 150 (November 2014), 118.

[29] Mark Woodward, "What is the State of Missions in Churches of Christ?," accessed on 1/26/2024, https://markwoodward.org/2013/05/01/2459/. My emphasis.

mission according to the following criteria: affordable, accessible, quantifiably impressive and motivating for the local church, and safe."[30] If churches are thinking in these terms, digital technology appears to have many benefits over embodied missions. Digital technology is affordable and accessible. For the cost of internet, anyone living in even the smallest American city can instantly connect with people all around the world. Expensive trips can be minimized. Best of all, it is hard to beat the safety offered by this form of disembodied missionary work. The suggestion is not to ignore or minimize the important role of digital technology in missions. Instead, the call is for theological educators to explore theological and missionally sound principles for making proper use of digital technology in a way that does not fundamentally ignore the inherently Christian need for incarnational missions.

How do we train and equip missionaries when, in the words of Tod Bolsinger, "the world in front of you is nothing like the world behind you"?[31] With so much change afoot, it is easy for ministers and missionaries to experience a sort of missional vertigo. No one knows what is up and what is down. This pundit says that, and that pundit says this. Without any societal complexity, what missionary does not already feel ill-equipped for the missionary call in front of them? How are missionaries to adapt and adjust to all these changes? The encouraging news is this: missionaries are often well-equipped for working in rapidly changing contexts. Missionaries expect to enter cultures they do not understand. They listen (on both a local and global level), discern, and seek to find points of connection between the kingdom and a culture. We should confidently expect good things from missionaries who enter this post-everything world.

Apart from these external changes and challenges, internal preparation is essential for missionary training. One of the central tasks of theological education is to help nurture and develop the spiritual life of the missionary. This is the only way a missionary will truly be

---

[30] Woodward, "State of Missions."
[31] Tod Bolsinger, *Canoeing the Mountains: Christian Leadership in Uncharted Territory* (Downers Grove, Il: InterVarsity Press, 2018), 17, Kindle.

prepared and equipped for ministry in unsettling times. In the Farewell Discourse (John 13–17), Jesus knew his disciples were on the precipice of some deeply disorienting days (John 14:1; 15:18-19; 16:4, 6, 20-22). Jesus also knew they needed encouragement, so he offers them a message of peace (John 14:27, 16:33). To equip his disciples, Jesus did not speak only of the coming challenges (John 15:18-19). Instead, he focused on the wellspring of resources available through his return to the Father and his ongoing presence through the Spirit. Through the Spirit he would be with them, in them, and work through them (John 14:17). The Spirit would work in and through the disciples to ensure God's will is accomplished. To be equipped for ministry, one must abide in Jesus. One cannot bear fruit alone (John 15:4).

Following the example of Jesus, theological education should focus on equipping missionaries for what Tod Bolsinger calls "leading off the map" and leading into "uncharted territory."[32] Missionaries in this post-everything era should be encouraged to know that he who is in you is greater than he who is in the world (1 John 4:4). The goal is not the proclamation of a pollyannaish doctrine. Instead, the goal is to offer a message of hope by tapping into the deep spiritual resources available in Christ.

Missionary work has always required individuals to depend on God's provision, humbly study a culture, and make necessary adjustments. As HST has been faithfully training and equipping students for the last 66 years, there are ample reasons to look forward with anticipation to what God has in store for the next chapter of the story of HST. As the school establishes herself in a new place, my prayer is that she will continue to reflect God's missionary heart as she trains and equips future generations for participating in the mission of God.

---

[32] Bolsinger, *Canoeing the Mountains*, 14.

CHAPTER NINE

Urban Mission

Jim Harbin

This essay reflects on the ways in which Harding School of Theology (HST) has impacted urban ministry in the city of Memphis, Tennessee and beyond. In my view, what has been accomplished in urban ministry would not have been possible without HST. This account of urban ministry, which begins in 1990 and continues through 2024, reveals the role of HST in educating urban practitioners who served in various capacities during this timeframe.

HST has blessed me tremendously. The Master of Arts degree that I obtained in 2002 at HST provided the necessary education I needed to plant an urban church, the Raleigh Community Church of Christ, and lead it successfully as the Senior Pastor for 27 years. Prior to attending HST, I worked in the Skin Biology Lab of Schering Plough in research and development producing Coppertone Artificial Suntan Lotions. I obtained a Bachelor of Science Degree from the University of Memphis with a dual major in Microbiology and Chemistry. Although I was working in my field, I had a strong desire to serve in ministry full time; however, I had no formal biblical education.

Because the tuition was free, I investigated attending a local school of preaching. While exploring this local school of preaching, I received a call from HST about their degree programs and decided to attend there. I have reflected many times on that decision and am certain I made the right one. I am convinced that what has been accomplished in urban ministry in Memphis through myself and my colleagues would not have been possible had I attended this school of preaching or another graduate school.

Prior to attending HST, my understanding of Scripture was shallow and permeated with traditions. With no formal biblical education, I learned by attending worship, listening to preachers, attending Bible class, and self-study at home. For twelve years, my wife, Beverly, and our four children, Joi, Jami, Courtni, and Jim IV, attended the Norris Road Church of Christ (formerly Vance Avenue Church of Christ). I sat under the feet of the prominent preacher, the late Nokomis Yeldell, learning the art form of African American preaching. At Norris Road, I learned to preach and was given many opportunities to preach on Sunday mornings and evenings, conduct eulogies, lead the youth ministry and prison ministry, and teach Bible class. I loved ministry, and Norris Road provided the opportunity for my family to actively serve the Lord.

When I enrolled at HST, I thought I understood the Bible pretty well until I was suddenly confronted with Greek, Hebrew, the exegesis of Scripture, and hermeneutics. The process of interpreting Scripture and understanding the Bible at a deeper level was unsettling. I was shocked and dismayed when I heard interpretations of biblical passages at HST that differed from the traditional ways I heard them preached or explained. Consequently, I committed myself to sticking with "the truth" as I knew it and regurgitating the answers on tests to successfully complete my coursework. Professors like Dr. Allen Black, Dr. John Mark Hicks, and Dr. Phil McMillan gently, yet persuasively, taught me the process to discover the truth for myself, but never told me what to believe.

HST provided a methodology that empowered me to separate the truth in Scripture from the traditions that I grew up with. Understanding this process, I became free and no longer experienced my perceived tension between truth, tradition, and error. In my newfound freedom, I could simultaneously embrace some traditions and still "stand on the truth." The greatest lesson I learned at HST was simple—I learned just how much I didn't know. From that point forward, I committed myself to being a life-long learner and sticking to my best understanding of Scripture.

In addition to the academic education, I was blessed to have mentors who were HST professors. During my time at HST and beyond, I was mentored by former Deans, Dr. Evertt Huffard and Dr. Allen Black. Dr. Stanley Granberg (MTh, 1993) provided training in church planting through Kairos. Dr. Harold Shank, (MAR, 1977), a former church planter and exceptional preacher, mentored me while I was in the process of planting the Raleigh Community Church of Christ. I spent seven years from 1991 to 1998 at Highland Church of Christ under the leadership of Dr. Shank as a deacon over the School Store and later on staff as a church planter. Dr. Shank taught me the day-to-day operations of Highland, a large, predominantly-white church, and how to lead, preach, and teach Bible class in that context.

The establishment of urban ministry in Memphis is the result of a carefully constructed web consisting of individuals, urban and suburban churches, and nonprofits, with HST as an interconnecting thread to each one. Those connected to HST were the catalyst for reaching the lost through urban ministry in Memphis. Dr. Evertt Huffard and Dr. Harold Shank were two prominent and influential voices for the poor in distressed neighborhoods of Memphis who convinced elders and churches to heavily invest in the city through church planting.

In 1991, Highland Church of Christ, led by Dr. Harold Shank and others, presented a proposal compiled by Ron Bergeron and Alan Madera to initiate the planting of an urban church with Highland as the lead church. At the same time, HST began a real effort to meet the urban challenge by hosting the first Urban Ministries Seminar led by Dr. Evertt W. Huffard to begin the education process.

The Highland Church of Christ elders formed a Highland City Missions Committee to provide leadership and focus to Highland's efforts to serve the city. One example of an early effort to serve the inner-city was the Highland School Store. At the Highland School Store, free school supplies were given to needy children in kindergarten through the sixth grade so they would be ready to start the first day of school. A family from Cleaborn Homes attended the School Store and requested a Bible study. As a result, a weekly Bible study was started in the community center in Cleaborn Homes.

The Highland City Missions Committee was responsible for the church planting ministry, which envisioned planting churches in the inner-city of Memphis. During the 1990s, there was also a migration of churches from the urban center of Memphis that moved into the suburbs, which was an impetus for inner-city church planting. Within a few years, the Highland City Missions Committee grew to become a collaborative effort among Churches of Christ and provided oversight of the newly formed Memphis Urban Ministry.

In 1990, Anthony Wood (DMin, 2002) was hired to help direct Memphis Urban Ministry (MUM). Financial support for MUM came from Highland Church of Christ, White Station Church of Christ, Sycamore View Church of Christ, Cordova Community Church, Missouri Street Church of Christ, and a host of other churches, individual contributors, and businesses. Through MUM, five urban churches were planted: Downtown Church of Christ, Raleigh Community Church of Christ, Frayser Mission Church of Christ, Wonder City Church of Christ in West Memphis, Arkansas, and Iglesia de Cristo.

In 1992, the 3rd National Conference for Ministries to the Poor and Homeless was held in Memphis and was coordinated by Dr. Shank. This was the first time Memphis hosted the conference. It was also the first time inner-city ministry directors met to discuss the conference and develop a network of support and ideas.[1] The Urban Ministry Conference continued as an annual event until 2006 when it was cancelled. In 2006, the conference was held in Montgomery, Alabama and coordinated by Jonathan Mosby, minister of the Inner-City Church of Christ. The group decided to end the conference altogether because some felt it was no longer useful to practitioners, so from 2007-2010 it was discontinued.

In 1992, the Downtown Church of Christ became the first

---

[1] Anthony Wood, email message to the author, "Urban Ministry Conference History," 2009.

MUM church plant. The building that housed the Downtown Church of Christ was located at 576 Vance Avenue, across the street from the former location of the Vance Avenue Church of Christ. This facility was known as the Annex and was the fellowship hall of the Vance Avenue church. The Downtown Church was strategically located in the heart of downtown Memphis and in an ideal location to minister to the generational poor in the neighborhoods of Cleaborn Homes, Foote Homes, and other parts of the city.

The goal included developing indigenous leadership from an indigenous membership. There was a heavy use of volunteers; however, volunteers could not become part of the church. The Downtown Church depended heavily on outside support for staff, facilities, and financial support. Apprentices from HST preached, led worship, and worked in the neighborhoods. Volunteers and staff taught Bible classes and conducted the outreach ministries, including the School Store, Turkey Store, and Christmas Store.

On June 6, 1996, my wife Beverly and I went to a Highland Church of Christ elders' meeting and presented a proposal to plant a church in Raleigh, the neighborhood where we lived. We asked the elders for two things: spiritual oversight and funding. After receiving both, the Raleigh Community Church of Christ was planted on Father's Day, June 15, 1997 in a storefront on Covington Pike.

In 2002, with financial support from the Highland Church of Christ, Raleigh Community constructed a new multipurpose building situated on 9.1 acres on New Allen Road. In 2005, two elders and eight deacons were appointed to lead the church into the future. Ministries focus on strengthening marriages and family. The congregation reaches into the community through a vibrant children's and youth ministry that includes power hours, basketball, and an exciting summer day camp. Through continued prayers and support, the church plans to continue to develop their campus into a center of worship and outreach for their neighborhood.

In 1998, Frayser Mission Church (FMC) was planted in the Frayser community by Ron and Ann Cook. FMC met in the East

Frayser Church of Christ building and another church building until December 2005.

The Wonder City Church of Christ (WCC) in West Memphis, Arkansas began as a satellite church planted by the Missouri Street Church of Christ (MOST) in 1999. Chris Mauldin (MDiv, 2005) led the Wonder City Church of Christ from 1999-2001. Later Mack McFarland (MDiv, 2004) became the minister for Wonder City. The Wonder City Church sought to learn how to embody the presence of God in the indigent community in West Memphis. Initially, Wonder City was located at 2314 East Broadway, West Memphis, Arkansas and its purpose was to address both the spiritual and social needs of the local community. When Mack McFarland resigned from WCC, Hamilton Archibald (MDiv, 2014) was hired by MOST. The name was changed to the Northside Church of Christ and they moved into a building purchased by Missouri Street Church of Christ at 201 N 8th Street, West Memphis, Arkansas.

During the 1990s nearly 100,000 Hispanics moved to Memphis. As a result of this continuous growing population, Iglesia de Cristo was planted in 1999 by Jim Holway (MAR, 1987). The church initially met in the Sycamore View Church of Christ facilities. In 2005, Jim Holway joined LAMP (Latin American Mission Project), a Miami church planting project and partnership among Christian universities and ministry-training schools. Holway planned to facilitate mission teams as they moved to South Florida to plant new churches or train for ministry in the Spanish-speaking world. In July 2005, the leadership of the church was handed over to Gonzalo Salinas. Gonzalo had preached the gospel in Nicaragua, Costa Rica, Honduras and Panama and helped to plant 27 churches. Currently, Iglesia de Cristo is part of the White Station Church of Christ, and Juan Meza (MDiv, 2018) serves as the minister.

By the year 2000, five urban churches had been planted through MUM and on March 1, 2006, Jim Harbin was appointed Director of MUM. On October 5, 2009, MUM became incorporated as a nonprofit in Tennessee and in 2010, MUM became a 501(c)3. MUM developed a new vision which stated, "MUM partners with churches, ministries, organizations, and agencies to reach and restore our community through church planting, outreach to the poor, leadership and community development."

These two texts, Luke 4:18-21 and Proverbs 21:13, were central to the vision, mission, and the theological basis for MUM:

"The Spirit of the Lord is on me, because he has anointed me to preach good news to the poor. He has sent me to proclaim freedom for the prisoners and recovery of sight for the blind, to release the oppressed, to proclaim the year of the Lord's favor." Then he rolled up the scroll, gave it back to the attendant and sat down. The eyes of everyone in the synagogue were fastened on him, and he began by saying to them, "Today this scripture is fulfilled in your hearing." (Luke 4:18-21, NIV)

If a man shuts his ears to the cry of the poor, he too will cry out and not be answered. (Proverbs 21:13, NIV)

Through a partnership with HST, MUM offered an urban ministry apprenticeship. The apprenticeship program was directly connected to the MUM's vision of leadership development. The apprenticeship provided field experience in urban ministry at a local church while students completed a Master's degree at HST. There was a mutual benefit for the local church and the student. During the approximate eighteen months of the apprenticeship, students received practical experience in serving in an urban church. Opportunities were provided for preaching, teaching Bible Class, engaging in evangelism, and serving in compassionate ministries.

Cynthia Turner, Jeremy Marshall, Jared King, Jonathan Strasser, Makoto Tateno, Dorn Muscar, Joshua McGough, Kristen Thomas, Aaron and Mika Roland, and Justin McCreary completed a MUM Apprenticeship at Raleigh Community Church of Christ. These HST students greatly impacted the Raleigh Community Church by helping to shape the vision and implementation of the mission as "boots on the ground." Raleigh Community Church impacted apprentices by providing opportunities to serve in ministry in real-time and put into practice what they were learning at HST. For example, it was obvious that some apprentices had never actually taught adult Bible Class. Through the apprenticeship, they not only taught adult Bible classes, but received constructive feedback from their field supervisor and congregants. A key area that needs to continually be addressed is the need for extended field training in an apprenticeship for students pursuing a career in ministry.

The impact of HST on MUM Apprentices is clearly visible through their successes in ministry. Former apprentice Captain Cynthia Turner is serving as Chaplain in the United States Army. Dorn Muscar served for eight years as the preaching minister for the University Park Church of Christ. Dorn is now the IMA to the Deputy Wing Chaplain in the United States Air Force.[2] Jeremy Marshall is the Family Discipleship Minister at the Brooks Avenue Church of Christ. Jared King is the Lead Church Planter and Pastor of Missio Church. Erika Carr now teaches at Yale University School of Medicine and directs programs for the Connecticut Mental Health Center.[3]

In 2009, Cynthia Turner, Dorn Muscar, and Mack McFarland organized a National Urban Ministry Summit (NUMS) in St. Louis to determine if the Urban Ministry Conference should be resurrected, and they reestablished a national network of practitioners for support and exchange of ideas. Surprisingly, there were ten different urban churches and nonprofits from eight states that attended. The group decided that a National Urban Ministry Association would be established and the association would be responsible for coordinating the annual National Urban Ministry Conference (NUMC). The first NUMC was held in 2011 at the Impact Church of Christ in Houston, Texas. Since 2011, the annual NUMC is held the third weekend in February. Because of COVID-19, it was held virtually in 2021. The NUMC provides a platform for HST and other institutions to present urban-ministry focused theological presentations and other presentations

---

[2] Dorn Muscar contributed chapter 13, on chaplaincy, to this volume.
[3] Erika Carr contributed chapter 10, on counseling, to this volume.

relevant to urban ministry. Dr. Evertt Huffard, Dr. Harold Shank, and Dr. Steve Cloer have delivered keynotes at the annual NUMC.

In 2004, significant transitions happened with MUM and most of the urban church plants. Anthony Wood resigned as the director and MUM was essentially left idle for about two-and-a-half years. Each urban church plant was on its own. In March 2004, Jeff Matthews (MDiv, 2004) resigned as minister for the Downtown Church and entered a chaplaincy program. Consequently, from March 2004 until October of 2005 there was no minister at the Downtown Church. Anthony Wood became the minister of the Downtown Church from December 2005 until July of 2006. Jim Harbin, new Director of Memphis Urban Ministry, filled-in with preaching and helping to guide members through this transition. From July 2006 until July 2007, I preached nearly every Sunday at the Downtown Church. I preached at Raleigh Community Church of Christ on Sunday morning, then drove to the Downtown Church to preach. However, the DTC needed a full-time minister, so William Smith was hired.

In December 2005, a decision was made by Ron Cook and members of Frayser Mission Church to close the ministry and merge with the Downtown Church. At that time, there were only a handful of members left. About eight of the members of Frayser Mission Church started worshiping with the Raleigh Community Church of Christ. Wonder City Church severed relationship with MUM and both the Downtown Church of Christ and the Frayser Mission Church closed. Although Raleigh Community Church of Christ, Northside Church of Christ (formerly Wonder City Church of Christ), and Iglesia de Cristo remained, some elders viewed MUM as a flawed venture because of the limited results for the total dollars spent. The MUM Board of Directors decided to dissolve it in 2011.

During this period, HopeWorks led by Ron Wade (MA, 1987) and Agape Child & Family Services (Agape) were thriving.[4] HopeWorks' mission is to "guide Memphians in need of a second

---

[4] For more information on HopeWorks, see https://www.whyhopeworks.org/. For more information on Agape Child and Family Services, see https://agapemeanslove.org/.

chance through essential education, counseling and career development programming to establish a relationship with God while building stability, confidence and a hope-filled future." MUM often partnered with HopeWorks, and some of their clients became members in the urban church plants.

In 2011, while continuing to serve as the minister of Raleigh Community Church of Christ, I was hired at Agape as a Site Coordinator for Powerlines Community Network (PCN) for Raleigh Frayser. PCN was embedded in apartment communities in Raleigh, Hickory Hill, and Whitehaven. PCN had space in apartments in Ashton Hills-Frayser, Summit Park-Whitehaven, and Autumn Ridge-Hickory Hill and provided afterschool programs, summer camp, and wraparound services to the residents.

Through PCN, Agape partnered with the Achievement School District in Frayser to provide wraparound services to schools. The model entailed embedding Agape staff called Stars Connectors in schools to improve student attendance, behavior, and academics. Using a two-generational approach and well over one hundred partners, Agape served both the child and the family in six schools in Frayser. This model was expanded to Hickory Hill and Whitehaven.

The approach of Agape fit the model of John Perkins' Christian Community Development Association of serving in the neighborhoods where people live. David Jordan, CEO and President of Agape envisioned a practical way to go to apartment communities where families live to serve them. In addition, David Jordan adopted an evidence-based model to provide social services to families in three impoverished areas of Memphis.

Another lesson learned from Agape is the importance of collecting data in a systematic way to demonstrate the effectiveness of the "theory of change" in programming. Agape used recognized computer databases to capture standard inputs based on logic models and would later analyze the data to determine if the program achieved its objectives. Because of this data-informed approach to service delivery, Agape was successful in obtaining grant funding from a variety of sources.

Agape demonstrated that grants were available to faith-based nonprofits that used models with fidelity and demonstrated effectiveness in programming. This means that social services can be funded with local, state, and federal dollars. Urban ministry is no longer trendy, so expecting all funding to come from the local church may be problematic.

Another important milestone in urban ministry was Agape's transition from apartment communities to churches, called Right Relationship Centers. Agape partnered with churches to have staff embedded in the church to provide social services during the week when typically, smaller churches are closed. For example, the Pursuit of God Transformation Center located in Frayser is considered a "hub church," and Agape staff have been given office space to serve families in the community. Agape has "hub churches" located in the other impoverished areas served by PCN. Agape has developed a model that provides resources to families through the local church.

In September of 2018, I resigned from Agape to focus on taking what I had learned and applying it to Raleigh Community Church of Christ. Briefly, we started using evidence-based curriculum in our children's ministry, collecting data, and hiring staff that was committed to serving in the church. We were able to obtain grant funding for our childcare ministry through the state. We partnered with United Way of the Midsouth Driving the Dream program to provide social services to the families we served.[5]

In 2020, Pastor Daniel Henley, former Chief Spiritual Health Officer of Agape, asked me to come back to Agape to lead their Becoming ONE Project, a marriage ministry. The Becoming ONE project targets 450 Memphis married couples over a five-year period in congregations located in neighborhoods of Shelby County to build healthy marriages. Agape received a substantial grant to serve married couples through the local church. For the last three years, I have served as the Project Coordinator for Becoming ONE. Through Agape, we have trained 94 facilitators to instruct couples in an evidence-based

---

[5] See https://uwmidsouth.org/category/driving-the-dream/.

curriculum, Prep 8.0.[6] Currently, 351 married couples have successfully completed the Becoming ONE Program. While Becoming ONE is open to the community at large, the vast majority of these married couples and facilitators are members of churches in Memphis.

What I have attempted to describe above in this historical framework is only a portion of urban ministry in Memphis. When urban ministry is viewed from above so that all the components can be seen, it is extremely complex. Urban ministry involves spreading the gospel and providing social services through funding, education, partnerships, collaboration, data collection, as well as continuous quality improvement through lessons learned.

Successfully serving in an urban church or urban ministry requires a theology for the city. A knowledge of the city and an understanding of the dynamics of the sometimes rapidly changing city is a key area that theological education must address. Cities have been impacted by changes in demographics in which city dwellers are displaced into surrounding areas when public housing is demolished and replaced with mixed income developments. "Six large public housing developments—Lauderdale Courts, Dixie Homes, Hurt Village, Lamar Terrace, LeMoyne Gardens and Cleaborn Homes—became mixed-income developments starting with the 1998 demolition of LeMoyne Gardens in South Memphis."[7]

The US Department of Housing and Urban Development initiated a plan called Hope VI in which mixed income developments replaced public housing. In 2010, Memphis Housing Authority developed Cleaborn Homes Hope VI, which included a supportive services plan to provide resources for the displaced public housing tenants. Memphis Housing Authority surveyed residents of Cleaborn Homes and found the following:

> The Needs Survey of the 413 target households indicates high levels of disability and illness and other barriers to

---

[6] See https://prepinc.com/.

[7] See https://www.memphisdailynews.com/news/2017/jun/1/long-awaited-demolition-at-foote-homes-begins/.

self-sufficiency. It is estimated that 135 households are receiving Social Security Income (SSI). Only 40 of 484 adults are employed and the median household income is $5,886. Forty-nine (49%) of all adults have less than a high school diploma or GED.[8]

The characteristics of these residents indicates a dire need for social services. Based on the data from the surveys, social services that are needed include GED completion, post-secondary education and training opportunities, services for people with mental and physical disabilities, counseling, employment opportunities, health resources and childcare resources.

You will recall that an urban church plant, the Downtown Church was located directly across the street from Cleaborn Homes public housing project. Many of the people who showed up to the Downtown Church on Sunday morning for worship and Bible class lived in Cleaborn Homes. These were the same individuals that needed post-secondary education, training, jobs, services for people with mental and physical disabilities, counseling, health resources, and childcare.

In my work with MUM and the Downtown Church, I discovered that some elders and other leaders clearly saw the need for a church plant and preaching the gospel, but did not understand nor embrace the need for providing the aforementioned resources to meet the individuals felt needs. For some churches, considerable theological tension exists between sharing the gospel and providing social services. Some churches believe that providing social services is not connected to the mission of the church. HST has a role in educating ministers, churches, and organizations so that an appropriate theological framework is developed to share the gospel and address the ongoing felt needs of people living in the city. Consequently, urban churches and urban ministries must have a wholistic theology that allows the gospel to be spread and the needs of those living in the city to be met.

---

[8] Document: MEMPHIS HOUSING AUTHORITY Cleaborn Hope VI. 4/9/2011/ VERSION I.

There are deep divisions on key issues in our country that cause other barriers within the church. The political climate in America is hostile and has become increasingly polarized in recent years. There are deep divisions within our country.

Democrats and Republicans hold starkly different views on various issues, including the economy, racial justice, climate change, law enforcement, and international engagement. The 2020 presidential election further highlighted these divisions, with supporters of Joe Biden and Donald Trump seeing their differences as rooted in core American values.[9]

Controversial issues like Black Lives Matter, LGBTQ+, "Being Woke," crime, the wars between Israel and Hamas and Russia and the Ukraine, immigration, the overturning of Roe v. Wade, and the economy are potential barriers that prevent people from attending church. What is the position of the church in the political unrest in our country? Academicians need to help churches process these real issues and develop a theology that addresses these potential barriers.

One lesson learned in urban ministry is the important of collaborative partnerships between churches, nonprofits, and community organizations. These collaborations may not all be partnerships between Churches of Christ or organizations affiliated with Churches of Christ. This type of collaboration raises theological questions that must be addressed.

The modern age requires the use of social media and other platforms on the internet to spread the gospel. This means going beyond streaming a "talking head" with an open Bible over the internet. During Bible classes, on a given Sunday or Wednesday, there are thousands of "talking heads." Consequently, which one do you pick? Churches must adapt because today's messaging requires the use of multimedia presentations that immerse a techno-savvy audience into the Word of God. A theology is required that informs churches

---

[9] See https://www.pewresearch.org/short-reads/2020/11/13/america-is-exceptional-in-the-nature-of-its-political-divide/.

that technology is a platform that can effectively be used to spread the gospel.

When these barriers are overcome and urban ministries are successful in spreading the gospel and providing social services, God is glorified because "oaks of righteousness" are produced. Like the servant in Isaiah 61, we are called "to provide for those who mourn in Zion—to give them a garland instead of ashes, the oil of gladness instead of mourning, the mantle of praise instead of a faint spirit. They will be called oaks of righteousness, the planting of the LORD, to display his glory" (Isa 61:3, NRSV).

CHAPTER TEN

Counseling

Erika Carr

Attending graduate school at Harding School of Theology (HST) was a unique and special time that helped proliferate a lot of questions I had in my life. I went to Harding University for undergraduate school. Though I had a lot of fun, learned more about God, got connected to a lot of amazing people, and engaged in many diverse intellectual pursuits, I left still feeling like I was not sure what I wanted to do with my life. I knew I wanted to help people and share God's love but was uncertain how and in which way. It felt like I actually got a degree in hopping majors in Searcy, Arkansas—yes, I was one of those students. Initially, I declared myself as pre-med (excelled in it) but later for many reasons changed to business, next to accounting, then pre-law, and then education (which I picked because most of my friends were in those classes—always an excellent reason for a life decision). Finally, I ended up with a BA in Communication, Sciences, and Disorders—Clinical, but by the end of four years I knew I did not want to pursue the sequential next-step, which at the time was a master's degree in speech pathology. By then I realized I had no money or scholarships left, so I needed to get out of undergraduate school, take some space, and help my soul and mind figure out what I really wanted to do with my life. Some people cannot figure out a life profession at the mature age of 18-21 years old, when everything sounds interesting and possible, and simultaneously there is always a constant stream of new people to meet, activities to do, summer ventures to plan, attractive young guys to date, and a big wide world at your feet. All of these experiences and the basic distractions and dialectic of the newfound freedom of self-autonomy and need for adulting, while trying to study and develop a profession that would actually pay my own bills one day, left me leaving Searcy still trying to figure out what to do with my life.

I ended up in Memphis, Tennessee after working some in missions in a few different places in the world, including with the Village of Hope in Ghana, West Africa. I tell my own story and narrative because this is the unique and special way that HST came into my life—as I think it may have for many—though it does not sound quite streamlined. Once again, with my indecisive self, I was at the crux of two decisions: going back to school for pre-medicine or thinking about a graduate degree in counseling or psychology. When I started at HST, it became apparent that I finally was tuning my soul, mind, and spirit into a place and purpose that was on a wavelength in sync with who I am as a person. It felt like I was coming home and could put my heart and intellectual effort into learning a skill and profession that conceptualized what my future could and would embody.

Special Talent and People of HST and the Counseling Program

My first few classes at HST were with Dr. Ed Gray, who was leading the Master of Arts in Counseling program and was an excellent professor, clinician, and supervisor. It was evident by how he made space in his classes for us to learn that he saw each of us for our strengths and capabilities. He was also praying for each and every student, as we were going to touch lives through our work in counseling in ways that we could not envision yet. I remember Dr. Gray starting or ending many classes with prayer, with his kind and unique calmness that evoked in me—and I believe in each of us—the fortitude, belief in ourselves, and trust that God would guide us through the necessary journey of studying, writing, and shaping clinical skills. This was so critical and wise of Dr. Gray, because it invoked in us our own confidence and trust that God was with us as we started to learn about becoming therapists and clinicians, where we would start the precious journey of what it is like to hold narratives that individuals are oftentimes too scared to hold themselves, much less speak those stories into existence to another human. Dr. Gray led the Counseling program with steadfastness, humility, kindness, and sincerity. He openly shared his supreme skill with us, so that we were ready to step into our practicums and practice the clinical skills he was teaching us with an ethical compass, unconditional positive regard, and strong theoretical orientation to help guide our theoretical conceptualization skills and therapeutic interventions. It was intellectually stimulating and fun to learn about the vastness of knowledge within the counseling field, as Dr. Gray taught us about different mental health issues and how to have strong clinical acumen—with diagnostic skills, theoretical skills, and intervention skills—while also showing the love and humility of a power beyond what comes from the medical field and the limits of its knowledge.

I must mention Linda Oxford, one of the most gifted, funny, smart, insightful, fierce, and talented professors I have ever met—across my master's program and doctoral degree at the University of Tennessee-Knoxville. Her leadership skills were incredibly evident as she was in leadership at Agape Child and Family Services and was an active leader in a counseling association in Tennessee. It was obvious that our graduate program was not the only place aware of her many gifts and seeking her time. She taught us about family systems and had the brilliant and fun idea to teach us how to recognize and understand family dynamics by watching movies that could equivocate the elements of family dynamics much better than we could by just talking about them didactically. I remember our class watching parts of these movies, laughing hilariously, and then discussing them as a group. We also felt liberated to laugh and comment about our own zany and ironic family dynamics that likely shaped our personalities to that day.

Linda Oxford called for high standards, which I loved. I remember one of her classes—one of the very first that I took in the program—and I got a wee bit of a substandard grade for me (or a bit worse actually). I knew I had not really applied myself in studying, given that I was balancing graduate school and working to pay the bills. Boldly, she asked to meet me after class—or I asked her; I cannot remember which. I remember feeling excited to speak to this vibrant teacher, and a bit terrified. What was strikingly wonderful was that she saw my intellectual skills, knew I could do better, and expected better.

She wholeheartedly called me to the table. She knew what I needed to know to be one of the best in this profession, and for that I am fully grateful—this was also after years of feeling a bit lost in undergrad with all the majors. Thanks to her fierceness, I did apply myself in more depth and started to love this profession. From there I went on to get my PhD, and now this is my life's passion. I am grateful to Linda for seeing her graduate students and holding us to high standards.

On a humorous note, this was a time in my life when I was full of big ideas, which I have not completely lost. I remember Linda calling me "grandiose" one night in class and I thought she had complimented me. I really did. I even went home and told my roommate, who was also studying in the graduate counseling program at the time, thinking that this was a great compliment. It was only after a few more classes and more practical application of my studies that I realized "grandiose" is more synchronous with someone who has inflated pretension or beliefs beyond the ordinary, and sometimes is found in people who have lost touch with reality. But touché, the comment was even better when I realized what it really meant, because I knew Linda was seeing me for what and who I could be at times, but also having fun with me. She also knew that one day I would be in a space where I could hear that, laugh about it, and laugh deeply. Linda was a bright light for me because she is loud, vibrant, and always lives life to its full, with God as her guide; that always meant so much to me as a single woman (at the time) who wanted to fully serve God with my life, find my niche, and also lead as a woman in the church.

The unique talent in the program also must incorporate the immense love, devotion, gentleness of spirit, and godliness that Dr. Bill Flatt imbued into each and every one of his courses. Dr. Flatt, by far, is one of the kindest and gentlest human beings I have ever met—on the same status, in my mind, with the holiness of my grandmother, who was always doing good for others and thinking of others as a farmer's wife, mother, and community member in a small town in North Carolina. Dr. Flatt had a beautiful smile and loved God with every inch of his body, which is apparent in his book, *Restoring My Soul: The*

Pursuit of Spiritual Resilience.[1] I remember reading this book cover-to-cover in graduate school, and it helped me as I thought about how to engage with clients who were facing depression, anxiety, and suicidal thoughts. Dr. Flatt was uniquely able to shed light on the power of resilience and face such difficult topics as suicidality and addiction, which are not often talked about in Christian circles other than to say, "Don't do it." He addressed these topics holistically, with great respect and love, and from a spiritual perspective. This intellectual knowledge remains incredibly powerful and a gift to any who read this book. Dr. Flatt also shared his family and the love he had for them with us. He made us feel special by hosting a holiday party or end-of-the-semester party, offering special greetings to each and every one of us, and always being mindful to tell each of us how special we were and to note our unique gifts. Honestly, Dr. Flatt has many spiritual gifts, but when we were with him it felt like he was shining and loving each of us with the love of Jesus, and that helped make us brighter and hopeful. I realize that this was a unique capacity he had to shine the love of God. But he knew that we also had the capacity and gifts to shine that love to others. We too would go into the world and bear witness of God's love by listening, hearing, and validating people's pain and troubles, while showing them they deserve to heal and that there is hope.

Wonderfully, we were required to take some courses that were taught by the Bible professors. Dr. Allen Black left a lasting impression on my life, as he allowed us as students to ask so many hard and difficult questions. He led us to the Word and what God might have to say to us about living the Christian life. This was a pivotal and impactful time in my life, as a single woman trying to find her way in ministry and whatever form that might be as God depicts and designs those elements for me. At the time, I was working with Memphis Urban Ministry at the Downtown Church of Christ with the youth, while balancing graduate school and a job to pay my bills. It meant the world to me and others that Dr. Black so kindly, respectfully, and judiciously opened the Word with so much equanimity and led us through how God valued the role of

---

[1] Bill Flatt, *Restoring My Soul: The Pursuit of Spiritual Resilience* (Nashville: Gospel Advocate, 2001).

women in doing the Lord's work. This was a gift and liberation that I can never be thankful enough for. I do not even know if Dr. Black understands to the depths it has touched me, as well as other women. Such influences are critical as we lean in to what God's design is for each of us and for our voice on this earth, whereas many women have only been silenced or taught to exist in the shadows. Dr. Black spoke and elucidated the truth and reality of God's Word that valued our voice, our presence, and our gifts as women. As I went on to pursue a PhD in Psychology, I have worked at interweaving my spiritual gifts across every encounter, and in the systems in which I work, by being a social justice change agent, as I believe to my core that Jesus would have me be. I know other women who have gone on to gain additional graduate degrees in theology and are in full-time ministry. Relatedly, all of these amazing people that have made up the school have in common great humility, vast intellectual and professional talent, and a genuine and straightforward light that shows us where all of this strength and talent comes from, which is God.

There were many talented professors that Dr. Gray asked to come and teach unique aspects of counseling, for which they were all gifted. Dr. Gray's skillfulness in reaching out to the surrounding city and bringing in teachers and clinicians who could teach us about specialties in counseling, in which we needed to be uniquely trained to meet the high standards of our profession, was notable and led to such a high-caliber training program—which was evident in my practicum experiences and those of my cohorts. I will incorporate just one such example. Mr. George Tsirgiotis was kind enough to teach our graduate student cohort about the challenge people have with substance use disorder, and it was a highly influential class for each of us. It contained stories that brought the work to life, strong theoretical and interventional elements that were pivotal for effectiveness with those who may experience substance abuse, and also many elements of pursuing this work that we otherwise may not have known. I was fortunate to work on a few practicum experiences with George at Lakeside Behavioral Health with adolescents helping provide individual therapy, family therapy, and multi-family therapy. This experience brought the world of therapy to life for me. It was an incredible opportunity to finally coalesce all the teachings, studying, writings, and prayer into sitting with people in distress in this world and work with George to be a healer and listener, as Jesus also exemplified for each of us. George was and is amazingly talented as a clinician. He was my first teacher in the room with clients and always remains my most poignant *in vivo* teacher as I envision myself shaping into a listener, a hope-holder, an encourager, and a believer in the strengths of humans to reach for what is good and most meaningful in this life. George has been hearing narratives and stories, while fostering healing through his clinical acumen, for longer than I know. I am always impressed by his resilience, fortitude, and reliance on God to continue to do this work that at times is heavy, joyous, heartbreaking, healing, and gut-wrenching. There are many stories that end well, that we as clinicians hold to our heart. There are others that we lift up as only God can hold them; such narratives have the ability to break our hearts as they bear witness to the pain and trauma that can occur on this earth we all tread.

Building Community

One of the other fundamental and unique elements of HST was the focus on building community. This occurred in many ways, but I know Dr. Gray always envisioned this as he led our program: he always found ways to help us laugh as we entered finals and submitted major papers; he welcomed us to his house every year with any alumni who had ever been through the counseling program; he fostered us, caring for each other and loving each other as we all had diverse lives and there were diverse types of students making it through the program. Dr. Gray would elicit prayer requests. Sometimes we prayed for someone to be able to pay their bills that month, for someone else who was fighting cancer and in a middle stage of life, for someone in a late career change in life as they worried about their adult son, or for some of us babies (early 20s) who were just trying to figure out love, what to do with life itself, and the pursuit of happiness. Dr. Gray held space for it all, and he expected us to hold space for it all too and love each other, and we did. Looking back, I reflect that he was simultaneously teaching us about being the church and community and God's kingdom here on earth—as we felt safe, loved, and supported through our spiritual connection—while also helping us earn a degree. Ironically, I remember getting to know a middle-aged man in class who had a son I had gone on a date with at Harding University a few years before. At the time of the date, this young man told me all about his amazing father who had breast cancer, and how much he was worried about him and his survival; and we prayed about it and gave it to God. As my HST classmate and I connected this story, I remember feeling chill-bumps that God works in mysterious ways because I had prayed for this man before I ever met him. God knew all along that I would meet him down the road.

I remember rooming with Missy (Suggs) Dabbs, who was also trying to figure out her life and the pursuit of happiness in her 20s. We prayed together, studied together, and got connected to this great group of diverse people together. I cannot remember every name of every person who went through the program with me, but I remember many such as John Kennedy, who switched careers as he felt God was leading him in a new direction, Mary Cunningham and her honest and sincere comments in class that made us all think, and K. C. Winters and the fun, deep, truthful, and tremendous friendship we shared. K. C. also attended my wedding. But above it all, I remember that our connection to each other was Christ and building a meaningful purpose and passion for the work we would do in this life.

Another amazing aspect of HST was all the connections it had to the community, both with churches and with outreach to the city of Memphis. I had been connected previously through a summer internship at White Station Church of Christ in Memphis as a youth intern while at Harding University for undergraduate school. This experience connected me to friends and spiritual mentors such as Tommy Drinnen, and mission work at the Village of Hope in Ghana, West Africa. Such connections were deep and wide in Memphis for HST. There were people involved and active at so many churches across the city, whether it was downtown at the Downtown Church of Christ (like me, among others), or at Highland Street Church of Christ, or out in Millington (a suburb), or at Sycamore View Church of Christ, or to the community out in Raleigh. The story of the cross, that we were imbued with, engrained in us that we were all fellow humans who needed Jesus; rich, poor, or middle class; Black, White, Latino, Asian, or Middle Eastern; across every area of the city. We all were in desperate need of the cross, and that was and remains to be the answer for humanity and for our existence. HST in many ways was an epicenter for those training in ministry or counseling to reach Memphis and the larger Mid-South area by sharing the love of the cross with our diverse talents, skills, and methods.

During my graduate training at HST, I was grateful to be supported to share God's love through Memphis Urban Ministry at the Downtown Church of Christ. It was life changing. I was able to work with and minister through my work with the young people at the Downtown Church of Christ under the supervision of Candi Wood at Agape Child & Family Services. This experience showed me very clearly how my life had been so different from the lives of many of these youth, who grew up in poverty and faced daily the consequences of racism and structural inequities. God taught me so much during these teaching moments when I was driving a church bus through those areas to pick up kids and have Wednesday night Bible study and hang-out time. These youth were also teaching me as a person, who grew up without a lot of funds but with the power that comes with White privilege and without the touch and impact of generations of racism. I am thankful every day for these young people, who are now adults and raising kids of their own to know Christ and his teachings.

Creating Meaningful Lives

There is a lot of research on the value of a meaningful life as a protective factor against mental health issues such as emotion dysregulation, depression, anxiety, trauma, and suicidal ideation.[2] From a

---

[2] M. Baquero-Tomás, M. D. Grau, A. R. Moliner, and A. Sanchis-Sanchis, "Meaning in Life as a Protective Factor against Depression," *Frontiers in Psychology* 14 (2023): 1-9; E. M. Kleiman and J. K. Beaver, "A Meaningful Life is Worth Living: Meaning in Life as a Suicide Resiliency Factor," *Psychiatry Research* 210, no. 3 (2013): 934-39; J. Singer, C. Cummings, S. A. Moody, and L. T. Benuto, "Reducing Burnout, Vicarious Trauma, and Secondary Traumatic Stress through Investigating Purpose in

greater, spiritual perspective, every human has to struggle with and/or make sense of their existence and inevitable mortality. This is no small feat for any human as they grapple with the truth of life and death, and the questions of if there is something bigger than us, and if there is a creator and spiritual realm. Science backs up the concept that having a belief in God serves as a protective and/or mitigating factor for anxiety, depression, stress, post-traumatic stress disorder, and suicidality, while also boosting self-esteem, strength, hope, capacity for forgiveness, and increased capacity to manage long-term disabilities.[3]

As I think about HST as a whole, and its community, it taught us those lessons of creating and building our own meaningful lives, not only with our spiritual connection and belief in God, but with each other, and with our choice of profession, activities, and everyday life. This was also a key uniting factor and theme across every counseling and Bible class I can think of that I took while attending HST. We had purpose and the capacity to build meaningful lives; we also shared that kindness and the belief that whichever individuals we were privileged to serve and collaborate with in counseling relationships were similarly valued and had that same ability to create a life of meaning and purpose. Further, there was no fire and brimstone teaching that felt painful and traumatic, which unfortunately are aspects of the teachings of some churches. Rather, the concept of loving people as Christ loved people was championed. We learned about showing love through validating people's experiences, helping honor them, and fostering healing as they faced life-

---

Life in Social Workers," *Journal of Social Work* 20, no. 5 (2020): 620-38; S. Song, X. Yang, H. Yang, P. Zhou, H. Ma, C. Teng, ... and N. Zhang, "Psychological Resilience as a Protective Factor for Depression and Anxiety Among the Public During the Outbreak of COVID-19, *Frontiers in Psychology*, 11 (2021): 618509.

[3] J. Hasanović and I. Pajević, "Religious Moral Beliefs as Mental Health Protective Factor of War Veterans Suffering from PTSD, Depressiveness, Anxiety, Tobacco and Alcohol Abuse in Comorbidity," *Psychiatria Danubina* 22, no. 2 (2010): 203-10; A. C. Salgado, "Review of Empirical Studies on Impact of Religion, Religiosity and Spirituality as Protective Factors," *Journal of Educational Psychology-Propositos y Representaciones* 2, no. 1 (2014): 141-59; D. C. L. Teo, K. Duchonova, S. Kariman, and J. Ng, "Religion, Spirituality, Belief Systems, and Suicide," in *Suicide by Self-Immolation: Biopsychosocial and Transcultural Aspects*, eds. César A. Alfonso, et. al. (Cham, Switzerland: Springer, 2021), 183-200.

changing trauma and mental health concerns. We also learned about holding hope and helping rebuild people's lives. These concepts have stayed with me across many more years of education and learning through my doctoral degree in psychology and as I have specialized in working with those who experience serious mental illness. Though my training and expertise are highly specialized now, with a focus on serious mental illness (SMI) and predominantly with people who experience psychosis, chronic trauma, post-traumatic stress disorder, and challenges with chronic suicidality, the roots of building meaningful lives of purpose remain strong and interwoven across every evidence-based treatment and mental health innovation I have expertise in and deliver. Ironically, such concepts also stand as the cornerstone and foundation of some of the absolute best empirically-based treatments for suicide globally available. For example, the conceptual and intervention element of building a meaningful life is central in Marsha Linehan's dialectical behavior therapy (DBT), an original treatment for borderline personality disorder, which has now segued into a transdiagnostic treatment within the mental health field.[4]

The Future of the Profession of Counseling

As we look to the future of the profession of counseling and related programs that seek to address the mental health concerns of those in our country, there are many critical, timely, and salient issues at hand. Harding can equip its emerging graduate students to help address and take leadership in ethical, evidence-based, and spiritually-driven mechanisms for addressing such concerns as the opiate epidemic in our country. This means investing in high-level training in terms of substance-use recovery. It also means engaging in national and local social justice efforts so that the medical field can continually be held to high standards regarding safe prescribing practices, and pharmaceutical companies, who have the opportunity to do justice or repeat past egregious actions that have caused the deaths and destruction of many

---

[4] M. M. Linehan, *Dialectical Behavior Therapy in Clinical Practice: Applications Across Disorders and Settings* (New York: Guilford, 2020).

lives, can be held accountable.[5] In only the last 20 years, the opioid epidemic has claimed more than 700,000 lives and cost more than 500 billion dollars in our economy.[6]

Other ways Harding can invest in building a national community that cares about how we treat those who experience mental illness in ways consistent with the teachings of Jesus, are by developing more practitioners to work with people who have serious mental illnesses. Many of these people also face chronic hospitalization or the impact of years of institutionalization, as well as involuntary treatment, involuntary medication, and the overuse of seclusion and restraints that cause sanctuary trauma within systems of care.[7] Ironically, though such graduate programs train practitioners at a high level, there are not as many highly-trained clinicians offering therapy, providing evidence-based treatments, and advocating for the rights of those with SMI within our state hospitals and public sector settings. Typically, this is where people are also facing the intersection of poverty, homelessness, years of trauma, racism and classism, and basically are impacted by the social determinants of mental health.[8] From the perspective of the cross, and as we envision where Jesus might hang out and sit and offer support to people, I envision Him listening, loving people, and also speaking out

---

[5] R. A. Delfino, "A New Prescription for the Opioid Epidemic: 360-degree Accountability for Pharmaceutical Companies and their Executives," *Hastings Law Journal* 73, no. 2 (2022): 301-70; A. Kennedy-Hendricks, S. H. Busch, E. E. McGinty, M. A. Bachhuber, J. Niederdeppe, S. E. Gollust, ... and C. L. Barry "Primary Care Physicians' Perspectives on the Prescription Opioid Epidemic," *Drug and Alcohol Dependence* 165 (2016): 61-70.

[6] R. A. Delfino, "A New Prescription for the Opioid Epidemic."

[7] E. R. Carr, "A History of the Community Mental Health Movement and Individuals with Serious Mental Illness: A Vision for the Future," *American Journal of Orthopsychiatry*, forthcoming.

[8] Carr, "A History of the Community Mental Health Movement and Individuals with Serious Mental Illness." M. Knapp and G. Wong, "Economics and Mental Health: The Current Scenario," *World Psychiatry* 19, no. 1 (2020): 3-14; J. Y. Nazroo, K. S. Bhui, and J. Rhodes, "Where Next for Understanding Race/Ethnic Inequalities in Severe Mental Illness? Structural, Interpersonal and Institutional Racism," in *Sociology of Health and Illness* 42, no. 2 (2020): 262-76; Mark Olfson, "Building the Mental Health Workforce Capacity Needed to Treat Adults with Serious Mental Illnesses," *Health Affairs* 35, no. 6 (2016): 983-90.

about these injustices in bold and prolific ways. Jesus showed us how to be a social justice advocate and change agent. He was not mainstream or status quo. To emphasize the urgency of change and to advocate awareness of conditions across inpatient psychiatric settings for those with SMI, a recent study examined a four-year span across 1,642 psychiatric hospitals, with findings of 7,416 rates of seclusion and 7,398 rates of restraint.[9] For both acute and long-term care, there were marked differences in the statistics for private and/or for-profit hospitals as compared to public sector hospitals, which serve the underinsured and those facing poverty, as well as more people of color. The public sector hospitals all had markedly higher rates of seclusion and restraint. Interestingly, 67% of hospitals had lower rates of seclusion and restraint use, while 10% of hospitals had rates that were 5-10 times higher than the other hospitals. These statistics show both the egregious and traumatic nature of some settings, and the possibilities of others. This knowledge base, with the empirical data showing the negative impact of seclusion and restraint for patients and staff, is a call for action.[10] For those who are equipped and have been given the talent for leadership in such systems of care, there is a desperate need for leaders who are godly, ethical, and willing to fight for systemic transformation of mental health organizations and the humane treatment of those with SMI in our country.

On another note, there are disparities in funding and sufficient mental health services for youth and their families across the nation, disproportionately affecting people of color, those who face poverty, immigrants, and those who endure the social determinants of mental

---

[9] V. S. Staggs, "Variability in Psychiatric Facility Seclusion and Restraint Rates as Reported on Hospital Compare Site," *Psychiatric Services* 71, no. 9 (2020): 893-98.

[10] M. Chieze, S. Hurst, S. Kaiser, and O. Sentissi, "Effects of Seclusion and Restraint in Adult Psychiatry: A Systematic Review," *Frontiers in Psychiatry* 10 (2019): 491; B. C. Frueh, R. G. Knapp, K. J. Cusack, A. L. Grubaugh, J. A. Sauvageot, V. C. Cousins,... and T. G. Hiers, "Special Section on Seclusion and Restraint: Patients' Reports of Traumatic or Harmful Experiences Within the Psychiatric Setting," *Psychiatric Services* 56, no. 9 (2005): 1123-33.

health in our nation.[11] Again, with the vision of the cross, this is where Christians can be the hands and feet of Jesus as we seek to serve those who face marginalization, racism, trauma, and disparities in access to care, which impact critical developmental years for youth and families, thus shaping the very trajectory of the lives of many individuals. We have to be a community that cares about our neighbor as Jesus taught us to, and that is a high calling. With the love of the cross streaming through us, though, it is possible.

Graduate degrees in counseling and related fields like psychology also train individuals in the competencies of consultation, teaching, advocacy, and research across many societal concerns, as such factors are social determinants of mental health and population health.[12] Harding's program has an opportunity to lead and be impactful in many societal issues and stressors, such as racism and building anti-racist and anti-oppressive communities; mitigating political conflict and turmoil that has divided the nation; addressing the rapid growth, benefits, and challenges of artificial intelligence, social media, and technology; and the shift in the workforce to over-usage of child labor in our country (and resultant deaths, lack of protections, and oversight), despite laws to protect underage individuals during their developmental years.[13]

As our own Dr. Gray wrote about in his dissertation, all stress is not bad, and it cannot be completely avoided as we think about ongoing life events and the human experience.[14] Life involves stress that is inevitable, but finding ways to mitigate the imbalance of too much stress-causing detrimental effects and mental health problems for

---

[11] Youth Mental Health Services Act (2023): https://www.apaservices.org/advocacy/news/youth-mental-health-research-act.

[12] C. E. Murray, A. L. Pope, and P. C. Rowell, "Promoting Counseling Students' Advocacy Competencies through Service-Learning," *Journal for Social Action in Counseling and Psychology* 2, no. 2 (2010): 29-47.

[13] L. Alhajji, J. E. Potter, and V. Padilla, "Labor Trafficking: A Mental Health Perspective," in *Psychological Perspectives on Human Trafficking: Theory, Research, Prevention, and Intervention*, eds. L. Dryjanska, et. al. (Washington, D.C.: American Psychological Association, 2024), 75-97: https://doi.org/10.1037/0000379-004.

[14] E. A. Gray, "A Holistic Analysis of Stress with Implications for Stress Management as a Function of Pastoral Counseling" (PhD diss., New Orleans Baptist Theological Seminary, 1981).

humanity is a worthy cause. This is especially salient as it seems like every day in our nation there are constant stressors in our school systems with gun violence, conflicts and wars across the globe, political upheaval, economic fluctuations, and the business of daily, normative stress, alongside personalized events that may cause more stress. Dr. Gray called for working with people from a holistic perspective. He put it beautifully with these statements that help tie our work to the mission of the cross as we think about the future:

> Jesus approached men in a holistic way. By his ministry we know that he was concerned about the total man as he ministered to those with physical disorders, social problems, and psychical problems, as well as sin problems. One's total being is directed not only toward God, but also towards one's fellow man. "You shall love the Lord your God with all your heart, and with all your soul, and with all your strength, and with all your mind; and your neighbor as yourself."[15]

In closing, I am greatly humbled and honored to be able to write this chapter. I have no pretenses about the future, but I will share what I am convicted of—God has and will do more than we can ever fathom and imagine through his people if we allow him to do his work through us. It is the story of the Bible, and it is also the story of my life and others I know who have gone through this program. It is God shining his light and healing through us. We are just human, but he can, will, and always does do glorious things. Get ready HST, hold on to your seats, because God has a story that he has written, and we can only imagine the possibilities of this program and the ways in which this new venture, and the dynamic and inevitable shifts that will occur in Searcy, will unfold. Lastly, this Bible verse seems most germane to me as we envision the future of HST, and us also seeking what God's plans are for the school. This verse is deeply meaningful to me as it was shared with me over 20 years ago on multiple occasions by a close friend and spiritual

---

[15] Gray, 59 (cf. Luke 10:27).

mentor. It always helps me know that our peace, future, and very life all rests in God's hands.

"For I know the plans I have for you," declares the Lord, "plans to prosper you and not to harm you, plans to give you hope and a future. Then you will call on me and come and pray to me, and I will listen to you. You will seek me and find me when you seek me with all your heart" (Jeremiah 29:11-13, NIV).

CHAPTER ELEVEN

Spiritual Formation

Grant Azbell

The mission of Harding School of Theology (HST) is to "challenge Christian leaders to develop deeper faith in God and higher standards of ministry and scholarship." This is done through theological education that is "characterized by integration, formation, faithfulness, community, and witness."[1] In this chapter, I will focus on the second item on the list, formation. However, I will pursue formation in a way that is consistent with the other elements of HST's mission statement.

How should theological seminaries approach the spiritual formation of their students? The answer to this question is important as the concept of spiritual formation has become more prevalent in theological seminaries. While spiritual formation has not always been a stated goal in Protestant seminaries, today it is in the common religious academic vernacular.[2] According to James Bryan Smith, the modern spiritual formation movement can be traced back to Richard Foster's 1978 publication of *Celebration of Discipline*.[3] Because the focus on spiritual formation is relatively new in seminary education, standards for the formation of seminarians can vary from institution to institution. While most seminaries seem to agree that spiritual formation is important, what that means among seminaries of various denominations differs with their theological commitments. Expectations for spiritual formation of seminarians will necessarily demand nuance and particularity to match

---

[1] https://hst.edu/about-us/mission/, accessed Feb 5, 2024.

[2] Kirsten Birkett, "Spiritual Formation: The Rise of a Tradition," *Churchman* (2019), 346-47.

[3] James Bryan Smith, "Dallas Willard's 3 Fears About the Spiritual Formation Movement," *Christianity Today*, last modified August 22, 2022, accessed February 6, 2024. https://www.christianitytoday.com/ct/2022/september/dallas-willard-fears-spiritual-formation-movement.html.

the expectations of each seminary's base of support.

In this chapter, I will address the spiritual formation I received at HST from the perspective of an alumnus and offer a path toward spiritual formation that will better serve HST, its students, and the congregations where students will likely serve in ministry. While the path I will attempt to chart should be applicable to seminaries associated with the Churches of Christ and might be applicable to a broader spectrum of Christian theological seminaries, my focus will be HST. There are two reasons for this decision. First, the history and trajectory of HST is the focus of this book and approaching the question of spiritual formation universally would be beyond its scope. Second, any proposed definition and process of spiritual formation that could be applied universally would either be too vague to be useful or too specific to be agreeable. Useful and agreeable ideas of spiritual formation must be found within the histories and theological commitments of particular seminaries and their denominational affiliations.

Even within Churches of Christ, there are differing theological bents among regions and congregations. Therefore, while this chapter will be applicable to Church of Christ-related universities in general, it will need to be particular to those churches, even within the Churches of Christ, that fall within the boundaries of HST's theological influence. To help locate appropriate spiritual formation practices for HST, I must briefly describe my own history of spiritual formation beginning with my home congregation, followed by my time at HST, and ending with my experience after HST.

The words *spiritual formation* were not used in the Church of Christ where I grew up, which was on the conservative edge of Churches of Christ within HST's circle of influence. Indeed, the phrase *spiritual formation* would have been met with suspicion if not outright rejection. In a church that strove to "call Bible things by Bible names," the words *spiritual formation* would have failed the test of entrance. However, the concept of spiritual formation, defined simply as the correct forming of Christian character, was a primary concern.[4]

---

[4] Gerald May, one of the earliest Protestant proponents of spiritual formation, defines

When one moves past semantics, all congregations are concerned with the spiritual formation of their congregants. My home church, like most Churches of Christ, sought to form congregants by focusing on learning and correctly interpreting Scripture, worship and Bible class attendance, and fellowship. My church placed its faith in these practices, believing that when they were faithfully attended to, healthy spiritual character would be the result. Even though the language of spiritual formation would not have been used, the practice of spiritual formation was both present and intentional.

I did not hear the words *spiritual formation* until I began seminary at HST in 2008, in Jim Hinkle's youth ministry class. Youth ministry, in the Churches of Christ, was ahead of the curve when it came to spiritual formation. Professor Hinkle assigned books on contemplative approaches to youth ministry such as *Presence Centered Youth Ministry* by Mike King, *Contemplative Youth Ministry* by Mark Yaconelli, and *Soul Shaper* by Tony Jones.[5] Students had to choose an ancient spiritual practice and adapt it to a youth ministry context (I nearly burned down the classroom building due to an incense mishap!). The words *spiritual formation* continued to come up during my time at HST. Eddie Randolph had us read *Conformed to His Image: Biblical, Practical Approaches to Spiritual Formation* by Kenneth Boa for Congregational Ministry.[6] Mark Powell opened many of his classes with contemplative practices and assigned St. Ignatius's *The Spiritual Exercises*, as well as his own book, *Centered on God*, which is both an "introduction to the Trinitarian vision of God" and a primer on

---

it as such: "Spiritual formation is a rather general term referring to all attempts, means, instruction, and disciplines intended towards deepening of faith and furtherance of spiritual growth. Gerald May, *Care of Mind, Care of Spirit: A Psychiatrist Explores Spiritual Direction* (San Francisco: HarperSanFrancisco, 1992), 6.

[5] Mike King, *Presence-Centered Youth Ministry: Guiding Students into Spiritual Formation* (Downers Grove, IL: InterVarsity Press, 2006); Mark Yaconelli, *Contemplative Youth Ministry: Practicing the Presence of Jesus* (Grand Rapids: Zondervan, 2006); Tony Jones, *Soul Shaper: Exploring Spirituality and Contemplative Practices in Youth Ministry* (Grand Rapids: Zondervan, 2003).

[6] Kenneth Boa, *Conformed to His Image: Biblical and Practical Approaches to Spiritual Formation* (Grand Rapids: Zondervan, 2001).

theological spiritual formation.[7] Evertt Huffard, in the class Spiritual Leadership, stated in his syllabus that one goal was for us "to discover principles of spiritual formation in our own lives in order to become more effective leaders and mentors." Clearly, spiritual formation was central to my experience at HST.

When spiritual formation was not a stated goal, it still happened anyway. Studying about God, writing about God, and being taught and mentored by godly professors are all avenues of spiritual formation. It would be dubious to think I was not spiritually formed in classes with Rick Oster, Allen Black, Phil McMillion, and David Bland, even though I do not remember the terminology of spiritual formation used in a formal sense. Clearly, I received teaching from them that was intentional toward spiritual formation. Likewise, I received informal spiritual formation training in a way that could have been received even in my conservative home congregation.

Two years after graduating from HST, I began the Doctor of Ministry (DMin) program at Lipscomb University. The focus of this program was missional theology and spiritual formation. The focus of spiritual formation at Lipscomb would send me on a journey of both formal and informal spiritual formation training that would include spiritual direction, Ignatian spirituality, identity formation, Immanuel prayer, and other forms of contemplative prayer and spirituality.[8] I began this training looking for tools to help me be a better minister. What I did not expect was that it would change the way I preach, study the Bible, and navigate congregational relationships. Everything

---

[7] St. Ignatius of Loyola, *The Spiritual Exercises of St. Ignatius*, trans. Anthony Mottola (New York: Doubleday, 1989); Mark E. Powell, *Centered in God: The Trinity and Christian Spirituality* (Abilene: Abilene Christian University Press, 2014), back cover.

[8] Immanuel prayer is a model of inner-healing prayer. The basic concept of inner-healing prayer is that our painful memories impact the quality of our lives. Without healing, these memories will continue to have an oversized impact on the quality of our lives, our relationships with others and our relationship with God. Inner-healing prayer is based in the belief that God is willing, through prayer, to help us heal the difficult memories of our past. The Immanuel approach to inner-healing prayer was developed by board certified psychiatrist Dr. Karl Lehman. Karl Lehman, *The Immanuel Approach*

I studied was applicable to ministry and theology. Suddenly, the tools I received at HST came alive.

Because of this experience, I am convinced that an intentional approach to spiritual formation is crucial for HST students. As much as I gained at HST, I believe that a more intentional strategy for spiritual formation is needed for the future. Congregational ministry is not getting easier and ministry burnout rates are at crisis level. HST has a responsibility to train ministers that can lead churches as effectively as possible while maintaining their own spiritual, physical, and mental health.[9]

As mentioned at the beginning of this chapter, spiritual formation has moved to the forefront of outcomes in seminary training.[10] The problem is that spiritual formation cannot be consistently defined across seminaries because worship, ecclesiological, and theological commitments demand differing approaches. Put simply, each seminary has a responsibility to form students who can thrive as ministers at the churches within that seminary's circle of influence. This is easier said than done. Seminaries must also form ministers who can lead churches toward congregational health and continued spiritual transformation rather than to the ever-growing infirmary of sick and dying churches. Sometimes the goals of staying employed and implementing healthy congregational rhythms are in tension. This means that the seminary's responsibility should not be

---

(Chicago: Lehman Immanuel Publishing House, 2016). Two other well-known and responsible models are The Life Model and Healing Care; see James G. Friesen, E. James Wilder, Anne M. Bierling, Rick Koepcke, and Maribeth Poole, *Living from the Heart Jesus Gave You*, 15th Anniversary Study Edition (East Peoria, IL: Shepherd's House Inc., 2013); and Terry Wardle, *Healing Care Healing Prayer: Helping the Broken Find Wholeness in Christ* (Abilene: Leafwood Publishers, 2001). The most familiar model to Churches of Christ is Freedom Prayer; see Andy Reese and Jennifer Barnett, *Freedom Tools: for Overcoming Life's Tough Problems*, revised and expanded edition, (Minneapolis: Chosen, 2015).

[9] It is worth noting that a recent study from Barna indicates that ministers' confidence in their calling has dropped over twenty percent since 2015. Barna, "Excerpt: A Rapid Decline in Pastoral Security" last modified August 15 2023, accessed February 5, 2024. https://www.barna.com/research/pastoral-security-confidence/.

[10] Cornelis van der Knijff, "Re-engaging Spiritual Formation in Online Theological Education," *Transformation* 38 (2021): 324-25.

taken lightly as ministers must maintain their own health while also helping congregations continue to grow and form spiritually.

The strategy I will lay out employs traditional spiritual formation techniques and attempts to translate those techniques to be accessible to congregations most likely to receive ministers from HST. While there is no one standard definition for spiritual formation, I propose four strategies that I believe are accessible and acceptable to congregations likely to be served by an HST graduate:

1. Intentionally forming students by approaching the text through *Lectio Divina* and imaginative reading.
2. Formalizing the link between seminarians and congregations through apprenticeships at HST.
3. Strengthening the bonds between students by intentionally forming spiritual learning communities.
4. More broadly implementing spiritual direction.

The first strategy is to focus on the practices of *Lectio Divina* and imaginative reading as a way of engaging Scripture. When one thinks of what is valued in Churches of Christ, knowledge of and application of Scripture leaps to the forefront. While much of the traditional Church of Christ hermeneutic has been rightly questioned and even rejected, the impulse both to know the text and apply it practically are healthy impulses that are among the most ancient Christian practices.[11] One simple and increasingly common practice for approaching the text is *Lectio Divina*, or divine reading. This is the practice of slowing the reading down while reading smaller portions of the text. The act of slowing and paying attention to each word and what God might be intending to say to us through it fits neatly within the Restoration commitment to the text. This can be implemented on the seminary level to help retain the wonder and devotional quality of the text even as students are engaging in high level critical study. It can also be added to the regular rhythms of seminarians by employing *Lectio Divina* in

---

[11] For a fuller criticism on the traditional Church of Christ hermeneutic (CENI), see Tom Olbricht's article in *Restoration Quarterly*. T. H. Olbricht, "Hermeneutics in the Churches of Christ," *Restoration Quarterly* 37 (1995), 1–24.

student community groups or cohorts (which will be addressed later). *Lectio Divina* also easily translates to the congregational context, particularly considering the posture of Churches of Christ toward the text. Adding new ways to read, study, and experience Scripture is desirable for congregants who are hungry for the word of God.

Likewise, imaginative reading of Scripture may also enhance spiritual formation. Churches of Christ, historically, have employed a modern, rationalist approach to the text.[12] Because of this rationalist commitment, anything other than a scientific approach may feel dangerous. It is likely that many church members believe they have never used their imaginations when reading Scripture and might not even consider themselves as having an imagination.[13] However, anyone who has memorized the text has both used their imagination and, in turn, allowed the text to form their imagination. Anyone who has read a verse and been moved emotionally has had an imaginative experience. Anyone who has imagined the way that Jesus, the apostles, the cross, the flood, the parting of the Red Sea, or any other biblical character or scene looked in their minds has had an imaginative experience. This is the primary way we teach our children to engage the text. The truth is that all manner of television, music, movies, and social media are having their say on the formation of our imagination. Paul himself, recognizing how important it is that we are intentional in what forms our imagination, tells us to transform the way that we think (Rom 12:2). We are told that the word of God is living and active, sharper than a two-edged sword (Heb 4:12). We are told to fix our eyes on Jesus, the author and pioneer of our faith (Heb 12:1-3). Over and over the text is asking us to engage our imagination. Approaching the text simply demands that we engage the text imaginatively.

---

[12] C. Leonard Allen and Danny Gray Swick, *Participating in God's Life: Two Crossroads for Churches of Christ* (Orange, CA: New Leaf Books, 2001) 37-57.

[13] I am defining imagination as the ability to create or hold an idea or picture in the mind. Gregory Boyd does an excellent job of illustrating how all people use their imagination and how essential imagination is to our relationship with God. Gregory A. Boyd, *Seeing is Believing: Experience Jesus Through Imaginative Prayer* (Grand Rapids: Baker Books, 2004), 71-80.

Along with *Lectio Divina*, imaginative reading should be a part of students' engagement with Scripture. While these approaches are foreign to many Protestants, they have an ancient history. For example, N.T. Wright hypothesizes that Paul was engaged in an imaginative reading of Ezekiel 1 when he experienced his conversion on the road to Damascus.[14] Ignatius's *Spiritual Exercises*, compiled in the fourteenth century, are primarily a way of engaging Scripture with the imagination. And while it might be difficult to use Ignatian terminology in many pulpits in Churches of Christ, my experience is that the principles of Ignatian imagination are well-received when effectively translated into a Church of Christ context. By training seminarians in an imaginative approach, seminaries help them form their imaginations against the many forces fighting for their attention. This can help students engage in healthy ministry while also equipping them to help their congregations form imaginations that can also withstand the countervailing forces of this world (Eph 6:12).

Churches of Christ emphasize the assembly, which is a primary space where much spiritual formation takes place.[15] Church of Christ-related seminaries tend to have professors who are not only academics, but faithful church members as well. The value of having professors who are invested in the local church cannot be overstated. However, the link between the seminary and the local church needs to be strengthened. Formation through healthy church attendance, a spiritual rhythm itself, could be formalized and emphasized on the seminary level. John Mark Comer describes spiritual disciplines as the practices of Jesus.[16] If anything Jesus did can be considered a spiritual discipline, then participating in the assembly is a spiritual discipline (Luke 4:16). Participating in community worship and service should continue to be formally expected and should also be part of seminary training.

---

[14] N. T. Wright, *Paul: A Biography* (New York: HarperOne, 2018), 51-53.

[15] John Mark Hicks, Bobby Valentine, and Johnny Melton, *A Gathered People: Revisioning the Assembly as Transforming Encounter* (Abilene: Leafwood Publishers, 2007), 9-16.

[16] John Mark Comer, *The Ruthless Elimination of Hurry* (Colorado Springs: Waterbrook, 2019), 100.

Connecting seminarians with healthy, experienced ministers could go a long way if HST wants seminarians to become healthy and long-serving ministers. Encouraging experienced ministers—who know what it takes to have a long career in ministry—to mentor seminarians is crucial. Ministers who have managed to lead effective ministries while also maintaining healthy families and rhythms of life may serve as models and inspirations for future ministers. Theological training for practical outcomes is necessary—and sometimes, the most practical training ground is not the classroom.

Connecting younger ministers to older ministers is an ancient practice of spiritual formation; examples of these relationships throughout Christian history abound. Most importantly, if we are going to base our spiritual practices on the practices of Jesus, then our method of training ministers should look something like Jesus's method of training ministers. Jesus clearly mentored and apprenticed his disciples. The original way of training ministers of the gospel is through apprenticeship. While the apprenticeship model is used in seminaries and many students at HST participate in apprenticeships, the practice is still underutilized. Having ministers apprenticed by skilled ministers to supplement their formal education is a necessary adjustment if the desire is to see more ministers enjoy long, healthy, and effective careers.

The need to model and teach seminarians healthy life rhythms should not be understated. Many ministers suffer from unhealthy work/life boundaries. There is no clock to punch, and many ministers take their work home regularly. They are often unable to give themselves to their family or friends and unable to engage in self-care. Sermons, rather than being formed through a healthy rhythm during the week, are often prepared in a rush on Saturday night. Personal prayer and Bible study can be almost non-existent as most study and prayer is geared toward preaching and teaching. Ministry that flows out of healthy spiritual and life rhythms is far more likely to produce healthy fruit.

Apprenticeships could potentially create stronger bonds between HST and the congregations HST serves. Relationships between HST students, experienced ministers, and congregations should be reciprocal. Congregations will benefit from having HST students attend and provide ministry, ministers will benefit from mentoring students (which would hopefully include training and structure from HST), and students will benefit from the relationships and experience. While connecting seminarians to churches and ministers will help students form spiritually, seminary education itself can also be more intentional in promoting healthy student rhythms.

One way schools are doing this is through cohort group-based learning. Both Lipscomb University and Rochester University, two schools associated with Churches of Christ, have developed innovative cohort learning models for advanced theological degrees. Because I received a traditional MDiv from HST and participated in a cohort style DMin at Lipscomb, I have experienced both styles of learning. While there are advantages and disadvantages to both, my personal experience is that the cohort model is much more conducive to healthy spiritual rhythms. The cohort learning model is comparable to a small faith community. The twelve apostles can be positively compared to a learning cohort in that they spent time together, prayed together, worshipped together, listened to the same instructions, and had common assignments. Learning cohorts allow students to engage in the rhythms of life and the classroom together. If everything Jesus did can be considered instruction for formation, then setting up learning communities that model the learning community set up by Jesus should be embraced by seminaries seeking to form students in the ways of Jesus.

A final critical part of spiritual formation for seminarians is training in the practice of intentional listening. According to Barna, the top three reasons people doubt Christian beliefs are: past negative experiences with religious institutions, the perceived hypocrisy of religious people, and the negative reputation of the church.[17] It seems the church has moved far from the church described in Acts 2 that grew in favor with both God and people. How might seminaries train church leaders to reverse these perceptions? One possible solution for seminaries is to train potential ministers in intentional listening.

---

[17] Barna, "Doubt & Faith: Top Reasons People Question Christianity," last updated on March 1, 2023, accessed on February 2, 2024. https://www.barna.com/research/doubt-faith/.

My spiritual direction training was the most important training I received in ministry.[18] Nothing has helped me become a non-anxious and non-judgmental presence like the intentional listening I learned through spiritual direction. But at HST, I had only one counseling class. While the class was both important and well-taught, it simply was not enough to prepare me for the daily rigors of ministering to a congregation. I do not think we need more ministers training as counselors, or spiritual directors for that matter, but we do need ministers who are good at listening. One of the early surprises of ministry was learning that my well-formed arguments rarely changed minds and rarely moved people toward the gospel. What does move people toward the gospel is feeling loved by God. We, as ministers, can serve as conduits of God's love through listening. "Being heard is so close to being loved that for the average person, they are almost indistinguishable."[19] If Ausberger is right, then the connection between listening well and loving well cannot be overemphasized.

While it is important for ministers to become listeners, it is also important that they, too, are formed by being heard themselves. Assigning seminarians to a spiritual director might help them become better listeners through the act of being listened to themselves; once someone experiences the power of being listened to, they are more capable of listening to others and to God.

HST has already taken some encouraging steps toward providing a program for spiritual direction. It is my hope that spiritual direction will be available and utilized by all students and that training in

---

[18] I was introduced to spiritual direction while pursuing my DMin at Lipscomb University. The DMin included an introductory class on spiritual direction and provided spiritual direction for students during our bi-annual retreats. I formally trained in spiritual direction through Lipscomb's Institute of Christian Spirituality (ICS) and eventually trained spiritual directors for ICS. Chapter 1 of Sue Pickering's book *Spiritual Direction* provides a good introduction and overview of spiritual direction. Sue Pickering, *Spiritual Direction: A Practical Introduction* (London: Canterbury Press, 2008), 1-34.

[19] The quote "Being heard is so close to being loved that for the average person they are almost indistinguishable" is widely attributed to David Augsburger, but its exact original source (such as a specific book, article, or speech) is not consistently documented.

spiritual direction remains available to any students who want to avail themselves of this ancient practice.

In the end, all the responsibility for the spiritual formation of HST students does not fall on HST. Students cannot be forced into healthy spirituality. However, if HST intentionally and regularly has students approach the text devotionally through contemplative and imaginative readings, formalizes and cultivates relationships between seminarians and local congregations through apprenticeships, strengthens the bonds between students by intentionally forming spiritual learning communities, and more widely implements spiritual direction, it will produce healthier ministers with well-attuned life rhythms through mechanisms inherent to the seminary education itself.

The focus on spiritual formation has been a welcome move for seminaries. What this focus entails can and should differ from seminary to seminary. Seminaries are responsible for forming ministers that can both lovingly serve the churches within their circle of influence and lead congregations toward spiritual formation. Training ministers to both love and lead their congregations demands knowing the types of congregations they will serve and loving those churches for both who they are and who they need to be to survive and thrive. Are there changes that need to be embraced? Absolutely! But we cannot healthily and effectively lead churches that we resent, nor can churches be led that do not trust our motives and methods. This give-and-take demands some degree of specificity from congregation to congregation. But it also demands more sensitive training from our seminaries. Seminaries in general, and HST in particular, must answer the question of who they are training and if it is working. Are our churches healthy? Are they being led by healthy ministers? Are seminaries part of the problem or part of the solution? I contend that ministers can learn and adopt healthier rhythms that will translate into the local congregation. But seminaries must be willing to teach and model those healthier rhythms and practices that our ministers and congregations need. This will lead to a theological education characterized by integration, formation, faithfulness, community, and witness.

CHAPTER TWELVE

African American Church Leadership

Edward J. Robinson

Published in 1915, Robert Frost's poem "The Road Not Taken" speaks of choices and decisions. His decision to move in a direction "less traveled by" dramatically shaped his destiny. Frost's poem, in some ways, captures the essence of my journey at Harding School of Theology (HST). Born and reared in Jacksonville, Texas, I graduated from Jacksonville High School in May 1985. Three months later, I enrolled at Southwestern Christian College (SwCC) in Terrell, Texas, where I earned a BA in Bible and Religious Education in 1988. Many of my classmates at SwCC went west to Abilene Christian University (ACU), Southern Methodist University (SMU), and other places, but in the words of Robert Frost, "I took the [road] less traveled by, and that has made all the difference."[1] I essentially stepped out on faith and went east of the Mississippi River, embarked upon an unknown path that has made all the difference.

A Black Man's Pilgrimage in Graduate Education

In the fall of 1988, a short, cordial, well-dressed White man with glasses arrived on the predominantly Black campus of Southwestern Christian College (SwCC) in Terrell, Texas. The White gentleman's name was Dr. Bill Flatt, a professor at HST, and he was on campus to recruit ministerial students who might be interested in pursuing graduate education in the state of Tennessee. Encouragement from Dr. Flatt and my future brother-in-law, Dr. Jefferson Caruthers, Jr., swayed me to take the road less traveled by. My girlfriend, Toni, and I married on October 28, 1988. After completing course work at SwCC in December, we

---

[1] Robert Frost, "The Road Not Taken," in *An Introduction to American Poetry*, ed. Lisa Swank (New York: Viking Press, 2015), 48-49.

drove 434 miles in my fully packed white Ford Pinto to the HST campus and took up residence in the married dorms. This would mark the beginning of a four-year eventful and arduous academic pilgrimage.

Having settled into the married dorms on campus with my good and supportive wife and determined to succeed, my first two classes were with Dr. W. B. West and Dr. Jack P. Lewis. Professor West taught the Book of Revelation enthusiastically, and Dr. Lewis zealously taught Advanced Introduction to the New Testament. The class with West encouraged me tremendously. He told funny stories from his preaching and personal experiences that kept class interesting. Students who took Dr. Lewis's introductory course often had to have notes prior to class in order to keep up with him. When the class started in January 1989, there were approximately thirty-five or more students; but by semester's end, the class had dwindled down to ten or less. Thankfully, I was one of those who persevered. I earned an A in the Revelation course and a B in Advanced Introduction to the New Testament. On the one hand, I was thrilled with my success; on the other hand, both classes opened my eyes to see that graduate study would be far more challenging than undergraduate school.

Taking Light to Darkness

Sometime near the end of the first semester, I applied for a preaching position in Greenwood, Mississippi, two hours south of Memphis, but I was determined to continue my studies at HST. Our three daughters—Clarice, Ashley, and Erika—were born in Greenwood. The ministerial post at the Barrentine and McLaurin Street (now Sycamore Street) Church of Christ in Greenwood proved to be a great blessing. I gained vital practical experience while acquiring rigorous theological training. I traveled from Greenwood to Memphis two times each week, and sometimes more. It was almost as if I went to HST each week to receive spiritual illumination; and I brought it back to help God's people and my people in the Mississippi Delta. As my biblical knowledge increased, I eagerly shared what I could with the church in Greenwood. I contributed articles to the local newspaper, the *Greenwood Commonwealth*. I conducted many home Bible studies, and the good Lord blessed the congregation in Greenwood to grow spiritually and numerically. Indeed, the church in Greenwood progressed so that the local White congregation took notice, and an affluent member gave us $75,000 to purchase land for plans to erect a new building.

The spiritual light I received from HST came from many sources. Don Meredith, HST's librarian, introduced me to the rigors and structure of academic research. Dr. Evertt Huffard taught me to be a "world Christian." Dr. Allen Black deepened my knowledge of koine Greek and Biblical Exegesis, while Dr. Rick Oster's New Testament World elucidated for me the background of the New Testament writings. I did not fully understand and appreciate how much Dr. Black and Dr. Oster enriched me until I earned a master's degree in Classical Greek at the University of Illinois at Urbana-Champaign in 1998.

I remember sitting at the feet of Dr. Slate, Dean of HST at the time of my tenure, in a practical ministry class. He shared significant moments from his evangelistic work in London, England. I distinctly remember Dr. Slate weeping in class over the swirling racial tension across the country because of the Rodney King riots in April 1992. He lamented the racial injustice that seemed to never go away. That was an unforgettable moment.

I am also thankful for other professors who touched me in some way: Dr. Harold Shank instructed me in Hebrew, Dr. John Mark Hicks stirred my interest in the theology of the Reformers, and Dr. James Thompson taught Advanced Preaching. I learned from Thompson that preaching is hard work. One must be willing to study hard, pray fervently, and research thoroughly in order to achieve effective preaching. HST taught me that "Saturday night specials" and extracting sermons from the internet will not get the job done. The secretaries, Jane Tomlinson, Ruth Herring, and Brenda Curtis, among others, were some of the nicest people I've ever met.

Furthermore, I met Dr. Richard Hughes one day in the HST Library. He was there doing research on what is now a classic,

Reviving the Ancient Faith: The Story of Churches of Christ in America.[2] I bought his book *Illusions of Innocence: Protestant Primitivism in America, 1630-1875*.[3] He signed my book and encouraged me to consider writing a history of African American Churches of Christ. In 2019, the good Lord blessed me to publish a history on Black Churches of Christ in the United States: *Hard-Fighting Soldiers: A History of African American Churches of Christ*.[4]

The Enduring Impact of Earl I. West

I thank God for all the foregoing, but the person who perhaps had the greatest impact on my graduate education at HST and beyond was Earl I. West. I took both of his Restoration Movement classes. In his Restoration Movement (Part 2) course, I did my research paper on the Black preacher Alexander Campbell (1862-1930), who helped launch the Jackson Street Church of Christ in Nashville, Tennessee. Campbell also inspired the preaching career of Marshall Keeble (1878-1968), the most influential evangelist in African American Churches of Christ. In the same class, Jerry Houston, a fellow alumnus of HST and currently the outstanding pulpit minister for the Dell Crest Church of Christ in San Antonio, Texas, did his research paper on S. R. Cassius (1853-1931). We exchanged papers. Twelve years later in 2003, I defended my dissertation on S. R. Cassius at Mississippi State University. My dissertation became my first book.[5] Brother Houston often jokingly says that I owe him royalties for his paper on Cassius!

Indeed, Jerry Houston, Ivan Harris (another African American student), and I took Earl West's Restoration Movement class at the same time. It was good and encouraging to be in class with some

---

[2] Richard T. Hughes, *Reviving the Ancient Faith: The Story of Churches of Christ in America* (Grand Rapids: Eerdmans, 1996).

[3] Richard T. Hughes, *Illusions of Innocence: Protestant Primitivism in America, 1630-1875* (Chicago: University of Chicago Press, 1988).

[4] Edward J. Robinson, *Hard-Fighting Soldiers: A History of African American Churches of Christ* (Knoxville: University of Tennessee Press, 2019).

[5] Edward J. Robinson, *To Save My Race from Abuse: The Life of Samuel Robert Cassius* (Tuscaloosa: University of Alabama Press, 2007).

students who looked like you and shared the same struggles and goals. Still, the good Lord showered his grace upon me by linking me with Earl West, who presided over my guided research paper on Alexander Campbell, the early Restoration leader, titled "Alexander Campbell and the Virginia Baptists in 1840." The project exposed me to the mechanics of scholarly research, and it allowed me to earn the M.A.R. in Church History in 1991. Two years later, I earned the M.Div. degree. Dr. West encouraged me to pursue academic research on African Americans in Churches of Christ. In fact, I dedicated my book on Annie C. Tuggle (1890-1976) to Earl I. West.[6] I owe a huge debt of gratitude to Dr. West and a host of other men and women who blessed my journey at HST and beyond.

Church of Christ Schools and the Plank of Segregation

Harding University, like most Church of Christ-affiliated schools across the South, was founded on a plank of racism and segregation. These institutions of higher learning never intended to welcome African Americans. Mark Lewis Taylor, professor of theology at Princeton Theological Seminary, recently observed: "None of us, especially in higher education—theological or otherwise—are free from the entanglement and web that slavery and white supremacy have spun."[7] My friend and scholar, Richard T. Hughes, confessed: "I am speaking, rather, of virtually all white Americans, including myself, for the myth of white supremacy is the very air we breathe, an ideology so deeply embedded in our common culture that we can escape the power it wields over our minds, emotions, and actions only with great difficulty, if at all."[8] During my tenure as an HST student, I sometimes felt that I walked beneath a dark cloud of suspicion. As a Black

---

[6] Edward J. Robinson, *I Was under a Heavy Burden: The Life of Annie C. Tuggle* (Abilene: Abilene Christian University Press, 2011).

[7] Mark Lewis Taylor, "Princeton Theological Seminary Announces Plan to Repent for Ties to Slavery: Conference Video Highlights," *Gather* 3 (Fall 2019): https://gather.ptsem.edu/conference-video-highlights/.

[8] Richard T. Hughes, "Resisting White Supremacy" in James L. Gorman, Jeff W. Childers, and Mark W. Hamilton, *Slavery's Long Shadow: Race and Reconciliation in American Christianity* (Grand Rapids: Eerdmans, 2019), 216.

student, I knew I had been allowed to matriculate at HST, but I did not always feel fully accepted. I learned that the credit hours of a White student from a White college or university transferred more easily than the credit hours of a Black student from SwCC. My training from SwCC was perhaps deemed to be inferior and inadequate. I recall a professor peering over my shoulder to make sure I was not cheating on a foreign language quiz or exam. I aced all the quizzes and exams because I relished foreign languages. You can't cheat on a language exam! Either you know it or you don't. Nevertheless, God's grace opened doors to me and other African Americans, and some of us have made the most of our opportunity.

In 2009, I became the first African American to receive the "Alumnus of the Year" award at HST. Dr. Willie Nettle, a distinguished preacher in Vicksburg, Mississippi, received the honor the following year. In 2022, Dr. Harold Redd garnered the award. Dr. Redd has left an enduring mark on African American students at HST, when he and the Midtown Church of Christ launched the M. A. Hull Scholarship for the support of Black students matriculating at HST. Shortly after I received the award, I was hired as an adjunct professor at HST to teach Restoration History. It was an honor to return to my alma mater and give back. I presently serve as adjunct professor at Harding University and teach History of Renewal Movements. Therefore, I have come full circle.

I am thankful that the good Lord blessed me to earn two degrees at HST, but the most important degree was the one my wife received. It was the PHT, that is, "Putting Hubby Through." I am grateful that HST awarded my wife and other spouses this honorary degree. Without my wife, I could not have made it through my graduate studies at HST. All three of my daughters have earned Master's degrees, and two of them have embarked upon terminal degrees. My thirst for knowledge has somehow rubbed off on them. To God be the glory!

African American Church Leaders

Next, I want to assess leadership profiles in African American Churches of Christ, paying special attention to specific challenges these leaders face. The development of leaders in African American Churches of Christ was unique in that it was forged in the crucible of chattel enslavement and legalized segregation. In the pre-Civil War era, Black church leadership often fell into the hands of Black preachers, who were often the only literate person and the most respected individual among enslaved people. W. E. B. Du Bois (1868-1963), a noted historian and sociologist, explained: "The Preacher is the most unique personality developed by the Negro on American soil. A leader, a politician, an orator, a 'boss,' an intriguer, an idealist—all these he is, and ever, too, the centre of a group of men, now twenty, now a thousand in number."[9] James Farmer (1920-1999), a civil rights activist, captured the significance in the view of most Black Christians: "The black preacher, especially in the South, is king in a private kingdom.... More than a priest, he is less only than God."[10]

S. R. Cassius

S. R. Cassius (1853-1931) was among the first known national leaders in African American Churches of Christ. Born into chattel enslavement in Prince William County, he converted to the Stone-Campbell Movement around 1881 and began preaching around 1883 in Illinois and Indiana. In 1891, Cassius relocated to the Oklahoma Territory and toiled there for three decades. While in Oklahoma, he toiled as farmer, Postmaster, civil rights leader, and Justice of the Peace of the Tohee, Oklahoma Territory. He was also an educator and organized the Tohee Industrial School, an educational enterprise modeled on the impressive Tuskegee Institute in Alabama, a school planted by Booker T. Washington in 1881. Cassius expressed his own philosophy of education in 1898, stating:

> The trend of the negro's mind can be changed in but one way; that is, to educate both mind and hands. Teach my people that the nation is looking forward to their boys and girls to make up the great industrial army of tomorrow;

---

[9] W. E. B. Du Bois, *The Souls of Black Folk* (New York: Penguin, 2012 [1903]), 162.
[10] James Farmer, *Lay Bare the Heart: An Autobiography of the Civil Rights Movement* (Fort Worth: Texas Christian University Press, 1985), 33.

teach them that an education consists of more than learning to read and write, and that industry means more than cooking and washing for the women, and barbering, preaching, waiting in hotels, and loafing for our men; teach them that the word 'education' means to develop both mind and matter—it means the strengthening of both the physical and intellectual part of man.[11]

Cassius's Tohee project began with enthusiasm, but failed partly because of insufficient monetary support but mainly because of the rise of the Colored Agricultural and Normal University (now Langston University).

Even though Cassius dabbled in multiple activities, his primary preoccupation was to advance what he believed was the "pure gospel."[12] Writing in 1898, he asserted: "The one object of my life since I confessed Christ has been that my race might be brought to a better understanding of God's revealed will, and to a higher appreciation of the gift of his only begotten son, that whosoever believeth in him need not perish, but have everlasting life."[13] Cassius did not oppose foreign missions, but he urged fellow Christians to make the evangelization of the Black man in America a high priority. "Brethren, why not clean up America," he thundered, "while we are trying to clean up the rest of the world? All of the above nations [Africa, China, Cuba, and Japan] are here and going to hell; and how can the church of Christ square itself with God about my people, who have been such a factor in the development of the United States?"[14]

Cassius found himself caught in a theological tug-of-war

---

[11] S. R. Cassius, *Negro Evangelization and the Tohee Industrial School* (Cincinnati, OH: Christian Leader Print., 1898); see also Edward J. Robinson, editor, *To Lift up My Race: The Essential Writings of Samuel Robert Cassius* (Knoxville: University of Tennessee Press, 2008), 39.

[12] In Cassius's view, the "pure gospel" consisted of adult baptism for the remission of sins, opposing instruments of music in worship, and evangelizing without missionary societies. See Robinson, *To Save My Race from Abuse: The Life of Samuel Robert Cassius*.

[13] S. R. Cassius, "Negro Evangelization" *Christian Leader* 12 (March 15, 1898): 4.

[14] S. R. Cassius, "Out on the Firing Line" *Gospel Advocate* 72 (July 10, 1930): 671.

between the so-called "progressives" (Disciples of Christ) and the so-called "loyals" (Churches of Christ). Although he appealed to both groups for monetary support, he sided eventually with the latter group, stating: "I condemn every attempt to substitute human forms, plans and ideas for the plain written word of God contained in the Bible, believing that God has given us a complete revelation of his will, and that he will not accept any addition to or subtraction from his word."[15] But Cassius found himself disappointed in his chosen fellowship because of the racism he encountered. He lamented: "I have had to win my way through religious prejudice in my own race, and race prejudice among brethren concerned of my own faith."[16] Cassius testified that racial segregation and racial discrimination did not originate in the world; "it was started by the church because the white members of the church did not think that negroes were good enough to worship God in the same house that they did."[17]

In short, Cassius was a "misfit" in Churches of Christ because of his preoccupation with the race problem and because he consistently injected social and political issues into the religious journals he contributed to. He used pen, podium, and pulpit to denounce the lynching of Black people and to rail against the "Birth of a Nation," a venomous anti-Black movie that portrayed Black men as rapists and glorified the Ku Klux Klan as the "savior" of White womanhood and White civilization. Cassius is the only known leader in Churches of Christ—Black or White—to protest the movie publicly.[18]

Because Cassius merged religion and politics, he often drew the ire of White leaders in Churches of Christ. Notwithstanding his mishaps and misunderstandings, Cassius left three decisive marks on African American Churches of Christ. First, Cassius influenced his son, Amos L. Cassius (1889-1982) to enter the preaching ministry. In 1922, father and son planted the Compton Avenue Church of Christ

---

[15] S. R. Cassius, "My Position on All Questions of Fellowship" *Christian Leader* 11 (September 21, 1897): 4.
[16] S. R. Cassius, "My Trip to the East" *Christian Leader* 36 (June 20, 1922): 12.
[17] See Robinson, editor, *To Lift up My Race*, 138.
[18] See Robinson, *To Save My Race from Abuse*, 135-55.

in Los Angeles, California, a congregation that continues to thrive.[19] Second, Amos perpetuated his father's work as an evangelist in that he went on to plant congregations in Hobbs, New Mexico, and Phoenix, Arizona. Third, Cassius brought to the attention of White Christians the spiritual needs of African Americans. He never garnered the monetary support that Marshall Keeble did. Yet, it can be properly and rightly conjectured that Cassius, by his frequent protests against racial injustice and because of his constant appeals for financial assistance to evangelize Black people in the United States, paved the way for Keeble, the premier evangelist in African American Churches of Christ.

Marshall Keeble

S. R. Cassius died in Colorado Springs, Colorado, in 1931. In the same year, Marshall Keeble baptized 166 people in a Gospel campaign in Valdosta, Georgia, resulting in the establishment of what is now the Woodlawn Forrest Church of Christ.[20] Generous White Christians sponsored Keeble's evangelistic sojourns across the South and beyond. Indeed, after baptizing a grand total of more than one thousand people, he proudly announced: "The white churches sponsored all of this work."[21]

The preaching success of Marshall Keeble raises two important questions. First, what accounts for his astonishing effectiveness as an evangelist? Without question, Keeble succeeded as a proclaimer of the Word because he possessed unique leadership skills. Further, both of his wives, Minnie who passed away in 1932 and Laura whom he married two years later, devoted their lives to helping him spread the Gospel.

Keeble modeled the leadership trait of teachability in that he willingly sat at the feet of both White and Black leaders. He learned from a White preacher, Joe McPherson (1861-1918), the art of sermon

---

[19] Calvin Bowers, *Realizing the California Dream: The Story of Black Churches of Christ in Los Angeles* (Calvin Bowers, 2001), 45-51.

[20] Ibid., 114.

[21] Marshall Keeble, "Sowing and Reaping" *Gospel Advocate* 74 (January 28, 1932): 124; Edward J. Robinson, *Show Us How You Do It: Marshall Keeble and the Rise of Black Churches of Christ in the United States, 1914-1968* (The University of Alabama Press: Tuscaloosa, AL, 2015), 73.

construction. When McPherson led an evangelistic campaign in Nashville in 1914, Keeble recalled: "I copied every lesson Brother McPherson preached; and though he is dead, I am still preaching his sermons, and these lessons are still bringing men to Christ." Keeble later added that McPherson "did more toward teaching me how to preach than any man I ever heard."[22] He also credited his father-in-law, S. W. Womack (1851-1920) and the Black preacher Alexander Campbell (1862-1930) in teaching him the "gospel plan of salvation."[23]

Keeble also learned from Womack, his most influential mentor, "how to get along with the white Southerner who exercised throughout the South both power and influence."[24] Significantly, Keeble, in an era of widespread racial tension, reached across racial boundaries to imbibe biblical and practical principles of leadership. Keeble understood that a fervent prayer life was a key ingredient to leadership proficiency. Therefore, he stressed the significance of "secret prayer."[25] Keeble further acknowledged that he incorporated "humor," a useful leadership tool, in his sermons.[26]

The second significant question regarding Keeble's leadership success is: How was a Black man, with only a seventh-grade education, able to garner extensive generous monetary support from White Christians? To dismiss Keeble's appeal to White believers to his being an "Uncle Tom" is an oversimplification.[27] Marshall Keeble was a complex man living in complicated times. Annie C. Tuggle (1890-1976), a close associate of Keeble's, explained: "Bro. Keeble was as brave as a lion and as humble as a lamb."[28]

The writer contends that Marshall Keeble demonstrated outstanding leadership qualities of tact and diplomacy, genuine

---

[22] Cited in Robinson, *Show Us How You Do It*, 15-16.
[23] Robinson, *Show Us How You Do It*, 2.
[24] J. E. Choate, *Roll Jordan Roll* (Nashville: Gospel Advocate, 1968), 18.
[25] Robinson, *Show Us How You Do It*, 2.
[26] Robinson, *Show Us How You Do It*, 2.
[27] Choate, 41, rightly acknowledges that some Black leaders and members of Churches of Christ leveled this criticism against Keeble.
[28] Cited in Robinson, *Show Us How You Do It*, 99.

humility, and the ability to reproduce other leaders. Keeble garnered something that Cassius never received—the consistent and sustaining financial support of White Christians. He achieved this feat by his ability to exercise tact and diplomacy. When preaching across southern communities, Keeble allowed the White leaders to baptize White candidates because he knew that a Black man baptizing White people in the Jim Crow South was an affront to White supremacy.[29]

Additionally, Marshall Keeble exhibited many other noteworthy qualities of spiritual leadership. In the writer's view, genuine humility might have been one of his greatest qualities. When preaching in west Tennessee in 1940, a White man in the audience came forward in response to Keeble's message and struck the Black preacher with a "staggering blow on the left side of his head with brass knuckles." Stunned temporarily, he recovered, got up, regathered himself, and "turned the other cheek."[30]

Another important leadership quality that Keeble demonstrated was his ability to reproduce other leaders. In his position as president of the Nashville Christian Institute (NCI), he mentored many young men, such as Fred D. Gray, Robert Woods, and Jack Evans, Sr., who accompanied him on his preaching excursions and fundraising tours. In a recent speech at the Keeble Symposium at Lipscomb University, Gray told the audience that Keeble taught him how to pack clothes to travel, how to speak before large crowds without fear, and how to answer a person's questions without volunteering information. Brother Keeble, Gray added, was a "wise religious man. He taught me so much more; most of which I have been using in my 68 years as a civil rights lawyer, destroying segregation wherever I could find it. You may say that Bro. Keeble played a major role in what I have done during the last 69 years as a civil rights lawyer."[31] An exceptional and skilled leader, Marshall Keeble poured his heart and soul into the lives of many young men and women at NCI, who went on to leave their mark on the world.

---

[29] Robinson, *Show Us How You Do It*, 2.
[30] Robinson, *Show Us How You Do It*, 106.
[31] The Keeble Symposium was held at Lipscomb University on September 21, 2023. Fred Gray's speech is in the writer's possession.

G. P. Bowser

Marshall Keeble was not the only African American leader who shaped the lives of Black youth in Churches of Christ. G. P. Bowser (1874-1950), a former Methodist preacher, converted to the Stone-Campbell Movement and launched various educational projects to train young people in African American Churches of Christ. The formation of the Silver Point Christian Institute (1907-1914) in Silver Point, Tennessee, the founding of the Bowser Christian Institute (1938-1946) in Fort Smith, Arkansas, and the launching of Southwestern Christian College (1948-present)—all attest to Bowser's desire to train and equip young leaders who could expand the kingdom of God. Therefore, he gathered around him young men whom he mentored. Four of these men included: G. E. Steward (1906-1979), Levi Kennedy (1899-1970), R. N. Hogan (1902-1997), and J. S. Winston (1906-2002). Indeed, Southwestern Christian College still stands today because "Bowser dreamed the dream, but his proteges, R. N. Hogan, Levi Kennedy, and J. S. Winston, executed his dream."[32]

The Perils of Leadership in African American Churches of Christ

African American Churches of Christ have found themselves conflicted over the place and power of elders and evangelists in local congregations. Esteemed White preacher and educator, Batsell Barrett Baxter (1916-1982), asserted that the "eldership is the highest place which man may achieve in the Lord's church. Everyone else, including preachers, is to serve under their guidance, for they 'exercise the rule' and have the care of souls (Hebrews 13:7, 17)."[33] African American preachers, such as R. N. Hogan disagreed with Baxter's position. Aware of the friction swirling between ministers and elders in Black congregations, Hogan argued that "both the evangelists and elders [should serve] as rulers in the Lord's church. Neither is over the other,

---

[32] Edward J. Robinson, *The Fight is on in Texas: A History of African American Churches of Christ in the Lone Star State, 1865-2000* (Abilene: Abilene Christian University Press, 2008), 113.

[33] Cited in Robinson, *Show Us How You Do It*, 132.

but are workers together in the Lord."³⁴ Here Hogan advocates for the teamwork model in that shepherds and preachers should work collaboratively.

Yet, Hogan resented the notion of having to submit to a wayward man whom he had converted off the streets. "[H]ere is a man out in the world," fussed Hogan, "living a filthy and ungodly life and I, an evangelist, go out there and preach the Gospel to him. He hears and obeys the gospel and I continue to teach him until he is thought to be qualified for the office of an elder. As an evangelist, I appoint him an elder and as soon as he is appointed, I have to crawl under him. Pshaw! The Bible teaches no such thing!"³⁵ Many Black ministers in Churches of Christ today hold tenaciously to Hogan's view even when there are well-qualified Black men working among them.

When Black leaders in Churches of Christ refuse to delegate authority among scripturally equipped men, they regrettably retard the spiritual progress of the local church and frustrate the emergence of gifted successors. Some promising leaders in African American Churches of Christ have withdrawn from Black congregations and found leadership roles among their White counterparts. Additionally, several African American preachers in Churches of Christ have died at the ministerial post without any succession plan.

Purity in the Pulpit

In the summer of 1940, Paul D. English, a promising preacher in African American Churches of Christ, was tragically killed by his own wife, Novella, in Harlem, New York. Mrs. English confessed to authorities that she shot and killed her husband for "boasting of his conquests with other women."³⁶ A brilliant and gifted preacher, English had recently established a Black Church of Christ in Harlem. Keeble, with this horrific incident in mind, warned fellow preachers

---

[34] R. N. Hogan, "The Relationship between the Evangelist and the Elder" *Christian Echo* (March 1990): 2, 7.

[35] Cited in Robinson, *Hard-Fighting Soldiers: A History of African American Churches of Christ* (Knoxville: University of Tennessee Press, 2019), 90.

[36] "Wife Slays Pastor Who Boasted of His Conquests" *Pittsburgh Courier* 31 (August 10, 1940): 1, 4.

against the dangers of sexual deviancy in a 1951 article, "Purity in the Pulpit." Keeble alerted Black Christians to the "danger sign of a preacher weakening," adding:

> When we begin to be successful and people begin to praise us, most of us are not able to stand it. We begin to dress in a way that makes us appeal to some weak sisters and they soon discover that we are trying to entice them. Now my advice to all preachers is to not try to dress so attractively, because in dressing in this way you make the wrong impression on both the brothers and sisters and cause them to lose confidence in you and your sermons will lose their power. When a preacher loses control of himself and begins to let weak sisters entice him, he not only loses power and influence but finally he will have to stop preaching because no one appreciates his sermons. Preachers are allowed in our homes at any time because the brethren have confidence in them. But when a preacher takes advantage of this confidence and betrays this trust and begins to flirt with the women, he begins the most dangerous thing he could allow himself to do, because it will surely destroy him.[37]

Here Keeble stands as unique in that he was not only concerned with doctrinal orthodoxy, but he was also preoccupied with moral and ethical purity in church leaders.

Women Leaders in African American Churches of Christ

Women also played a valuable role in the history of African American Churches of Christ. One noteworthy person was Annie C. Tuggle (1890-1976). A former Methodist, Annie received baptism at the hands of Robert Burton in 1908 and soon began teaching members of her family. Because there were virtually no Black Churches of Christ

---

[37] Marshall Keeble, "Among the Colored Brethren" *Gospel Advocate* 93 (May 17, 1951): 317-18; Robinson, editor, *A Godsend to His People: The Essential Writings and Speeches of Marshall Keeble* (Knoxville, Tennessee: University of Tennessee Press, 2008), 47.

in west Tennessee, Annie organized an all-women congregation, the Smyrna Church of Christ in Germantown, Tennessee.

In 1932, in the throes of the Great Depression, White and Black leaders convened a meeting at the Union Avenue Church of Christ in Memphis, Tennessee, to discuss the $800 indebtedness on the church building occupied by Black members of the Iowa and Lauderdale Church of Christ. Most of the men recommended that the Black preacher be terminated and his salary be used to pay off the debt.[38] Tuggle, however, stood up and stated: "The gospel is the power of God to save. I suggest instead of turning off this minister, send and get another one in the person of Brother Marshall Keeble." The White and Black men in the meeting endorsed Tuggle's suggestion and invited Keeble and his song-leader, William Lee, for a one-month Gospel campaign. The effort resulted in 100 baptisms. Tuggle testified that the Keeble-meeting "shook Memphis from center to circumference."[39]

Tuggle was an ordinary woman whom God used to accomplish extraordinary works. Not only did she leave her mark on African American Churches of Christ as a counselor and educator, but she was often called on to read Scripture in public worship when no literate men were present.[40] Additionally, she possessed a historical consciousness in an ahistorical fellowship in that she painstakingly recorded and documented important narratives related to African American Churches of Christ. Tuggle married, but later divorced. She dreamed of having at least six children, but she had none. Yet, as moral and spiritual counselor as well as an educator at the NCI, she birthed many spiritual sons and daughters in the faith. Fred D. Gray, Robert Woods, R. N. Hogan, and many others came under her godly influence.[41] The story of Annie C. Tuggle reminds us that God can use not only men to mold and shape lives, but that He can use women as

---

[38] Annie C. Tuggle, *Another World Wonder* (n.p., n.d.), 113.

[39] Ibid., 114-115. See also, Edward J. Robinson, *I Was under a Heavy Burden: The Life of Annie C. Tuggle* (Abilene, Texas: Abilene Christian University Press, 2011), 72-73.

[40] Tuggle, 112.

[41] See Robinson, *I Was under a Heavy Burden*, 63-81.

well. Additionally, God often uses imperfect people, even divorced people, to accomplish His perfect will.

The story of African American leadership in Churches of Christ is both complex and complicated. It stands replete with highs and lows, successes and failures, strengths and weaknesses. African American leaders in Churches of Christ generally toiled within an environment of racial restrictions and social limitations. Yet, their greatest weaknesses proved to be their greatest strengths. The great apostle testified that he boasted in "weaknesses, insults, hardships, persecutions, and calamities. For when I am weak, then am I strong" (2 Corinthians 12:10).

CHAPTER THIRTEEN

Chaplaincy

Dorn Muscar, Jr.

Before moving to Memphis from Maryland, I had not visited the HST campus. I remember when my father and I first drove into the city. We drove past Cherry Road on Park Avenue and went down to Orange Mound before realizing we had missed our turn to campus. This was before GPS and back in the days of MapQuest printouts! I remember thinking, "Where have I agreed to live for the next three years to study theology and ministry?"

Little did I know how much I was going to learn in, and through the people who lived in, communities like Orange Mound throughout the metro-area of Memphis; specifically, Raleigh, Frayser, Downtown, and Uptown. The Lord used this little campus as a peaceful place of refuge for my years of the "ministry of study," as Dr. Lewis so aptly challenged us to see our time as students.[1]

In this chapter, I will reflect on my time at HST and the impact it has had on my ministry experience in chaplaincy. I have served as an Air Force chaplain in the Reserves since 2016, but the following insights apply to other contexts for chaplaincy such as hospitals, prisons, campuses, first responders, and the marketplace.[2] My experience has

---

[1] I grew up in Maryland and came to Memphis after four years at Ohio Valley University. I lived on the HST campus as a single student from 2003 until 2008, when I graduated with my MDiv. While working with Memphis Urban Ministry (2006-2011), I began my DMin program in 2010 and completed the degree in 2017. Many important opportunities came to me as an HST student: a practicum in Albania, a Bible lands tour with the Huffards, extensive urban ministry experience, and best of all meeting my wife, Carolyn, through my roommate. It is safe to say that HST in Memphis has played a formative role in my development as a child of God, minister, and chaplain for the Church of Christ.

[2] Jim Browning and Jim Spivey, eds., *The Heart of a Chaplain: Exploring Essentials for*

taught me that an effective chaplain is theologically grounded to be calm in a crisis, listen actively, show genuine interest in others, be a team player, be empathetic, and speak with hope. This posture equips and prepares a chaplain to create the kind of space for the hurting to find solace during hardship, and to be personally resilient while walking alongside the hurting time and time again.[3] The following true story is representative of common encounters for chaplains.

Example of the Need

It was the middle of the day, and I was in my office having a sandwich for lunch. Suddenly, I had a colleague in the chapel pop their head in and say, "Chaplain, are you available for a 'walk-in'"? This meant, "Are you ready to sit with someone who is struggling and needs support to wade through what is burdening them?" I said, "Definitely." I wrapped up my sandwich, cleared up my desk a bit, and then made sure the chairs were ready for counseling. I proceeded to take a deep breath and ask the Lord to help me before I proceeded to welcome this burdened soul into my office. As I stepped out into the hallway, here came toward me a tall, broad-shouldered, young airman, in his early twenties, who smiled as we approached each other. I introduced myself, asked him to come into my office, and showed him his seat. I asked him, "What brings you to the chapel today?" He immediately, without a word, sunk into his chair, folded his head down into his hands on his lap, and said, "I just can't take it." He then wept aloud for a couple of minutes without saying another word. Once he completely poured out his built-up tension in tears, he began to reveal just how much stress he had been tucking-in and carrying with him over the years. In about an hour and a half, he shared a lot and we came up with some solutions to help him relieve stress moving forward. I had never met this airman before and never saw him again, but I was called upon to sit with him in a moment of great despair

---

Ministry (Birmingham: B. H. Carroll Theological Institute and Iron Stream Media, 2022) has a great bibliography on chaplaincy for further reading.

[3] Chaplains provide comfort not by being able to answer the tough questions suffering produces in those seeking support, but by providing a "safe presence of one who understands the question." Alan Baker, *Foundations of Chaplaincy: A Practical Guide* (Grand Rapids: Eerdmans Publishing: 2021), 21.

and heartache. He probably does not recall anything I said or even everything he revealed, but he will remember he reached out for help on a day he was overwhelmed and a chaplain sat with him, listened, cared, and helped him find hope to move forward. However, he may also see that conversation as a turning point in his life, where he found new strength to endure a difficult season and a Christian chaplain was there for him. Again, the basic posture of a chaplain is to care for the hurting. The calling and capacity to sit with people who are hurting, accept them as they are, hear them out, encourage them to walk through their adversity, and speak words of fortitude is foundational in the ministry of chaplaincy.

Theological Reflection for Chaplain Resiliency

The calling and capacity of a person to "sit with people who are hurting" is not rooted in the needs of the hurting person, or in the chaplain holding a position or a degree, receiving a promotion, or even acquiring certain ministry skills or experience. It is rooted in the chaplain's theology. Chaplaincy is a ministry not first born out of a chaplain's desire to serve people in need, but in being a person who has found refuge in God and longs to serve God.[4] Lasting and fulfilling chaplain ministry must be rooted in three places: (1) in response to the chaplain's need for God, (2) in an understanding of God's closeness and nearness to the brokenhearted, and (3) in the chaplain's desire to heed God's call to be conduits of God's comfort and grace to the hurting.

The service member mentioned above, and all those who face the wear and tear of military service or the hardships of life, must be met by a chaplain who is rooted in a theology like that found in Psalm 34. This wonderful psalm could very well be called The Chaplain's Psalm.[5] The

---

[4] Jim Spivey, "Spiritual Formation and the Call," in *The Heart of a Chaplain*, 12-13, states, "The chaplain's world is not for the faint-hearted with unclear or weak convictions. It pulls us in contradictory directions and pushes us to the very boundaries of our theological frameworks. ... it is imperative to be well-grounded in our faith and committed to our confessional beliefs. ... Yet, we should remain flexible and avoid the kind of dogmatism that incapacitates and prevents us from doing ministry in places parish pastors rarely go."

[5] Psalm 91 is known as the Soldier's Psalm. It focuses on the protective presence of

theology of Psalm 34 provides the perspective, wisdom, and calling to help a chaplain maintain a resilient foundation for effective and lasting chaplain ministry.

I propose the following outline for how Psalm 34 can provide a theological footing for those serving as chaplains to the hurting.[6] Again, this examination and application of Psalm 34 is put forth to ground the chaplain in theology rather than in their ministry or the person in need.

34:1-7   Chaplain's motivating personal experience with God (past, present, future)

Verse 8 is a hinge from personal to professional calling

34:8-18   Chaplain's focus and goals in ministry to others

Verse 18 is a hinge from professional back to personal calling

34:19-22   Chaplain's confidence in their call to ministry[7]

The presence of the Lord in the life of the psalmist, as we see in Psalm 34, provides a relevant emphasis on the power of the Lord's presence in the life of a chaplain. The Lord, and not one's ministry, must be the focus of one's life. Initially, the focus that draws a chaplain to ministry is the reality of the significant impact the Lord can have on others through them. At some point, a subtle shift can occur in which the chaplain's focus becomes the needs of others and the chaplain's competence to help them, with less thought of the Lord's hand to redeem and heal. In time, the chaplain's energy for their ministry soon

---

God in one's life and echoes the confidence that no harm will come to the one who trusts in God. Psalm 34 is a great compliment to Psalm 91 because when things do not turn out as Psalm 91 indicates, it will be the chaplain, inspired by Psalm 34, who will be there to encourage and wait patiently with the member for ultimate deliverance.

[6] This is an important exercise not only for military chaplains but all of those who serve as ministers in any context. When we approach the Scriptures, we often look to see what the message is for others rather than seeking to discern what passages have to say to us in our ministries.

[7] Spivey, "Spiritual Formation and the Call," in *The Heart of a Chaplain*, 12, provides three vital questions of ongoing reflection for chaplains: "What is my call (and do I have more than one), what is my role (and do I have more than one," and what is my image?"

withers. They then will either burn out or turn again to see the Lord's gracious presence. This psalm calls the chaplain to focus on the Lord who is sufficient to minister through them and strengthen them through the care of souls in need.

Three verses in Psalm 34 demonstrate the quality of resilience a strong theology, informed by the Word of God, gives a chaplain (34:18, 8, 5).

34:18 "The Lord is close to the broken-hearted and saves the crushed in spirit."

There is a powerlessness that chaplains feel when stepping into the heartache, pain, and grief of another that is both important to grasp and difficult to accept.[8] Chaplains are called to be present and provide support, but there is ultimately a limit to what a chaplain can do to bring about healing or resolution to the situation presented. An important theme of biblical theology, represented in Psalm 34:18, is that it is the Lord who is close and able to save those who are broken-hearted and crushed within. Chaplains are not called by God to be the saviors or healers of the broken. We are called to be present and represent the ever-present grace of God to hurting persons.[9] We sit with them as one who knows the Lord is near and able to lift them up. Not only does this verse state that the Lord is with the one the chaplain is supporting, but it also proclaims that the Lord is close to the chaplain whose heart breaks and is crushed in ministry to the hurting. The Lord heals and builds up the chaplain to continue to go out and sit with one hurting person after another. Without the Lord, this capacity is limited and will take an exacting toll. The impact this

---

[8] Michael Jaques, *A Chaplain's Battle: Transcending Powerlessness in an Explosive World* (Self-published, 2022), 24-25;. Delores Bergen, *The Sword of the Lord: Military Chaplains from the First to Twenty-First Century* (Notre Dame: University of Notre Dame Press, 2004), 24.

[9] One of the most important theological models for chaplaincy is an incarnational model that drives chaplains to "incarnate the love and presence of God in their work." Andrew Todd, "A Theology of the World," in *A Christian Theology of Chaplaincy*, edited by John Caperon, Andrew Todd, and James Walters (Philadelphia: Kingsley Publishers, 2018), 22.

theological foundation has on the resilience of a chaplain must not be underestimated.

34:8 "Oh, taste and see that the Lord is good! Blessed is the man who takes refuge in him!"

With a firm focus on the Lord's closeness to those who come to the chaplain for help, it is also vital for the chaplain to constantly remember the goodness of the Lord to them personally.[10] Several spiritual disciplines help children of God stay rooted in the goodness of God, but they all must be regularly practiced to provide the protective factors a chaplain needs. One wonderful time for this reflection is during the Lord's Supper in worship each week. This is a moment to recall the ultimate act of goodness toward us in Christ and then take refuge there, as the psalmist testifies, so that a state of blessedness can be secured for the one who takes refuge in the Lord. When a chaplain is required to hear the hardships of others, deliver devastating news to loved ones, or lead groups of people through grief, the heart of the chaplain must find a place of rest in calling to mind the goodness of God. There are certainly countless heartaches in life, but there are also countless testimonies to the goodness of God. The chaplain simply must make the time to go there for refuge. The chaplain leads others on this journey to rest in the goodness of God, but also must do this with and for themselves.

34:5 "Those who look to the Lord are radiant and their faces shall never be ashamed."

Psalm 34:5 explains that this reflection on the goodness of God and the corresponding resilience leads to the radiance of the chaplain. Chaplains go into their ministry with great light to bring to others, and others expect to see this light shine brightly from a chaplain. However, through ministry to the hurting this light can become dim. The good news, just mentioned, is that remaining mindful of the goodness of God restores the joy, the hopefulness, the confidence in God's healing power, and the calling of the chaplain to continue to go out to serve. In

---

[10] Peter C. Craigie, *Psalms 1-50*, Word Biblical Commentary (Waco: Word Books, 1983), 279.

trying to help, there is the risk that a chaplain may feel ashamed for not being able to help someone find a resolution to their hardship, hope in their despair, or purpose in their adversity. The chaplain may not be able to save a marriage or persuade a person about reasons for living. These experiences of powerlessness are inevitable for a caring chaplain. The only way through them is to remember that it is the Lord who is close to the broken-hearted and able to deliver those crushed in spirit.

Psalm 34 helps the chaplain stay firmly rooted in the realities that: (1) chaplains are personal recipients of grace from God, (2) this grace is also for all, (3) one is called to share and carry this grace of God to others,[11] and (4) the grace of God continues to sustain a chaplain to serve. This encounter with God and confidence in God, as represented in Psalm 34, sustains a chaplain's interest in building relationships and creating transformational encounters "in which the chaplain stands as the manifestation of God's love, even—perhaps especially—in places where hopelessness seems to dominate."[12] Equipped with a Psalm-34 theology, a chaplain is ever-empowered to enter these places and conversations, not as a stranger or one who is alone, but as one who is familiar with being broken-hearted and now joins God's ministry to the broken-hearted and crushed in spirit.

Spiritual Leadership

Chaplains are spiritual leaders and religious ministry professionals who are ecclesiastically endorsed and represent a Department of Defense-recognized faith group.[13] As spiritual leaders, chaplains should embody the values of a servant leader since they are visible reminders of the Holy.[14] There are two sides to this coin of spiritual leadership: religious

---

[11] Harold Shank, *Listening to His Heartbeat* (Joplin: College Press, 2009), 237.

[12] Ben Ryan, "Theology and Models of Chaplaincy," in *A Christian Theology of Chaplaincy*, 98.

[13] The following link shows the list of Department of Defense-approved faith groups that can have their religious ministry professionals serve as chaplains employed by government agencies. https://prhome.defense.gov/M-RA/MPP/AFCB/Endorsements/

[14] Ken Blanchard, "Principles of Servant Leadership," in *Concepts of Air Force Leadership* (Maxwell AFB: Air University Press, 2008), 217, writes, "Servant leadership

and spiritual.[15] The religious side would be the role of competently and confidently leading others in religious practices like prayer, preaching, worship, communion, baptism, and marriage or funeral services. It would also include being an expert on broader religious matters and the religious needs of unit members for the commander, such as in the case of the need for religious accommodation. The other side of the spiritual leader's role is the broader sense of spirituality that focuses on the purpose, beliefs, and development of perspective that is foundational to spiritual fitness. Leading in this area would mean briefing on topics related to spiritual resiliency and providing short "thoughts of the day" to large groups that have a focus on purpose and inspiration for living out service branch core values.[16] In reflecting on my time at HST and its impact on my ministry as a chaplain, I grew in my appreciation of the power and significance of leading others in prayer and through preaching.

One of my favorite times during my MDiv coursework was the first few minutes of class with Dr. Mark Powell leading his class in prayer.[17] I never wanted to be a second late to miss this time of spiritual formation. Dr. Powell prayed in a soft and thoughtful tone. His prayers were filled with rich theology and sincere praise for God's faithfulness and pleas for our growth in faithful response to our gracious God. His voice in prayer led me to the throne of God. These were brief and quiet moments that reminded me of the power of prayer, of what it can mean to those being led in prayer, and what theologically-informed prayer entails.

---

asserts the belief that the sheep do not exist for the sake of shepherd, but rather the shepherd exists for the sake of the sheep."

[15] Jim Spivey, "Spiritual Foundation," in *The Heart of a Chaplain*, 36, differentiates between religious care, pastoral care, and spiritual care. He writes, "Religious care addresses the needs of a chaplain's specific faith group.... Pastoral care meets the practical and emotional needs of anyone in the institution.... Spiritual care deals with existential matters: introspective questions such as personal identity, connectedness with others, destiny, transcendental issues and relationship with the divine."

[16] Air Force core values are "Integrity First, Service Before Self, and Excellence in All We Do".

[17] My other favorite time that proved to be spiritually formative was the first week of each semester when Dr. Huffard preached in chapel on the annual theme. His wise, thought-provoking, deeply theological, global, and biblical sermons reinforced to me the power preaching has on the lives of God's people.

Prayer is a big part of the ministry of a military chaplain. We are looked to for appropriate, thoughtful, and concise prayers. These prayers are of several varieties: liturgical, public, and intercessory. By liturgical, I am referring to the prayers that chaplains offer in worship services. These are the kinds of prayers a chaplain would pray in their faith group worship services that are expected to have the emphasis or quality as if in a religious assembly with like-minded believers. We are also called upon to pray at a variety of public gatherings and ceremonies for promotion, changes of command, and retirement. These prayers require a bit more ecumenism and are not the same as prayers a chaplain would pray in a worship service.

The intercessory prayers are offered with those who come to us for support in their time of need. These prayers require empathy, boldness, and confidence to pray because these are not prayers written-out ahead of time, and you only know what the members have revealed about themselves. A chaplain, in most cases, should offer to pray with the individual seeking help. Some accept and some do not, but this is one dimension we bring to the member that other helping agencies do not offer.

Generally, chaplains' prayers ought to be "ecumenical" in nature, though the religious prayers will be the same prayer you would lead in a church service off base. By "ecumenical," I mean a prayer that makes room for a broader grouping of people to pray to God. It is not hard to be biblical and ecumenical with addressing God as "Almighty God," "Sovereign Lord," "Most High God," or "God of the Nations," for example. Here is an example of a prayer I recently prayed at a public event with community members after a 2023 Innovative Readiness Training (IRT) mission in Dayton, Tennessee called "Healthy TN."

> Please join me as I pray. Almighty God, thank you for today. Thank you for the Sequatchie and Tennessee Valleys and the people who call this area home. What a beautiful area you have created. We feel blessed to have a positive impact on Bledsoe and Rhea counties. Please bless them for the warm reception, respect, and hospitality they have shown to us. Please, also, continue to give us what we need

to complete the mission. Fill us with increased energy, patience, and joy to serve well together. We pray the care we are providing will inspire community members to take even better care of themselves and their families. We continue to place this IRT in your hands for you to use it for your glory and the good of everyone involved. May your will be done on earth as it is in heaven. May your will be done in the Sequatchie Valley as it is in heaven. All this we humbly ask, Amen.

This is a public and ecumenical prayer, but I also believe it is faithful to the biblical witness of prayer that honors the God of the Bible and seeks God's help. I did not say the words "in Jesus's name," but I believe I prayed in the character and message of our Savior requesting God's will to be done on earth as it is in heaven. A prospective chaplain should be comfortable praying in such a fashion and be comfortable with such an ecumenical-style of prayer in public gatherings. These prayers are not the end-all or be-all. These invocations are opportunities to not only lead people to God, but to build credibility and trust to do even further ministry among those you are called to serve as chaplains.

The theologically informed prayer I learned at HST in the classroom, in chapel, in student housing nights of prayer, and in the local church, has served me well both personally and professionally as a chaplain.

Cross-Cultural Ministry

One of the lasting legacies and contributions HST has made for God's kingdom is training ministers in a context where cross-cultural ministry opportunities are abundant and transformative. In our ever-increasing urbanized world, ministers are going to find themselves called by God to minister to people in urban communities and multi-cultural ministry contexts that require cross-cultural competencies.[18] One of those diverse ministry contexts is chaplaincy. I can say unequivocally that studying ministry and theology at HST, in an urban context with the

---

[18] Norma Guitierrez, "Cultural Competencies," in *Professional Spiritual & Pastoral Care: A Practical Clergy and Chaplain's Handbook* (Woodstock, VT: SkyLight Paths Publishing, 2013), 409.

opportunity to have an urban ministry apprenticeship, was formative and foundational in my willingness and interest to accept a call to serve in a multi-ethnic congregation and the AF Chaplain Corps.[19] The fertile ground HST in Memphis provided for rich cross-cultural, urban ministry experience for graduate ministry students will be missed and hard to replicate. There is hope that students will continue to be shaped by these unique urban experiences through Harding's new initiative through the Center for Church and Community Engagement, based in Memphis and led by Dr. Steve Cloer.

Before I even served on staff as a minister with Memphis Urban Ministry (MUM), I was a member of the Raleigh Community Church of Christ for two and one-half years. I was a minority in this community of faith, but I was accepted, loved, encouraged, mentored, and challenged.[20] The cherished relationships I developed helped me become more comfortable and relatable in diverse ministry contexts. Chaplaincy is a ministry context in which a minister must be comfortable relating to and connecting with people of various backgrounds and belief systems. This comfort comes through doing life and spending time with people from various backgrounds that contrast one's own.[21] I did not have to go far to find this experience in Memphis, introduced by HST, and I am better as a chaplain for my years at MUM and Raleigh Community Church of Christ.

One of the unique aspects of chaplain ministry, as compared to congregational ministry, is that you are called to interact with and

---

[19] I spent eight and one-half years as a preaching minister for the University Park Church of Christ, which is located on the Prince George's County side of the DC Metro area and is the most populace black majority county in the United States. Our congregation was seventy percent non-Caucasian and had members born in over a dozen other countries.

[20] I was a minority in culture and race, but not in faith. I was in fellowship with brothers and sisters in Christ.

[21] Lingenfelter & Mayers, *Ministering Cross-Culturally: A Model for Effective Personal Relationships*, 3rd ed. (Grand Rapids: Baker Academic, 2016), 6, discusses that no two people are alike and each has their own personal cultural heritage that is initially shaped in their family of origin and then further shaped through that person's unique enculturation experience. So, thoughtfully approaching each person with attentiveness to their unique personal culture is of great value to a chaplain.

provide religious ministry support to people from various faith backgrounds and all parts of the world.[22] A minister could simply be overwhelmed and miss many opportunities without formative cross-cultural ministry experiences, which HST provided countless students either through apprenticeships, internships, practicums, or urban ministry fieldwork opportunities. These opportunities create and nurture internal and external dialogue that is invaluable. The internal dialogue informed by cross-cultural experiences leads a future chaplain to greater self-awareness and confrontation with unconscious bias that comes when you are serving people from various backgrounds and belief systems. I had numerous humbling conversations and encounters that helped me, upon self-reflection, to expose and strip away unconscious bias that would have hindered me from faithfully and effectively serving as a minister and chaplain. The external dialogue with those from other backgrounds requires the development of a listening posture. Effective chaplain ministry is developed by being interested in and willing to deeply listen to those we are called to serve. Especially when dealing with people with different experiences and backgrounds, it is vital to listen carefully and actively.[23] This attentive listening and conversation builds one's "cross-cultural intuition" through one interaction after another in a secular and diverse ministry context. I learned so much about connecting with people cross-culturally and was gifted opportunities to have my listening skills enhanced, both in the classroom on Cherry Road and in the classroom of life in the city of Memphis.

---

[22] Chaplains are employed by secular institutions and invested with position and authority based on their ecclesiastical credentials. However, working outside of one ecclesiastical familiarity increases the need for a chaplain to be interested and able to show "genuine care for souls within their purview, regardless of how different they may look, act, think or believe." Jim Browning, "So, You want to be a Chaplain?" in *The Heart of a Chaplain*, 5.

[23] This consistent and active listening hones a chaplain's intuitiveness about people and how to care for them. This intuitiveness is a vital soft skill for chaplaincy. Scott Collins, "Called Together into Ministry," in *The Heart of a Chaplain*, 137. George Yancey, *Beyond Racial Division: A Unifying Alternative to Colorblindness and Antiracism*, (Downers Grove: InterVarsity Press, 2022), 159, provides a thoughtful approach of "mutual accountability" with those from different backgrounds from our own which requires a commitment to intentionally seeking out interracial relationships with a humble and collaborative communication style.

Additionally, Robert Vickers explains that chaplaincy moves chaplains into "new cultures" by virtue of the various secular organizations that employ them.[24] Not only is there a need to have cross-cultural comfortability on an interpersonal level, but also to demonstrate "institutional awareness" on an organizational level. The skills gained in the formative MDiv years can and should foster a greater ability to form a contextually appropriate chaplain ministry in these institutions. Vickers also states that a chaplain must be rooted in their identity, calling, and theology to function well in these new and different organizational cultures.[25] In several respects, cross-cultural experience and comfortability, which I gained while pursuing graduate theological education, are vital for lasting and effective chaplain ministry.

Ministry Formation During MDiv Learning

Twelve chaplains—seven military and five hospital/other, either currently or formerly employed and endorsed by the Church of Christ—responded to a survey with two questions regarding their MDiv experience.[26] The first was: "What was most helpful in your MDiv program or experience to prepare you for your chaplain ministries?" The second was, "What would you suggest would strengthen an MDiv program's impact for students to thrive in future chaplain roles?" In addressing these questions, it is helpful to remember there are two primary groups of chaplains that a school of theology is educating. Some enter graduate studies knowing they would like to serve as a chaplain, which requires them to obtain an MDiv. Others have not thought of pursuing chaplaincy, but several years into their coursework or post-MDiv ministries realize they would like to explore one of the many contexts for chaplain ministry.[27]

---

[24] Robert Vickers, "Institutional Life," in *The Heart of a Chaplain*, 76.
[25] Ibid., 77.
[26] We currently endorse 60 chaplains. The Fairfax Church of Christ, in Fairfax, Virginia is the endorsing congregation and Dr. Gary Payne, (Army Chaplain, Lt. Col, retired) is the Chairman of the Chaplain Endorsement Committee which is made up of several elders from the Fairfax congregation(http://fxcc.org/ and chaplains@fxcc.org).
[27] The Association of Theological Schools has found that schools of graduate theological education are having more students enroll in the MA program instead of the MDiv. Some schools are also facing the challenge of shortening the MDiv. It is important

The surveyed chaplains expressed the tremendous value of the broad scope of the MDiv, especially for developing skills in exegesis, homiletics, church history, and counseling. These areas were of particular value because of the amount of preaching, working with people from other faith traditions, and carrying a significant load of pastoral counseling that chaplain ministry demands. Ministry opportunities through practicums or internships are seen as important, as well as the mentorship received from seasoned ministry leaders who either teach or network with students while they are in graduate school.

Regarding how MDiv programs could be strengthened to enhance preparation for chaplain roles, it is probably not a surprise that respondents emphasized the practical ministry side of the program. A significant number of recommendations included giving clinical pastoral education (CPE) opportunities within the MDiv program. It was suggested to either require one or more units of CPE, or offer credit for CPE. Additionally, the improved development of people skills, specific training in solution-focused therapy, incorporating seasoned chaplains to teach chaplaincy-related courses or modules, and ensuring students are involved in learning through internships or apprenticeships beyond the shorter required practicums, were all mentioned. There are several wonderful military chaplain candidate program options for MDiv students, which allow students who have an interest in military chaplaincy to get their feet wet and discern, through practical engagement with supervision and feedback, if military ministry is a good fit for them. Graduate programs must make this option known to students in the first few semesters of their studies so they can enter one of these programs before they get too far into their studies and no longer qualify to enter the program.[28]

---

to advise students that if they think they would ever like to pursue chaplaincy, especially in the military, they need to have at least a 72-hour graduate theological degree. Two thirty-six-hour degrees are not accepted. In my time recruiting chaplains for the AF Reserves, I saw a great number of our applicants being pastors/ministers in their 30s who are looking for something else to do for the Lord.

[28] There are numerous benefits to both the graduate school and the student by a student's participation in a chaplain candidate program. The following article outlines several of these benefits: Dorn Muscar, "Air Force Chaplain Candidate Program offers

A final word regarding the improvements MDiv programs could make to prepare future chaplains, whether students are pursuing chaplaincy upon graduation or not, would be for graduate schools to introduce all students to what chaplaincy could look like for them. From my personal experience and years in recruiting, many ministers are at risk of burnout and leaving ministry altogether, or are looking for some other ministry to invest themselves in outside of local church ministry. I credit staying twice as long in ministry at a specific local church to having the outlet of serving as a Reserve Chaplain. The days of chaplain ministry provided me with a break from my routine to go on an "adventure" in ministry. These adventures allowed me to have new conversations in a different environment, gave me another ministry team to serve alongside, provided leadership development opportunities, and then sent me back to the local church with renewed energy. Knowing that chaplaincy, specifically part-time chaplaincy roles, could be a way to keep future ministers in ministry longer, should be sufficient reason to give chaplaincy more attention in MDiv programs.[28]

Conclusion

Sitting with people who are hurting, accepting them as they are, listening in confidentiality, encouraging them so they can walk through adversity, and then speaking hopeful words of fortitude are central to the heart of chaplaincy. The Lord used my MDiv experience at HST to develop in me the capacity to provide this kind of ministry through coursework, the presence of faithful spiritual leaders, an accepting urban congregation, and cross-cultural ministry with members of the Memphis community. My prayer is for HST to continue to be a place where future spiritual leaders, some of whom will serve as chaplains, can further grow in the grace and knowledge of our Lord Jesus Christ and continue to cherish investing themselves in the ministry of study.

---

benefits to seminaries and students" (*Colloquy Online*, May 2022, https://www.ats.edu/files/galleries/air-force-chaplain-candidate-program-offers-benefits-to-seminaries-and-students.pdf).

CHAPTER FOURTEEN

Campus Ministry

Chris W. Buxton

Remember your Creator during your youth, when all possibilities lie open before you and you can offer all your strength intact for his service. The time to remember is not after you become senile and paralyzed! Then it is not too late for your salvation, but too late for you to serve as the presence of God in the midst of the world and the creation. You must take sides earlier—when you can actually make choices, when you have many paths opening at your feet, before the weight of necessity overwhelms you.[1]

Jacque Ellul's paraphrase of Ecclesiastes 12:1-2 so well expresses what energizes and sustains those who work among college and university students in the kingdom mission called campus ministry. As students leave home, often for the first time, as they begin to form friendships with people who often become their lifetime inner circle, as they determine their vocational path, as they hear competing narratives from some of society's most-educated people and begin to form the worldviews that will inform and frame their life's values and priorities…will they remember their Creator?

Having worked as a public-university campus minister for twenty-two years and having experienced campus ministry during my own time as a public-university student, I am convinced that one of the most crucial variables that determines if students remember their Creator during their collegiate experience is whether their lives intersect with devoted, committed people of God who are willing to

---

[1] Jacques Ellul, *Reason for Being: A Meditation on Ecclesiastes* (Grand Rapids: Eerdmans, 1990), 282-83.

journey with, teach, and mentor them through one of life's most crucial and transformational seasons. Campus ministry exists for such intersections. Whether it is a prominent organization with a large staff, facility, and budget or a professor teaching a simple Bible lesson to a handful of students in a tucked-away classroom, campus ministry possesses incredible capacities to make disciples and transform lives.

On the macro level, it is easy to see how campus ministries are strategically positioned as powerful tools for kingdom expansion. In Acts 19:8-10, the apostle Paul and his companions entered the synagogue in Ephesus and "spoke boldly there for three months." But when some of the Jews "refused to believe," Paul relocated to the lecture hall of Tyrannus. Luke tells us that for two years, Paul taught daily there, and as a result "all the Jews and Greeks who lived in the province of Asia heard the word of the Lord." As a center for business and trade and home to the temple of Artemis, Ephesus drew people from across the province. Many of the drawn were taught by Paul, then returned to their homes with knowledge of Jesus.

Today, every college campus in the USA is an Ephesus and every campus ministry a lecture hall of Tyrannus. As if it were breathing, the university draws in, then sends out. The broadly held belief in American culture that a college degree is the primary path to success drives a steady flow of young hearts and minds every year to our nation's colleges and universities. "Our society views college not as a consumer product at all, but as both a surefire, can't-lose financial investment and, even more crucial than that, a moral imperative."[2] During their college years, campus ministries walk with students during one of the most crucial and pivotal seasons of their lives. They are then sent back into the world, transformed.

Or consider this. In Acts 2, on the day of Pentecost, the church began in earnest with the pouring out of the Holy Spirit, the apostles' sermon, and the conversion of three thousand people. But why did God choose that particular place and time? Acts 2:5 says "there were staying

---

[2] Professor X, *In the Basement of the Ivory Tower: Confessions of an Accidental Academic* (New York: Viking, 2011), 119.

in Jerusalem God-fearing Jews from *every nation under heaven.*" This in-gathering of nations ostensibly allowed the apostles to preach to all the world at once. Today, that dynamic is repeating itself every year in the form of international students descending from around the world on our college and university campuses. I believe there exists for the modern church no greater missional opportunity than the one million-plus international students coming annually to the USA for higher education. It is the Great Commission in reverse: all the world is coming to us.

Charles Habib Malik, former Harvard University professor, diplomat, and president of the United Nations General Assembly, summarizes well the macro-level impact American colleges and universities have, not only on American society, but on the globe:

> The University is a clear-cut fulcrum with which to move the world. The problem here is for the church to realize that no greater service can it render both itself and the cause of the gospel, with which it is entrusted, than to try to recapture the universities for Christ on whom they were all originally founded. One of the best ways of treating the macrocosm is through the handle of the universities in which millions of youths destined to positions of leadership spend, in rigorous training, between four and ten years of the most formative period of their life. More potently than by any other means, change the university and you change the world.[3]

On the micro level, the case for campus ministry's immense potential is also clear. When Jesus began his ministry, he went to the seashore, called out to the Galilean fishermen Peter and Andrew and asked them to follow him. Jesus said to them, "Follow me, and *I will make you become* fishers of men" (Mark 1:17).[4] Jesus declared to two of his

---

[3] Charles Habib Malik, *A Christian Critique of the University* (Downers Grove: InterVarsity, 1982), 100-01.

[4] The Greek word here translated "men" is *anthropos*, which can refer to men or women. The NIV translation of Mark 1:17 is: "Come, follow me," Jesus said, "and I will send you out to fish for people." For my use, however, I prefer the ESV or NASB renderings of this text because they better convey the literal Greek phrasing in which we clearly see the force of Jesus's intention, through his mentoring influence, to "make" the apostles into very different people.

most important future apostles that he was going to "make you become" people they would have otherwise never been. Three years with Jesus would radically and permanently alter the course of their lives.

Many potential Peters and Andrews are studying every day on our college campuses, open to mentors who can "make" them into something and someone they would otherwise never become. I believe there exists nowhere in the modern church a mission so resembling the mission of Jesus—and one so filled with latent potential—as the one occurring on American college and university campuses. Distanced for the first time from childhood restraints yet unfettered by many of the responsibilities of adulthood, old enough to handle advanced and complex concepts yet young enough to possess pliable, moldable hearts, university students represent a "sweet spot" of flexibility and receptivity. They are, perhaps, our society's most available, teachable, and send-able members.

Also on the micro level, consider the number of crucial, life-altering decisions the typical student makes during the college years. It is often during this time when students will form the close friendships that will endure for decades or even for the rest of their lives. It is often during this time when students find a spouse, begin the path toward a life-long vocation, and build a worldview that will establish the vantage point from which they will interpret all of life. Very few students enter college with a fully-formed worldview and very few students leave college without one. Vocation, spouse, closest friendships, and worldview: are there any factors that have more bearing on the trajectory and quality of a person's life than these?

For most American young people, these decisions are made during the window of time we call the college years. This brief but intense window during which immense life-transformation can occur is not unlike the three years Jesus spent with the apostles. The question is not *whether or not* college students experience huge transformation. They almost certainly will! The question is *how* will they be transformed, *who* will be there to help guide them, and how will those who guide them have been prepared for the task?

The Culture of Higher Learning

All of today's Ivy League institutions except Cornell were established for two purposes: to train ministers and to bring glory to God. When the first of these schools, Harvard College, was established in 1648, its Puritan founders were "committed to a rigorous, demanding education," that would shape their students' minds *and* souls.[5] Through the Civil War era, most American colleges and universities understood their task similarly. As late as 1890, most public universities required their students to attend daily chapel services and some even required Sunday church attendance. Through the mid-twentieth century, "it was not unusual for spokespersons of leading public schools to refer to them as 'Christian' institutions."[6] Today, however, the public university has left such things behind. With little more than naturalistic explanations as the raw materials from which to construct ethical and moral foundations, "the secular academy has... lost its ability to deliver on this central part of its mission."[7]

While institutions of higher learning are committed to the acquisition, expansion, and dissemination of knowledge, today's secular higher education climate often arrays itself and its considerable influence against God in ways that can frequently be dismissive of faith, or even radically opposed to it. Those who are called into the life of ministry to college students are called into demanding and complex circumstances.

In the fall of 1998, I became the director of a campus ministry serving Arkansas Tech University.[8] I recognized early on that, for the sake of the mission, I needed to become more academically and intellectually equipped. It was my first ministry job. I was young, and I lacked any substantive experience or training. The son of a preacher, I probably understood ministry life better than most, and I had

---

[5] John R. Thelin, *A History of American Higher Education*, 2nd ed. (Baltimore: Johns Hopkins University Press, 2011), 24.

[6] Thelin, *A History*, 3.

[7] George M. Marsden, *The Soul of the American University: From Protestant Establishment to Established Nonbelief* (New York: Oxford, 1994), 430.

[8] Arkansas Tech University is a public university located in Russellville, Arkansas. The campus ministry I led is called Renew College Ministry: https://www.renewatu.org.

experienced campus ministry as a college student. But I lacked many of the hard and soft skills needed to lead a ministry—or myself. I had little sense of the job's complexity and difficulty. I sought guidance through books (the scant few I could find), conversations with older ministers, and conferences. These were not enough; I needed an education that would help equip me.

In the synagogues, among the Jews and God-fearing Greeks, as well as in the marketplace, Paul "reasoned" with his audiences (Acts 17:17). When the Epicurean and Stoic philosophers took him to a meeting at the Areopagus, he presented one of the Bible's most important rationalizations for the one true God, built partially on the Athenians' philosophical presuppositions. It was a masterful display of knowledge, wisdom, and logic that approximates the intellectual challenges facing the present-day campus minister. But I was no apostle Paul. Early on, I began to face the usual college student issues: conflicts with roommates/friends/parents, sexual sin, alcohol and drug abuse, vocational discernment, or far deeper meaning-of-life questions. I heard Jesus saying to me as he did to Nicodemus: "You are [your students'] teacher and do you not understand these things?" (John 3:10).

Today's campus minister must have an "alert" and "sober" mind (1 Pet 1:13; 5:8) and be able to "demolish arguments and every pretension that sets itself up against the knowledge of God," and to "take captive every thought to make it obedient to Christ" (2 Cor 10:5). The campus minister must speak cogently and compellingly for and about God within some of the world's most intellectually stimulating and curious—but often combative—environments. I knew I needed to be far-better-equipped. My students were interacting daily with some of the best-educated people in our culture. I wanted to be able to teach Scripture at the same level my students' professors expounded on other fields of study. I needed to be able to compete more effectively within the university's marketplace of ideas. I needed to grow as one "who correctly handles the word of truth" (2 Tim 2:15).

So, after three years of learning much about what I did not know, I began my Master of Divinity journey with Harding School of Theology. Early on, I learned from Don Meredith principles of proper research that I still rely on today. In his class, I wrote my first truly graduate-level paper in which I explored from Romans 2 a question about salvation that had troubled me since childhood, and one that would occasionally trouble my students. I took the course on campus ministry with Tim Stafford, who earned his Doctor of Ministry from HST and served at the time as a campus minister at the University of Memphis. I remember the fascination I felt as our class explored my profession from scholarly perspectives I had previously never considered. I remember quickly applying Ed Gray's Counseling Skills course as I sat with students navigating issues such as failed dating relationships, addiction, or the death of a parent. Although I was not a preacher, Dave Bland's Congregational Ministry introduced me to practical skills in areas such as my relationship with elders, navigating conflict, and organizational leadership. Bland's Sermon Development and Delivery helped me more carefully and effectively craft my words as I prepared to teach Scripture—a task I grew to see as the true centerpiece of my work.

While I was a reluctant student of languages, Allen Black's Greek courses drew me into the New Testament text in fascinating new ways. Rick Oster's Paul's Prison Letters not only advanced my understanding of how to read Paul but specifically helped me navigate some practical questions surrounding our ministry's worship gatherings. John Mark Hicks' Christian Worship also contributed greatly to the same, shaping my theology of worship and helping me navigate more effectively the questions—and occasional strong challenges—I encountered.

Mark Powell's Reformation and Modern Church helped me more fully develop my theology of atonement as I wrestled with the teachings of the sixteenth-century Socinians. Kevin Youngblood's Minor Prophets illuminated some of the Bible's most mysterious texts and inspired me to teach those books to my students in a series that became one of their favorites. I can say the same for Black's Gospel of John course. And the systematic theology training I received from Hicks and Powell helped equip me for myriad conversations, Bible lessons, and sermons.

Two courses, however, stand out as having had the greatest impact on my journey as a campus minister. The first was Hicks' Providence and Suffering, a course that wrestled with perhaps humanity's most troubling theological question: the problem of evil. Hicks' grief-filled personal story that he so graciously shared, and his desire to hold in tension his deep faith and deep loss, powerfully illuminated texts like Job and helped equip me with far better perspective and language to navigate many future conversations regarding my students' loss, pain, and confusion. One morning during our class week, with the story of Job, our questions and doubts, and details of his personal loss all fresh on our minds, we sat down for chapel. From the row directly behind him, I watched as Dr. Hicks raised his hands and his voice in praise to a God whose ways we cannot fully comprehend. That moment was the most important part of the course.

The second was Evertt Huffard's Spiritual Leadership. The centerpiece of the class was a Leadership Emerging Pattern (LEP) project, a sort of biographical overview in which students deeply examine their lives to determine "bent in life," "gift mix," "spheres of influence," and all the "process items" that were most transformative. As I spent months processing parents, major events, mentors, and ministry successes and failures, my life began to come into sharper focus than perhaps ever before, and I began to understand myself in ways I had previously failed to comprehend. As a direct result of the project, I was convicted of some destructive attitudes I had held for many years, and God called me to repentance. Obeying that conviction led to needed confession and to crucial healing that, in turn, readied me for a significant new challenge I did not know was coming.

That challenge was to return to my alma mater, Arkansas State University, in January of 2010.[9] The campus ministry I had been a part of as a student had recently ceased operation. A group of supporters

---

[9] Arkansas State University's main campus is located in Jonesboro, Arkansas. The revived ministry at Arkansas State is called Wolflife Campus Ministry: https://asuwolflife.org. The name is a combination of A-State's Red Wolves mascot and the abundant life we are offered through Jesus (John 10:10).

and alumni rallied and asked me to come back to lead the rebuilding efforts. God made it clear I was supposed to do just that. During the following ten years, by God's grace, my wife Monica, and I, joined by many others, built a new ministry on the foundation of the old one. God allowed us to raise a large sum of money to build a beautiful new facility on campus, empowered us to launch an apprenticeship program to train and send future campus ministers, blessed us to begin a highly fruitful ministry to international students, and allowed us to send a team to plant a new campus ministry at the University of Washington.[10] Looking back, I am convinced God was working upstream, using HST to prepare me for the journey.

The Future of Campus Ministry

Today, I teach campus ministry to students on the undergraduate and graduate levels, and as a campus ministry consultant, I mentor and coach young ministers across the country. I hope the ones I coach and teach today will be walking among college students for decades to come. But what will the terrain of the American university and its students look like at that time? While we cannot know for sure, the current trajectory is clearly toward decreasing religiosity[11] and increasing cultural complexity.

If campus ministry was ever in Jerusalem, its home is now in Athens. Current and future campus ministers face a growing list of intricate topics: navigating social media, LGBTQ issues, climate change, political polarization, faith deconstruction, and the daunting task of how to share Jesus when the range of acceptable speech is in constant flux. Additionally, the current generation, commonly known as "Gen Z," is the most atheistic and religiously unaffiliated generation

---

[10] The University of Washington is located in Seattle, Washington. The ministry the students from Arkansas State University launched is called Sojourn Campus Ministry: https://www.sojournuw.org.

[11] Becka A. Alper, Asta Kallo, Justin Nortey, Michael Rotolo, Gregory A. Smith, and Patricia Tevington, *"Religious Nones in America: Who They Are and What They Believe,"* Pew Research Center, Jan. 24, 2024, accessed Feb. 21, 2024: https://www.pewresearch.org/religion/2024/01/24/religious-nones-in-america-who-they-are-and-what-they-believe/.

in American history—our nation's first truly post-Christian generation.

Even among college students who claim Christianity, their moral framework is all-too-often some form of what has been labeled moralistic therapeutic deism. "Moralistic" refers to the call to be "good." For some, "good" is a sort of Kantian reduction of Christianity to ethics, and among those who would not call themselves Christians, "good" is a nebulous term primarily defined by secular culture. "Therapeutic" means our anxiety and guilt are assuaged by a God who forgives without consequences and wants us to feel good about ourselves. "Deism" refers to a God who exists as Creator but is not particularly involved in the details of our lives, interceding lightly, if at all.

We must also remember that as these newer issues emerge, ministry on college campuses continues to face all the traditional challenges, temptations, and opportunities for moral compromise. Students who come to college as believers fall away from God, faith, and church at alarming rates. In fairness, it should be noted that this is typically not the result of the secular university "stealing" a student's faith but instead highlights the student's lack of substantive faith from the start. It should also be noted that some who drift away will return later in life—often around marriage or the birth of their first child. But the fact remains that students who come to college as Christians frequently walk away from their faith. Even those who return later often make some of their most crucial decisions and possibly some of their most devastating mistakes while away from God.

The founders of the original Ivy League colleges would be perplexed and dumbfounded in the extreme to see today's higher education landscape. Professors and administrators believe the realms of morality, spirituality, or even what constitutes a meaningful life are outside their scope. Only a small minority of university faculty see themselves as having either the competence or the duty to address issues of morality. Since they have relegated the One True Source of such answers to the extreme margins, the typical American university has left itself precious little to draw from to guide students in their most fundamental questions of meaning, purpose and transcendence.

In spite of all this, there is reason for God's people to have great hope. To the student who is intellectually honest and spiritually open, the naturalistic explanations for life's questions are eventually exposed as hopeless, the pursuit of moral darkness turns vapid and empty, and the constantly shifting sand of rudderless culture leaves them exhausted. From this void often arises a deep spiritual hunger, a longing for a solid rock on which to stand. Because of this hunger, many students are often never more spiritually receptive than during their collegiate experience.

The window of opportunity is wide open on today's college campuses. But will God's people see the campus as a place where they must be, and will kingdom efforts on campus be led by people who are adequately prepared for the challenge? Below are three crucial ways I believe institutions like HST can most significantly aid our future mission to help college students know the Lord.

First, theological schools should make campus ministry a standard part of their curricula. As of this writing, most theological institutions affiliated with Churches of Christ do not offer a single course in campus ministry on the undergraduate or graduate levels. Perhaps this is because so few faculty members have any experience in or passion for campus ministry. Or perhaps it is the result of some misguided sense of competition between Christian and public universities. Whatever the reasons, I find the lack of course offerings in campus ministry not only highly disappointing but a true dereliction of duty. Students at such schools who are training for ministry are not only unable to receive specific training in campus ministry, but in many cases are thoroughly unaware such a thing as campus ministry exists. As young people are preparing for a life in ministry, campus ministry is often not even presented as an option. This must change.

Second, theological schools must respond to the seismic shift in our collective moral worldview, a shift that is abundantly clear on secular college campuses. In previous generations, a strong majority of Americans shared a knowledge of and a basic allegiance to at least a form of nominal Christianity. Most American citizens possessed the moral and theological "dots" that could be connected to form common language and understanding. No longer is this true. Any sense of a shared moral code is gone. No longer is there a broadly held assumption that we are all sinners, and that sinners need salvation. How does a campus minister communicate the gospel to a student who may believe in God but does not believe in the concept of sin or the need to be saved from it? How do campus ministers persuade students who believe in the Freudian assertion that the most important source of truth is not external but internal—people whose devotion to expressive individualism leads them to follow their hearts before all other sources of truth or authority?[12] Theological schools must equip future ministers for this starkly different cultural context.

Third, theological schools should find ways to require, or at least encourage, more substantial forms of ministry mentoring. This need, of course, is not exclusive to those entering campus ministry. But the complexities of the university make it particularly important for them. Campus ministries tend to take seriously the need to raise up and train their own future leaders from within. Theological schools should also help students experience life-on-life mentoring and ministry outside the classroom. Within the academy, unless an undergraduate or graduate student intentionally seeks mentoring, it most likely will not happen. Many faculty members are not interested in mentoring their students, and the "field" education most seminaries require is helpful but inadequate.

Even those who have earned the Master of Divinity—the gold standard for ministry education—may graduate having never actually worked, to any significant degree, with real people in real ministry situations or experienced mentoring relationship that allows the kind of transparent and personal shepherding that a classroom experience can rarely provide. Skills such as evangelism, teaching, organizational

---

[12] Canadian philosopher Charles Taylor explains the belief system that has come to be known as expressive individualism this way: "Issues where we were meant to accept the dictates of authority we now have to think out for ourselves. Modern freedom and autonomy centres us on ourselves, and the ideal of authenticity requires that we discover and articulate our own identity." Charles Taylor, *The Ethics of Authenticity* (Cambridge, MA: Harvard University Press, 2018), Kindle edition, 81.

leadership, fundraising, and conflict management can be taught but are often more readily "caught" from a master practitioner.

I trust that all our theological schools will rise to meet these challenges because campus ministry has never been more crucial. American public colleges and universities represent a cultural epicenter, reflecting society but also leading it. They are drawing in and raising up tomorrow's worldwide leaders during one of their most transformational seasons of life. During their collegiate experience, students make crucial decisions relating to issues such as faith, worldview, spouse, friendships, career, and more. They establish beliefs, behaviors, and relationships that will largely set the trajectory for the remainder of their lives.

Those who are serious about the mission of Jesus cannot afford to ignore our colleges and universities; they are simply far too critical to the mission. Yahweh selected Canaan to be Israel's homeland precisely because of its position between Egypt and Mesopotamia—at the literal crossroads of the ancient world—to be a light to the nations (Ezek 5:5; Isa 51:4). American colleges and universities and the campus ministries that serve them also exist at one of the world's most significant crossroads. College students desperately need committed, prepared people of God to meet them there.

CHAPTER FIFTEEN

Bivocational Ministry

R. Mark Wilson

Bivocational ministry is the current, common term for those expressly working in secular employment to financially support their involvement in various kinds of religious work (for example, preaching). Formerly, this arrangement was usually termed *vocational ministry*, or more colloquially, *tent-making*.[1]

This brief, autobiographical saga demonstrates how late-in-life, graduate-level theological education empowered a robust response to a latent "divine call" to special religious life. It launched a previously unimaginable, extremely rewarding, bivocational Christian adventure, outside the normal channels of academia and full-time church ministry, beneficial for many churches, my community and the kingdom of heaven at large.

Harding School of Theology professors and staff must have wondered—as surely did my secular professional associates in the Department of the Interior, my church, and sometimes I myself as well —why a 50-year-old Supervisor of the United States Fish and Wildlife Service (FWS) office in Helena, Montana, would enroll in a graduate theological studies program. Missing from the long list of the curious were immediate members of my Missouri family and my closest friends. From the very earliest days of my life, relatives and friends observing my childhood interests and behavior were thinking (or saying), "Someday Mark is either going to be a preacher or a

[1] Inspired by Acts 18:3.

conservation agent."[2] Aptitudinal signals evident in the first decade of my life signaled a career trajectory trending toward either religion or natural resources conservation.

Unfortunately, nobody back then seemed to understand (neither family members nor church teachers ever expressed it to me) that it didn't necessarily have to be an "either/or" choice. Religion is about truth; the exact intersect with my early interest in natural science. The extraordinarily intrinsic alignment of theological and ecological aspects of God's magnificent creation should have been practically self-evident. The beauty of creation shouts our Creator's providence. The aesthetics and complexity of the natural world evokes inherent awe in humans. It's a normal expression of Christian virtue to fuse reverent wonder with sensible, practical concern for the well-being of the magisterial creation.

Consider how common it is for people who have hiked to a high vista to observe the wonders of God in a spectacularly beautiful place (for example, Glacier National Park), to feel so profoundly overcome with emotion that they describe it as a "religious experience!" Humans, as images of God, innately share in the author of the universe's joy and satisfaction with the "very good" creation (Gen 1:31). Scripture itself is the only rival to the awesome spectacle of our natural world as a revelation of the Creator to human hearts.

In the Stone-Campbell Movement, fostering wonder and reverence for God's glorious creation is primarily relegated to children's Sunday and Vacation Bible School classes. Rarely is the topic of creation care presented in either adult Bible classes or pulpit sermons. I never heard a single sermon or Bible class lesson on caring for God's creation until asked to do one myself, while working in Tennessee in the late 1980s. Our faith movement's infrequent, inadequate teaching on this subject reflects poorly developed, unbiblical eschatology dating back to the early 20th century. It leaves our adherents uneasy and sparsely equipped to cope with existential issues pertaining to the

---

[2] This is what game wardens with the Missouri Department of Conservation are called.

protection of our natural world (for example, global warming related to fossil fuel use, biodiversity loss, and natural resources depletion).

My religious upbringing was deep within the conservative Missouri Churches of Christ of the mid-20th century. Religious sentience fell upon me at about age 12 or 13, during my junior high school years. Early interest in the Bible caused me to read every tract in the racks in the church foyer. This was also roughly the point in my life where simultaneous, opposing, vocational counter-forces of natural resources conservation and religion began yanking me in different directions.

People usually assume *vocation* infers a type of job or field of endeavor. However, the Merriam/Webster Dictionary defines it as a summons or strong inclination, "especially a divine call to the religious life."[3] That divine call to religious life was tugging at me early on, but not exclusively. Career aspiration to natural resources conservation work was equally compelling. I didn't understand until later that both incoming calls originated in the same divine area code.

Much of the preaching/teaching that I remember from my childhood era (1960s) dealt with proper scriptural church formation and governance. The focus seemed to be upon elders and deacons, their proper qualifications, and sometimes, what roles were appropriate for women in the church. But I always wondered why preachers were hardly ever mentioned when discussing church governance and operation. This seemed a glaring, ironic omission. All the churches we attended in my lifetime had at least one professionally employed church minister/preacher. And the larger congregations had youth ministers, family ministers, and more.

As a teenager, observant family members and church teachers often encouraged me to consider becoming a preacher (that is, opt for the vocation of church preacher). This prospect created ambivalence for a couple of reasons. First, there was the opposing allure of natural resources conservation work. Second, my adolescent, patternistic understanding of the first century church resulted in some uncertainty

---

[3] "Vocation." Merriam-Webster.com Dictionary, Merriam-Webster, https://www.merriam-webster.com/dictionary/vocation. Accessed 10 Jan. 2024.

about preachers *per se*. Although congregationally employed preachers were evident everywhere in churches throughout our movement (and other faith traditions), they weren't equivalently depicted in the New Testament that scrupulous Churches of Christ used as "the pattern" for church governance and activity.

First Timothy 3:1 specifically says "if any man aspires to the office of overseer [that is, elder, bishop or pastor...but not *preacher*], it is a fine work he desires to do." Whenever my teenaged friends and I discussed taking part in future church leadership, it was always potentially as a preacher; never an elder. I can't remember any young person ever aspiring to the role of church elder. Not that becoming an elder was not worthwhile; rather, it was preachers who seemingly had all of the visibility and influence. Preaching seemed to be where the action and opportunity to genuinely do the most good lay within the church.

Years of Bible study, listening to sermons, and reading church tracts (usually during the sermon) resulted in a youthful disquiet. Our 1960s church leadership arrangement seemed incongruent with what was scripturally depicted in the first century. At the time, I wasn't aware that this had previously been a serious concern for 19th century American Restoration Movement churches too. Later (in the mid-1980s), I happened across Earl West's *Search for The Ancient Order* in the Manhattan (Kansas) Church of Christ's library. Therein, I discovered that Restoration-era church leaders often had been similarly troubled.[4] According to West,

> ...many concluded that a located preacher was to be tabooed. The idea was slow taking hold that a preacher

---

[4] It was a significant event in my spiritual life to discover that not only had other Christians wrestled with the same issue bothering me, but also to ascertain that this subject was a hotly debated and divisive issue in the mid through late 19th and early 20th centuries. One of my favorite classes at HST was Edward Robinson's "American Restoration History," which was of immense help in coming to understand this, and many other longstanding church issues, especially through the assigned reading of Richard Hughes' *Reviving the Ancient Faith*. I so wished I could have had access to a resource such as this much earlier in my life. My term paper for that class involved a deeply interesting, curiosity satisfying dive into the Restoration-era pastor system controversy surrounding located preachers.

might possibly establish himself in a certain area for a lengthy period of time and preach the gospel under the oversight of a scriptural set of elders without assuming the function of those elders.[5]

In 1974, Southwest Missouri State University (SMSU)[6] awarded me a bachelor of science degree in biology. Having always planned to attend graduate school, the time was ripe for a decision to pursue either divinity or natural resources conservation as an advanced field of learning. If divinity, it had to be an academically classical theological education, of the type offered at HST. At the time, HST had the reputation as the principal center of higher theological education for the Churches of Christ. Some of my friends at the Church of Christ's Christian Student Center on the SMSU campus were headed there. Ultimately, the draw of natural resources conservation prevailed. My affinity was tighter with peers oriented towards forestry and fish and wildlife management than with those wanting to study theology and to become ministers. So, I pursued a graduate degree in biology at the University of South Dakota, still harboring significant remorse that I was unable to study theology at HST.

Over approximately the next 30 years, I was involved with school, my career with the FWS, my family, and the Church of Christ congregations we attended wherever I was stationed. As was common for federal employees at the time, our family relocated often. We lived in six different states while I ascended through the ranks of the FWS. Wherever my family resided throughout the course of my career, I always taught adult Bible class, led singing, occasionally preached and sometimes was a presenter at church camps and various special events for Church of Christ congregations in those locations.

A significantly transformative, mid-career event occurred in about 1990, when the elders of the Collegeside Church of Christ in Cookeville, Tennessee, asked me to make an environmental

---

[5] Earl I. West, *The Search for The Ancient Order. Vol. 2: A History of The Restoration Movement 1849-1906* (Indianapolis: Religious Book Service, 1950), 453.

[6] Now Missouri State University, since 2005.

stewardship presentation. This was in connection with a program the church offered to the community of Cookeville, featuring experts in various fields who spoke about various, broadly applicable aspects of good stewardship (financial, health, family, etc.). Members of the community heard beneficial advice for life, while hopefully also coming to the realization that the presenting experts were Christians, conveying biblically based guidance.

The topic of environmental stewardship was well received. People expressed sincere gratitude upon learning that there was an underlying basis in scripture for the spiritual uplift they often experienced during immersive outdoor activities (such as fishing, gardening, golf, and camping). People's appreciativeness to my earliest attempt at creation care teaching ignited a tiny flare of insight that glowed dimly in my subconscious for a few more years.

In 2000, at the turn of the 21st century, I became the FWS Field Office Supervisor in Montana's capital city, Helena. From the standpoint of conservation work it was one of the FWS's highest profile stations. Wolf reintroductions, grizzly bear recovery, and many other issues were highly contentious regionally, even if supported at the national level. From a career standpoint, those first few years in Montana were highly stressful and it was a difficult transition adjusting to the challenging workload.

A few years later, in December of 2003, my family happened to attend the annual Church of Christ Rendezvous in West Yellowstone, Montana. Evertt W. Huffard, then Dean of HST, was a featured speaker. As he always did at speaking events, Evertt offered "an invitation," encouraging potentially interested people to consider pursuit of the advanced theological or counseling degrees offered at HST. At the conclusion of his presentation, I walked down and introduced myself and queried Evertt about programs of study for people like me whose employment precluded attending on-campus classes. Evertt smiled, casually reached into his sport jacket pocket, and pulled out a brochure. He handed it to me with these words: "We just started a new online program of study for people like you. Get in it!"[7] I thanked him and then appeared to return to my auditorium seat in the ordinary way, although my feet never touched the ground!

After nearly 30 years of dormancy, my seemingly relinquished dream of advanced theological study unexpectedly seemed potentially within reach. I was finally on the verge of entering a program of formal theological study—at HST, no less!

This extremely happy moment in my life simultaneously occurred during a period of personal despondence related to church difficulties in Helena. To prevent adding fuel to the fire, I temporarily sidelined myself from church involvement. The low-spirited biologist who initially entered HST in the summer of 2004 instantly experienced a sensation of belonging. In conservation terminology, it seemed a sort of reintroduction into my natural habitat.

Through lectures, reading, and term paper research, my soul was overwhelmed with interesting, helpful and uplifting information. It was the proverbial "drink from the firehose!" Between my full-time government job and graduate theological studies, there (literally) wasn't any spare time to fret about church problems. Theological studies at HST felt like an Alice in Wonderland "drop through the rabbit hole"; reality reconfigured around me. I was so prayerfully grateful to God that the internet had unlocked this awesome learning opportunity!

Boarding a rocket-sled of developing new insight, I hurtled past church conflict-related despondency. Theological graduate study refilled in "good measure, pressed down, shaken together, and running over; it was put into my lap." And then, at maybe the happiest time of my life, when I was bursting at the seams with excitement, joy, enthusiasm and gratitude, God swung open the floodgate and *really good stuff started happening!*

One especially good thing occurred while taking Dr. Duane Warden's class on the prison epistles. Preparation for the class included

---

[7] This was the Master of Arts in Christian Ministry (MACM) degree program designed for distance learners.

reading a short biography of the Apostle Paul.[8] Though unfamiliar with the author at that time, his writings later upended my Christian worldview. It is impossible to read anything written by N.T. Wright and miss his compelling, new-creational, eschatological outlook. Though there was only the vaguest whiff of new creation mentioned in that short biography of Paul's life, I pursued the faint scent nevertheless. It seemed to take forever to finish my term paper so I could subsequently grab a copy of the (then) latest book written by Wright, *Surprised by Hope*.[9]

Reading N. T. Wright (twenty-one is the recent count of his books in my library) especially corrected my eschatological outlook, intensifying my Christian joy in the process. A formerly unscriptural, dualistically gnostic, overly spiritualized, eschatological outlook exploded into a robust, biblically sound, materially manifested, renewal-of-creation perspective of eternity. Everything became resoundingly more genuine, meaningful, and joyous.

My secular work in natural resources conservation changed into simultaneously sacred and secular effort—though not exclusively. All endeavors meant to make the world more just, healthy, beautiful, orderly, or inviting are in keeping with a kingdom-of-heaven lifestyle.

Conservation and protection of fish, wildlife, and their habitats turned into mitigating the adverse effects of sin upon creation, and showcasing the unimpaired creative work of God. The on-the-ground conservation work remained the same, but the underlying incentive became preparatorily ushering in new-creational aspects of the eternal kingdom of heaven, re-infusing the broken earth with the pristine character of God's primordial conception.

Over the course of my career, I attended many public hearings, conferences and workshops that dealt with controversial, natural resources conservation issues. The testimony and presentations at these events were crammed with appeals to authorities and political

---

[8] N. T. Wright, *Paul: In Fresh Perspective* (Minneapolis: Fortress Press, 2005).

[9] N. T. Wright, *Surprised by Hope: Rethinking Heaven, the Resurrection, and the Mission of the Church* (New York: HarperCollins, 2008).

decision-makers to respect "the God-given rights" of various groups and individuals who felt resource management decisions might adversely affect them. Sadly, there were never any church or religious representatives who spoke to remind government policy officials about the divinely endowed, human responsibility to act as wise, conscionable stewards on behalf of the resplendent creation that God entrusted to human care. It haunted me that concern for our beautiful world seemed only expressed from a secular, rather than sacred, perspective. So, one afternoon, neglecting to adequately reflect upon the potential for adverse consequences, this cavalier beneficiary of several years of advanced theological study took matters into his own hands.

At a fluvial Arctic grayling[10] symposium in 2005, I impulsively (preferable adjective to *foolishly*) put myself out there and gave a presentation that briefly referenced sacred imperatives for protecting rare species, in addition to usual legal and moral obligations for protecting rare species. Many in the audience were caught off-guard by this tactic, and squirmed in their seats, staring back at me in confusion and disbelief. Most seemed unprepared to contend with a divine mandate for responsible ecological stewardship, though a few subtly thanked me afterward. Later in the evening, when the crowd had thinned down and most of the influential representatives had departed, the Montana governor's chief-of-staff quietly motioned me over to a secluded corner. Only then, did I think "uh-oh," as the realization sank in concerning what I had said, and what it might portend relative to continued employment.

Unexpectedly, the governor's representative used this Nicodemian meeting to privately convey his personal gratitude to me for evoking a "divine rationale" for guiding natural resources conservation decisions. He explained that when he was a boy, his father had often instructed him to be mindful of the sacred Christian responsibility for good stewardship of the wondrous natural resources Montana had been blessed with. Feeling slightly faint from relief, I sincerely thanked one of

---

[10] A rare fish occurring only in the Big Hole River system in Montana that was under consideration for being listed as a threatened species under the Endangered Species Act.

the state's most politically powerful people for expressing his love of Montana's beautiful natural wonders and acknowledging its Creator!

Another especially notable benefit resulting from my graduate theological education includes a continuing friendship with Steve Brehe, the Helena-based mentor/supervisor that HST assigned to oversee my practicum project. A retired Episcopal priest (DMin) and a former religion page reporter for the *St. Louis Globe Dispatch*, Steve deftly guided work on my proposal for a Saturday-edition religion page that would be incorporated into the *Helena Independent Record* newspaper. The newspaper adopted my report and plan eleven years ago. I continue to schedule local religion writers, from across all faiths, who provide a weekly religion column for the newspaper. Most religion column contributors belong to the Helena Ministerial Association that I worked closely with during my practicum.

In 2013, I completed my 36-year, conservation-based career with the FWS, and retired in Helena, Montana. My theological graduate degree credentials subsequently facilitated many new, post-retirement, ministry and teaching opportunities that wouldn't ordinarily be available to most Christians. Some examples include: lectures in the Carroll College theology department's ethics classes (Biblically Based Creation Care);[11] summer community theology classes (co-taught with Steve Brehe); new-creation themed articles in *The Christian Chronicle*; many interim ministry (sometimes ecumenical) assignments; assistance with new minister selection for multiple Churches of Christ in the Pacific Northwest; a fly fishing pro/counselor position at an ecumenical church camp; and the opportunity to coauthor *Embracing Creation* with John Mark Hicks and Bobby Valentine.[12] The future promises many more exciting ministerial and teaching opportunities yet to be revealed.

Now, my joyful religious life is especially characterized by evoking humanity's innate reverence for God's creation, teaching that

---

[11] Carroll College is a four-year, Catholic liberal arts college located in Helena, Montana.

[12] John Mark Hicks, Bobby Valentine and Mark Wilson, *Embracing Creation: God's Forgotten Mission* (Abilene: Leafwood, 2016).

God still values and intends to save what he formerly pronounced "very good," and encouraging Christian efforts to accomplish Jesus's prayer to make earth seem like heaven (Matt 5:10). Decades of natural resources conservation work, in combination with six years of late-in-life graduate theological study at HST, seems to have wrought a Church of Christ version of "St. Francis of Assisi."[13]

That completes the overview of my call to special religious life, and how graduate theological education sensationally enhanced my career in natural resources conservation. Now I would like to turn briefly to some pressing issues that educated bivocational ministers like myself could help churches to address.

Church of Christ congregations across the country are currently in steep decline. In 2023, *The Christian Chronicle* reported that in the past three decades, the number of adherents has declined to 1,447,271 —down 237,601, or 14 percent. The number of congregations has fallen to 11,965—down 1,209, or 9 percent. There is also anecdotal evidence that the decline may be steeper than what has been reported.[14] This issue is widespread, also affecting other faith traditions. In the 1990s, one-third of America's church pastors were under the age of 40, whereas today, that number is 16 percent.[15]

The closure of Austin Graduate School of Theology and the graduate theology program at Oklahoma Christian University, and the transition of Harding School of Theology to Searcy, are reflective of the sharp decline in students currently seeking advanced theology degrees. This situation is ominously portentous for churches who will soon be coping with impending shortages of skilled ministers. Theological education for bivocational ministers, especially at the graduate level, is a natural solution to the problem of a looming minister scarcity. It

---

[13] In 1979, Pope John Paul II declared St. Francis of Assisi the patron saint of ecologists.

[14] Cheryl Mann Bacon. 2022. "Church Closing Trend Began Before Covid-19." *The Christian Chronicle* March 30.

[15] Tim Alberta, *The Kingdom, the Power and the Glory: American Evangelicals in an Age of Extremism* (New York: HarperCollins, 2023), 439.

might also present a principal tool our faith movement can utilize to mitigate some of the current church fractiousness.

Today's preachers struggle to address divisive, highly politicized social issues while maintaining congregational unity. Every preacher knows that prophetically preaching about controversial topics can be tantamount to career martyrdom. And yet, church failure to address society's fears and concerns risks further decline in the public's opinion of both church and religion's relevance. Religion that is unable to address kingdom-of-heaven morality issues moots its witness and value to society.

The professional risk for preachers who address controversial moral issues isn't new, even if some of today's ethical issues are existentially more calamitous.[16] In the first century, perceived connections to pagan idolatry caused church leaders to struggle with what foods Christians could consume, and what holidays could be celebrated. In the 19th century (almost two millennia later), American Restoration Movement churches often failed to adequately address the issue of slavery and racial equality even as our congregations flourished in the regions where slave ownership was most prevalent.

In the 20th century, Churches of Christ remained mostly racially segregated and we still usually avoided preaching on racial equality, even while many cities were literally on fire because of racial unrest, protesting, and riots.[17] In the early 21st century, as worried atmospheric scientists gravely warn about anthropogenically induced,[18] planet-wide, temperature increases that may threaten much of the earth's life with extinction, evangelical Christians (which would include Churches of Christ) are among the most skeptical about the existence of this problem. For example, in a 2022 Pew Research Center survey

---

[16] Existential concerns involving potential human ability to destroy the earth's capacity to sustain human life (for example, nuclear war and global warming) are new.

[17] Maybe our attention was diverted because of the unnerving sound of our sisters' voices calling for women to share a more prominent place along with their brothers in the kingdom of heaven.

[18] The result of heavy reliance upon carbon-based fossil fuels (particularly coal) and other industrial activities that put excessive amounts of waste greenhouse gases (especially carbon dioxide) into the earth's atmosphere.

about how religion affects the American public's views about environmental matters, the pollsters determined that about 70% of the general public believes the earth is warming because of human activity (including 90% of atheists and 78% of agnostics), but only 32% of Protestant Evangelical Christians do.[19] This is a controversial matter that many of our preachers feel ill-equipped to address and reluctant to step up to because of the politically contentious nature of the topic. But, if the church is unable to name and prophetically speak straight to the moral issues of our day (or any day), is it any surprise that people might look elsewhere for divine guidance and social association?

It isn't necessary for Church of Christ ministers *per se* to become experts in climatic science, infectious disease, or other controversial issues *du jour*. Why not theologically educate and unleash the experts already among us who can prophetically teach and model Christian ethical thinking and behavior across the range of human experience and endeavor? Similar to my earlier example of the Collegeside Church of Christ in Cookeville, Tennessee, we should utilize the expertise existing within our congregations, all across our faith movement, to address various Christian stewardship obligations. A broader cadre of dually educated experts could supplement and relieve some of the pressure upon preachers who seem to always get corralled into addressing society's controversies.

This isn't a novel concept. Churches already occasionally ask gifted teachers or experts to instruct church classes on complex or controversial matters. What we don't do enough, though, is promote supplemental, higher-level theological education, in order to supercharge the understanding, and kingdom of heaven capabilities, of the experts residing within our ranks. This could provide churches with more insightful, beneficial discussion on controversial matters, even if the issues remain unsettled. Such folks can capably and knowledgeably address complex, controversial matters without exposing our congregational preachers to employment-related risks resulting from having to address sensitive topics outside their area of expertise.

---

[19] Pew Research Center, November 2022, "How Religion Intersects With Americans' Views on the Environment," p. 83.

We shouldn't acquiesce to a simplistic, rigidly literal, or sanctioned biblical narrative that flies in the face of what multiple disciplines of scholarly reasoning indicate cannot possibly be true. Our world is complex because God is intricate and complicated. Isaiah 55:9 states this: "For as the heavens are higher than the earth, so are my ways higher than your ways and my thoughts than your thoughts." Christian educators, especially those involved at the higher, graduate levels, must courageously confront anti-intellectualism and promote respect for the results of legitimate inquiry in all valid fields of study. Bear in mind the most prevalent biblical directive from God, angels, and Jesus: "Do not fear!" Promote theology as the "queen of sciences" (*regina scientiarum*) once again.[20] We must consider the magisterial intricacy of the Creator himself to properly filter meaning from all human endeavors and fields of learning.

Providing advanced theological education to an assortment of experts not directly employed by church congregations offers flexibility and potential solutions for a variety of church issues, not the least of which are having good teachers and preachers more broadly available, and safeguarding against backlash and the risk of employment loss arising from preaching on highly controversial topics. Other potential benefits include:

5. Providing teachers and preachers with a diverse range of skill, experience, and potentially improved acceptance within the faith community.
6. Helping smaller congregations with limited finances have greater access to high-quality Bible teaching.
7. Infusing more people's lives with the joy that comes from a better understanding of their rightful purpose and place within the kingdom of heaven.

Bivocational ministry isn't an all-purpose fix for every problem in the church. Full-time ministers have more time to devote to pastoral work, counseling, funerals, weddings, attending retreats and camps, and

---

[20] G. van den Brink, "How Theology Stopped Being Regina Scientiarum—and How Its Story Continues," *Studies in Christian Ethics* 32(4) (2019): 442-54.

more. Less than full-time ministry might also be unsuitable for empathetically inclined ministers who particularly enjoy the counseling and pastoral aspects of their work. However, in view of foreseeable future problems arising from hyper-political polarization and declining numbers of churches, universities affiliated with the Churches of Christ should consider addressing this situation by promoting bivocational degree program options. Such programs could probably track closely with those aimed at missionary preparation.

In summary, the learning and associations resulting from my years of study at HST provided benefits beyond anything I could have previously imagined. New creation eschatology especially has caused all of the Bible to make more sense, and I am a much better teacher for it. My career-related ecological protection work was infused with sacred perspective, increasing the joy I received from creation care pursuits. Finally, I have become far more valuable to the church at large as a teacher, preacher, and church administrative resource, especially for smaller congregations in the Pacific Northwest. I live in constant gratitude for the learning and capability that came with my degree from HST.

CHAPTER SIXTEEN

HST and the Changing Landscape of Theological Education
Mark E. Powell

The transition of Harding School of Theology from Memphis to Searcy comes during a time of fear and anxiety in the church, in the academic world, and in society at large. In the church, there is concern over steep declines in worship attendance and church membership, coupled with the growing influence of secularization, especially in the West.[1] Churches are closing, and fewer young people are going into ministry.[2] In the academic world, universities are experiencing declining enrollment as college is no longer the clear choice for high school graduates, as online and distance programs continue to proliferate, and as the number of potential students is decreasing with a sharp decline in the U.S. birth-rate. In society at large, there is political polarization due to varying views on the economy, sexual ethics, racial justice, ecological issues, immigration, gun violence, and more. The world at large is still reeling from the effects of the COVID-19 global pandemic and ongoing conflicts in Gaza and Ukraine.

Turning to educational institutions in Churches of Christ, there is the recent closing of Ohio Valley University in Vienna, West Virginia (2021); Lipscomb University's Austin Center (formerly Austin Graduate School of Theology) in Austin, Texas (2022); and

---

[1] See, for instance, Jim Davis and Michael Graham, with Ryan P. Burge, *The Great Dechurching: Who's Leaving, Why Are They Going, and What Will It Take to Bring Them Back?* (Grand Rapids: Zondervan, 2023); and Andrew Root, *Churches and the Crisis of Decline: A Hopeful, Practical Ecclesiology for a Secular Age* (Grand Rapids: Baker Academic, 2022).

[2] See Stanley E. Granberg, *Empty Church: Why People Don't Come and What to Do About It* (Self-published, Excel Book Writing, 2022).

Oklahoma Christian University's Graduate School of Theology in Oklahoma City, Oklahoma (2023).[3] All of these events easily lead to speculation as to why HST is transitioning from Memphis to Searcy and what this transition might mean for the future. In this brief chapter, I will not presume to predict the future or offer a complete explanation for HST's transition. Rather, I will suggest how the transition of HST fits within the changing landscape of theological education. Every school has its own story, and we need to carefully attend to individual stories as we also seek more comprehensive narratives.

In the case of HST in Memphis, two developments are particularly significant: (1) students have more graduate theology programs to choose from, and (2) improvements in educational technology have made distance learning an attractive option, especially for graduate students. These developments bring both opportunities and challenges for theological schools.

The Increase of Graduate Programs in Theology

First, students have more schools to choose from, both within and outside of institutions associated with Churches of Christ. Since HST was accredited by the Association of Theological Schools (ATS) in 1997, there has been a 32% increase in the total number of ATS-accredited schools in a 25-year period. There are currently five ATS accredited schools in Churches of Christ: in addition to HST, there is Abilene Christian (ACU, accredited in 2002), Lipscomb (accredited in 2011), Freed-Hardeman (FHU, accredited in 2017), and Faulkner (accredited in 2018). Further, there is one school with associate status: Heritage Christian (HCU).[4] In the states of Alabama and Tennessee

---

[3] See Cheryl Mann Bacon, "Harding School of Theology set to leave Memphis," *Christian Chronicle* (August 24, 2023): https://christianchronicle.org/harding-school-of-theology-set-to-leave-memphis/; and Cheryl Mann Bacon, "Oklahoma Christian University closing its Graduate School of Theology," *Christian Chronicle* (November 18, 2023): https://christianchronicle.org/oklahoma-christian-university-closing-its-graduate-school-of-theology/.

[4] Interestingly, Pepperdine has never pursued ATS accreditation. Oklahoma Christian University's Graduate School in Theology was an associate member of ATS,

alone, there are four ATS accredited schools associated with Churches of Christ and another one with associate status. Most of these programs can trace their academic ancestry—at least at the graduate level—back to HST, and their very existence is a win for HST's original mission to improve the training of ministers. The opposition that George Benson, W. B. West, and HST's first faculty encountered when beginning a graduate theology program in the 1950s has been replaced with an eagerness to start similar programs.

This many graduate programs in a limited geographical area brings both opportunities and challenges. On the positive side, this number of programs breeds creativity when it comes to degree offerings, curriculum, and educational methods. HST has kept up with what our sister schools are doing, has pursued our own innovations, and has focused more carefully on our brand and what we do best. The challenge, of course, is that more programs mean fewer potential students for each program. HST in Memphis is still the largest theological school in Churches of Christ east of the Mississippi River and second to ACU overall, but our enrollment has declined by one-half since I arrived in fall 2002: from 225 total students to 112 in fall 2023.

Improvements in Educational Technology

The second significant development, improvements in educational technology, has made distance learning an attractive option for students. This is especially the case for graduate students. Undergraduate students still desire a coming-of-age college experience—if they can afford it. Graduate students, on the other hand, tend to be young adults who are ready to begin a career or adults who are already settled in a job and geographical location. Distance learning provides students with more options when choosing a program and allows them to remain in their current ministry context.

When I first came to HST in 2002, we were already offering asynchronous, text-based online classes. These online classes replaced older classes that were offered by cassette tape and extension classes

---

but in fall 2023 university leaders announced the closing of the graduate theology program.

offered in satellite locations. Beginning in fall 2016 (four years before COVID-19), HST began offering synchronous online classes through video conferencing, a format we call HST LIVE (Live Interactive Video Education). Video conferencing allows HST to have on-campus students and distance students participating in the same class at the same time.[5] Recorded class sessions also allow us to offer courses asynchronously for students with approved exceptions.

Currently, ATS does not mandate a residency requirement for degrees. HST still requires some residency (nine-hours for the MDiv degree and six-hours for the MA and MACM degrees) to promote community among faculty, staff, and students. Most students meet residency requirements through week-long intensive courses, which include daily chapel and shared lunches. The DMin degree is fully residential and all courses are offered in a hybrid format that includes intensive-course meetings. Our students describe these intensive courses as a retreat or a camp for ministers. HST believes that some residency requirements are important for building community and nurturing the educational, spiritual, and ministerial formation of students. A combination of online distance classes (in either an asynchronous or synchronous format) and intensive on-campus meetings (either entire courses or a portion of a course) appears to be the way forward for many theological schools.

Improvements in educational technology bring both opportunities and challenges. HST's reach is more national and global than ever. Our fall 2023 student body includes students from 20 states and 16 other countries. Distance students are able to remain in their current ministry context and immediately apply their education to their ministry. In many ways, this model is superior to one where students leave their context for a 2-3-year period (or more) and study in isolation from

---

[5] HST's synchronous online classes are less convenient for students than asynchronous online classes, since students must participate in the class during the time it is offered. The faculty, however, believes that HST LIVE classes promote community better than asynchronous classes and allow students to engage complex material with others in real-time. With distance education, though, students often make decisions based on convenience rather than the quality of the academic experience.

their ministry context. The biggest challenge is building an educational community where faculty and students learn from and support each other during their studies and throughout a lifetime of ministry. The rise in distance education also brings financial challenges for schools like HST. Distance students are almost always part-time students, so students take less semester hours and there is less need for student housing.

Distance education is also a better option for most second-career students. My hunch is that the age for shoulder-tapping potential ministers has increased. When I was in high-school, the minister at my church and several older members encouraged me to go into ministry. Their encouragement made a big impression on me. Even in the heyday of undergraduate Bible enrollment, professors had to shoulder-tap potential ministers from the general undergraduate student body. A story is told at Harding University about Jerry Jones's first year as chairman of the Department of Bible, Religion, and Philosophy in 1975. The department normally graduated around 50 students, but that year only 10 incoming freshmen declared a major in the department. Stunned, Jones went to the registrar, only to learn that every year only about 10 incoming freshmen declare a Bible major. Most of those who graduated with a degree in Bible were recruited during their undergraduate studies. It appears that, today, shoulder-tapping happens even later in life, when church members see potential in a person who fills-in to preach, volunteers with the youth, or serves in some other capacity.[6] When the church needs a minister, they ask this person to serve full-time in their ministry role. In cases like this, distance education allows second-career ministers to remain in their current ministry context and receive much-needed training on a part-time basis.

---

[6] From our current student body, I am thinking of people like Sammie Young, who left a career in law to be a youth minister; Brett Rimer, who left a career in academic administration to be a youth minister; Hailey Pruitt, who has been a high school English teacher and is an editor for University Communication and Marketing at Harding, and actively serves in youth and women's ministries; Ubong Okorie, who is a medical researcher in Nigeria pursuing a theological education; and Clay Fowler who worked in graphic design before serving in ministry roles in churches and non-profit organizations.

The Impact on Graduate Programs in Theology

Today there are more graduate theology programs with a higher number of total students, but students are taking less classes. HST's highest enrollment was in 1982, with 282 credit students taking 2343 semester hours (for an average of 8.3 hours/student). This is substantially more than the 2023 enrollment of 112 students taking 481 semester hours (for an average of 4.3 hours/student). When one considers, however, the five graduate programs associated with Churches of Christ in Alabama and Tennessee, there are a total of 385 credit students taking 2035 hours (for an average of 5.3 hours/student) in 2023. Comparing 2023 to 1982, then, there are 103 more students taking 308 less hours—more programs with more students overall, but students are taking less hours.

Total Headcount[7]

	HST	Lipscomb	HCU	FHU	Faulkner	Total
1982	282	—	—	—	—	282
2002	225	87	13	73	—	398
2005	191	80	13	76	18	378
2010	161	97	28	61	17	364
2015	129	131*	33	67	54	414
2020	116	119	40	69	37	381
2023	112	69	88	73	43	385

---

[7] These statistics were provided by representatives of each school. I focused on schools east of the Mississippi River (those in Alabama and Tennessee) because they likely have the greatest impact on HST's enrollment. Faulkner University in Montgomery, Alabama is the furthest away from HST in Memphis at 325 miles (a five-hour drive plus stops, according to GPS). In general, HST's student population has decreased significantly, though it is still the largest school of the group; Freed-Hardeman's and Lipscomb's student population have remained steady; Faulkner's and Heritage Christian's student population have grown significantly. These statistics provide a general picture of developments over time, but there are many variables that are difficult to take into account. For instance, HST had a Master of Arts in Counseling

Total Semester Hours

	HST	Lipscomb	HCU	FHU	Faulkner	Total
1982	2343	—	—	—	—	2343
2002	1219	516	51	411	—	2197
2005	1002	414	72	418	174	2080
2010	887	547	144	388	162	2128
2015	656	859*	186	399	438	2538
2020	591	738	258	348	257	2192
2023	481	372	438	414	330	2035

Based on a conversation with a Lipscomb representative, these numbers are likely inflated and include non-credit students.

These two developments, and the results of these developments, provide a context for the decision to transition HST from Memphis to Searcy. Many factors were at play in the decision, but more graduate theology programs and improvements in educational technology decrease the need for a centrally-located, distinct seminary campus with student housing. Context matters, and much will be lost when the school moves from Memphis; but there will be gains when HST is in Searcy. There will be new opportunities, as well as new challenges.

In Acts 13:1-3, the church at Antioch was worshiping, fasting, and praying, and the Holy Spirit called Barnabas and Saul to leave Antioch for a new work. I became dean of HST in July 2021 during the COVID-19 pandemic and at a time of institutional transition at

---

program from 1995-2016 that is now under the College of Education in Searcy, but the counseling student numbers are included with the total numbers for those years.

ACU's Graduate Program in Theology was unable to provide total semester hours, but their total headcount has gone from 296 (their highest in 2003), to 213 (2005), 168 (2010), 141 (2015), 162 (2020), and 162 (2023). In 2023, 162 students took 795 hours (for an average of 4.9 hours/student). Like HST, ACU's enrollment has dropped considerably, and ACU has experienced a decline in local students and an increase in online/distance students.

Harding University. I am convinced that the first thing God's people should do, especially during a time of uncertainty, is to worship, fast, and pray. This is what the HST faculty and staff did for two whole years leading up to the Board's decision, and I trust that the future of HST and the future of theological education is in God's hands. The HST faculty and staff continue to worship, fast, and pray as we discern, not only where God is leading the school, but where God is leading each of us individually as well.

It is important to remember the past and to celebrate the good things that God has done. But God is a God of the present and the future, not just a God of the past. God is "the Alpha and the Omega ... who is, and who was, and who is to come, the Almighty" (Rev 1:8, NIV). It is not good when God's people dwell too much on the past and miss God's present working. We can become like Israel when they were wandering in the wilderness; they longed for the past in Egypt when God was leading them to the promised land. From where I sit, we live in changing but exciting times, with many opportunities to train Christian leaders on a global scale and help churches participate more fully in God's work in the world. Clearly, God is doing a new thing in our time, and I pray that God will give us eyes to see and a willingness to prayerfully and faithfully follow.

E. H. Ijams Administration Building

L. M. Graves Memorial Library

HST seal

HST's first graduating class, 1959

George Benson, W. B. West, Jr., and Annie May Alston at library groundbreaking, 1964

Jack P. Lewis

*Jane Tomlinson with four deans: Philip Slate, Bill Flatt,
Harold Hazelip, and Evertt W. Huffard*

Annie May Lewis and Richard Oster.

Don Meredith worked in the HST library for 49 years.

Administration, Faculty, and Staff

Administration

Vice-presidents: Evertt W. Huffard (2006-2013), Jim Martin (2014-2024)

Deans: W. B. West, Jr. (1952-1972), Harold Hazelip (1972-1986), C. Philip Slate (1986-1992), Edward P. Myers (1992-1993), Bill Flatt (1993-1999), Evertt W. Huffard (1999-2015), Allen Black (2015-2021), Mark E. Powell (2021-2024)

Associate Deans: Don Kinder, Vernon Ray, Steve McLeod

Faculty (full-time)

Allen Black, Richard Batey, Dave Bland, Douglas E. Brown, Steve Cloer, Bill Flatt, Ed Gray, Carlus Gupton, Lance Hawley, Harold Hazelip, John Mark Hicks, Evertt W. Huffard, E. H. Ijams, Joel Johnson, John F. Kennedy, Don Kinder, Jack P. Lewis, Mac Lynn, Phillip McMillion, Keith Mask, Carroll D. Osburn, Richard Oster, G. W. (Bill) Patterson, Jr., Mark E. Powell, Eddie Randolph, Vernon Ray, Jack Reese, Paul Rotenbury, John A. Scott, Kevin Shelby, C. Philip Slate, Donald R. Sime, Jack Vancil, Thomas Warren, Earl West, Velma West, W. B. West, Jr., James Zink

Library

Library Directors: Annie May Alston Lewis (1962-1983), Don Meredith (1983-2017), Bob Turner (2017-2021), Jessica Holland (2021-2024)

Librarians: Bonnie Ulrey Barnes, Carisse Berryhill, Don Meredith, Sheila Owen, Melanie Pennington, Bob Turner

Library Staff: Joy Carter, Charla Hinson, Pat Hughes, Evelyn Meredith, Tina Rogers, Pamela Shelby, Billie Thomason, Sherma Workman

Staff

Robert Adams, Jeannie Alexander, Bob Amis, James Anders, Larry Arick, Linda Beard, Roberta Bender, Jerry Blair, Robert and Gail Brady, Vee Brasfield, Barbara Brown, Susie Buford, Clara Clements,

Belinda Curtis, Brenda Curtis, Sammie Daniels, Cora Epperson, Glendol Grimes, Amy Hagedorn, Mary Hamm, Sandra Hawk, Sherry Hedden, Rachel Hemphill, Ruth Herring, Peggy Hilbun, Glaman and Pat Hughes, Evelyn Humphreys, Daphne Logan, LaCresha Longwell, Jocelyn McField, Catherine Mars, Tracey Mason, Veronica Matthews, Bethany Moore, Oscar and Katie Moore, Greg Muse, Marian Nunnally, Sandra Palmer, Mark Parker, Vernon Perry, Lynn Puckett, Dave Robbins, Art Roberts, Brenda Sain, Jean Saunders, Darlene Shook, Nedra Sparks, Barbara Stubblefield, Trina Thiesen, Jeannine Thweatt, Cecil Tomlinson, Jame Tomlinson, Marcella Trevathan, Dave Walker, Kelly Ward, Catherine Wilcoxson

Alumnus/Alumna of the Year

1973	Jimmy Moffett	1999	Robert Stephens
1974	C. W. Bradley	2000	Jimmy Adcox
1975	Paul Rogers	2001	Oliver Rodgers
1976	Jimmy Allen	2002	Jack Reece
1977	Bert Perry	2003	Larry Stephens
1978	Harvey Floyd	2004	Linda Oxford
1979	John Simpson	2005	Matt Carter
1980	William Woodson	2006	Annie May Lewis
1981	Charles Coil	2007	Lynn Anderson
1982	Neale Pryor	2008	Leon Sanderson
1983	Dowell Flatt	2009	Edward Robinson
1984	Arlin Hendrix	2010	Willie Nettle
1985	C. F. Myer, Jr.	2011	Dwight Albright
1986	F. Furman Kearley	2012	Edward Short
1987	C. Philip Slate	2013	Rodney Plunket
1988	Clarence Sparks	2014	Monte Cox
1989	Bill Flatt & Glendol Grimes	2015	Randy Harris
1990	Maurice Hall	2016	Bill Bowen
1991	David Underwood	2017	Jim Woodroof
1992	Mac Lynn	2018	Ashby Camp
1993	Annie May Alston Lewis	2019	Terrell Lee
1994	Clyde Woods	2020	Ron Wade
1995	Enoch Thweatt	2021	Evert W. Huffard
1996	Eugene Goudeau	2022	Harold Redd
1997	Terry Dempsey	2023	Lynn McMillon
1998	Don Meredith	2024	Brenda Curtis

Alma Mater

1. Near the banks of the river that flows down thru our land is a school for Christian service; foreever may she stand. She welcomes all who hear the call of ministry and love, and so we sing her praise to God who reigns above.

2. Framed by those who prayed and dreamed and looked beyond their peers; shaped by ever faithful servants she continues through the years. Builders true of more than brick and stone, she lives to mold the future years for servants yet unknown. O God you are our God, may you ever lead the way, for those who seek the Lord and gladly serve him every day. Through all that you have taught us; to seek, to learn, to be. May the Word of Life flow through us like a river to the sea.

3. We came as your students because we heard the call; we go throughout the wide world to share God's grace for all. Still tied to one another by the Word of God so true, we stand and face tomorrow for we owe so much to you.

Majestically

WORDS: Don Kinder, Bill Flatt (2011)
MUSIC: Leon Sanderson (2011)
©2011 by Leon Sanderson

Contributors

C. Leonard Allen, PhD is Dean of the College of Bible and Ministry at Lipscomb University in Nashville, Tennessee. (MA, 1975)

Grant Azbell, DMin is Preaching Minister at the Magnolia Church in Florence, Alabama. (MDiv, 2014)

Carisse Mickey Berryhill, PhD is Special Assistant to the Dean for Strategic Initiatives at Brown Library, Abilene Christian University in Abilene, Texas. (MA, 2001)

Garrett Best, PhD is Chair of the Department of Bible and Ministry and Associate Professor of Bible at York University in York, Nebraska. (MDiv, 2014)

Nathan Bills, ThD is Head of the Theology and Ministry Department and Lecturer at Heritage Christian College in Accra, Ghana. (MDiv, 2006)

Chris W. Buxton, DMin is Founder and Executive Director of ULife Consulting, a college ministry consulting and planting organization. He lives in Bono, Arkansas. (MDiv, 2010)

Erika Carr, PhD is Associate Professor of Psychiatry at Yale University School of Medicine and Director of the Behavioral Intervention Service and Director of the Inpatient Psychology Service at Connecticut Mental Health Center in New Haven, Connecticut. (MAC, 2005)

Steve Cloer, DMin is Assistant Professor of Ministry and Director of the Doctor of Ministry Program at Harding School of Theology in Memphis, Tennessee. (MDiv, 2006)

Craig Ford, DMin is Minister at the Billings Church of Christ in Billings, Montana. (MDiv, 2006)

Jim Harbin is Senior Minister at the Raleigh Community Church of Christ in Memphis, Tennessee, and President of the National Urban Ministry Association. (MAR, 2002)

Matthew D. Love, PhD (cand.) is Preaching Minister at the Beebe Church of Christ in Beebe, Arkansas. (MDiv, 2019)

Dorn Muscar, Jr., DMin is an IMA Chaplain to the Deputy Wing Chaplain at Little Rock Air Force Base in Jacksonville, Arkansas. (MDiv 2008, DMin 2017)

Mark E. Powell, PhD is Dean and Professor of Theology at Harding School of Theology in Memphis, Tennessee.

Carson E. Reed, DMin is Vice President of Church Relations, Executive Director of the Siburt Institute for Church Ministry, and Dean of the Graduate School of Theology at Abilene Christian University in Abilene, Texas. (MDiv, 1988)

Edward J. Robinson, PhD is Associate Professor of History and Religion at Texas College and Pulpit Minister at the North Tenneha Church of Christ in Tyler, Texas. (MAR, 1991; MDiv, 1993)

R. Mark Wilson is retired after 36 years with the United States Fish and Wildlife Service. He lives in Helena, Montana, and does interim ministry and teaching throughout the northwestern United States. (MACM, 2010)

Made in the USA
Middletown, DE
07 December 2024